Additional Praise for *Systematic Fixed Income: An Investor's Guide*

"Systematic investing – driven by models and data – has made major inroads in equity investment, but not in fixed income. This book is long overdue, and Scott Richardson is the ideal author. Combining his clear grasp of theory, coupled with his long practitioner experience, it is a 'must read' for fixed-income investors."

— Stephen Schaefer, Professor, London Business School

"This book is a must read for any serious investment professional or aspiring student interested in systematic fixed income. Scott Richardson is one of the most experienced hands-on global professionals in this space bringing a unique combination of insights that span both academia and industry."

— Andrew Jackson, Head of Research,
Vinva Investment Management

Systematic Fixed Income

Founded in 1807, John Wiley & Sons is the oldest independent publishing company in the United States. With offices in North America, Europe, Australia and Asia, Wiley is globally committed to developing and marketing print and electronic products and services for our customers' professional and personal knowledge and understanding.

The Wiley Finance series contains books written specifically for finance and investment professionals as well as sophisticated individual investors and their financial advisors. Book topics range from portfolio management to e-commerce, risk management, financial engineering, valuation and financial instrument analysis, as well as much more.

For a list of available titles, visit our Web site at www.WileyFinance.com.

Systematic Fixed Income

An Investor's Guide

SCOTT A. RICHARDSON, PhD

WILEY

Published by John Wiley & Sons, Inc., Hoboken, New Jersey.
Published simultaneously in Canada.

For general information on our other products and services or for technical support, please contact our Customer Care Department within the United States at (800) 762-2974, outside the United States at (317) 572-3993 or fax (317) 572-4002.

Wiley also publishes its books in a variety of electronic formats. Some content that appears in print may not be available in electronic formats. For more information about Wiley products, visit our website at www.wiley.com.

Library of Congress Cataloging-in-Publication Data

Names: Richardson, Scott (Accounting professor), author.
Title: Systematic fixed income : an investor's guide / Scott Richardson, Ph.D.
Description: Hoboken, New Jersey : John Wiley & Sons, Inc., [2022] |
    Series: Wiley finance series | Includes bibliographical references.
Identifiers: LCCN 2022010444 (print) | LCCN 2022010445 (ebook) | ISBN
    9781119900139 (cloth) | ISBN 9781119900238 (adobe pdf) | ISBN
    9781119900191 (epub)
Subjects: LCSH: Fixed-income securities.
Classification: LCC HG4650 .R53 2022 (print) | LCC HG4650 (ebook) | DDC
    332.63/2044—dc23/eng/20220302
LC record available at https://lccn.loc.gov/2022010444
LC ebook record available at https://lccn.loc.gov/2022010445

Cover Design: Wiley
Cover Image: © KTSDESIGN/Getty Images

SKY10034055_033122

To İrem
and
Sean

Contents

Preface

I wrote this book to help fill a void between theoretical fixed income asset pricing and the practicalities of investing in fixed income securities. Fixed income is a ubiquitous component of asset owner portfolios. Fixed income markets are enormous (well in excess of $100 trillion USD) and have traditionally been seen as a powerful diversifier alongside equity market allocations. To date, incumbent investment approaches for active risk taking in fixed income are typically discretionary. These discretionary approaches tend to be dominated by reaching for yield (spread) behavior that dampens the strategic diversification benefit of a fixed income allocation. With the advent of improved data sources (from pre- and post-trade price transparency to enhanced fundamental data insights for issuers of debt) systematic investment approaches can now be feasibly applied to fixed income markets. The potential for asset owners is enormous: a way to preserve the diversifying potential of fixed income as an asset class and add excess returns via security selection.

This book lays out a framework for identifying the relevant sources of risk and return in public fixed income markets. After a comprehensive analysis of the strategic and tactical roles that fixed income can play in asset allocation, the book covers the systematic return sources for rate and credit sensitive fixed income assets across developed and emerging markets. Armed with an understanding of return drivers, the book then explores the implementation challenges (e.g., liquidity, risk) that need to, and can, be overcome to successfully build a systematic fixed income portfolio. Putting it all together, the reader will appreciate the powerful diversifying potential of a well-implemented systematic fixed income allocation.

Although the book is primarily targeted to institutional asset owners and investors with an interest/responsibility for the fixed income asset class, the content is also suitable for advanced-degree students and other investment professionals looking to expand their knowledge of fixed income investment approaches.

Acknowledgments

There are many people to thank for the content of this book. It is the result of a dual career spanning academia and the investment community. Without excellent mentors and peers in both spheres I would not be where I am today.

On the academic side, my advisor, Richard Sloan, has always been and continues to be a source of inspiration and sound guidance. Over the years academic colleagues from University of Sydney (undergraduate days), University of Michigan (formative PhD years), University of Pennsylvania (assistant professor days) and London Business School (tenured professor life) have continued to support and challenge all my research. I thank them all.

On the investment side, there are too many individuals to thank individually. My formative investment years at Barclays Global Investors (BGI) were amazing. I am thankful for the opportunity to have been part of the original large-scale effort for systematic fixed income investing at BGI. The breadth of research talent across asset classes (stocks, bonds, currencies, and commodities) was truly breathtaking. Internal research seminars were on par with the quality of seminar attendees and critical discussion at the top business schools of the day. Over the past decade, I was fortunate to work with an excellent set of colleagues at AQR, where, again, the breadth of research talent across asset classes and the willingness to collaborate across asset classes was fantastic. After BGI, I thought I would never find a similar group of smart, engaged people to work with, but I was wrong. The founders, Cliff Asness, David Kabiller, and John Liew, helped cultivate that curiosity and collaboration. A special thanks for the time and resources provided to me at the end of 2021 and early 2022 to complete work on this book.

Thank you to all my co-authors over the years on the many academic and practitioner-oriented research papers focused on fixed income. That material, and the associated discussions/experiences, is the collective knowledge base of this book. I thank you all, especially Navneet Arora, Attakrit Asvanunt, Jordan Brooks, Maria Correia, Peter Diep, Andrea Eisfelt, Tony Gould, Johnny Kang, Ronen Israel, Stephen Lok, Diogo Palhares, Lukasz Pomorski, İrem Tuna, and Zhikai Xu.

At both BGI and AQR I had the opportunity to develop systematic fixed income businesses and do so in an environment that appreciated the diversification benefit of such an investment approach. If I can communicate that opportunity and create a new set of believers in this opportunity through this book I will be happy.

I also thank the entire publication team at Wiley, with special thanks to Bill Falloon, Samantha Enders, Purvi Patel, and Samantha Wu for their efforts in streamlining the publication process and making this process enjoyable. And to William Allen, Alfie Brixton, Michael Doros, Atif Ellahie, Antti Ilmanen, Thom Maloney, Jon Peress, and Kevin Rauseo, thank you for the discussions and feedback over the past few months in helping this book come to life.

About the Author

Scott Richardson is a senior advisor (former principal) at AQR Capital Management, where he was the co-head of fixed income and a senior member of the Research and Portfolio Management team. He was also involved with the equity research team for the firm's Global Stock Selection group. Prior to AQR, Scott held senior positions at BlackRock (Barclays Global Investors), including head of Europe equity research and head of global credit research, where he oversaw research and investment decisions at BGI for both total return and absolute return products across credit and equity markets. Scott is a professor of practice at London Business School, where he teaches graduate-level classes, including systematic investing in fixed income (an elective whose materials this book is based on). He began his career as an assistant professor at the University of Pennsylvania. He is an editor of the *Review of Accounting Studies* and has published extensively in leading academic and practitioner journals. In 2009 he won the Notable Contribution to Accounting award for his work on earnings quality and accruals. Scott earned a BEc with first-class honors from the University of Sydney and a PhD in business administration from the University of Michigan.

CHAPTER 1

Setting the Stage

OVERVIEW

This chapter defines key terms that will be used throughout the book. I start by describing fixed income securities and the size of the global fixed income markets. I introduce the term *systematic* and distinguish it from *quantitative*. All fixed income market participants are quantitatively aware; after all commonly used analytics like duration and convexity require a little more than elementary school mathematics. However, not all fixed income investors are systematic in how they translate their investment narratives into portfolios. That is what it means to be a systematic investor: prespecifying your investment hypotheses (narrative) and then converting that to an algorithm that generates trades and ultimate portfolio positions. We will explore the key ingredients of that algorithm as we proceed through the book. Finally, while this book is designed for fixed income investors and not financial engineers, resulting in minimal mathematical proofs, it is still important that commonly used analytics like yields, durations, and convexity are well understood. We will cover the intuition of these concepts, and their limitations, in detail.

1.1 WHAT IS FIXED INCOME?

This book is focused on understanding the investment opportunities available to asset owners from the fixed income markets. We need to define what makes a financial asset a fixed income security. But let's first start with a brief discussion of what a financial asset is to help set the stage for what is to come later in this chapter. All financial assets provide the owner a right to share in the cash flows generated from ownership. The price of a financial asset today will reflect expected cash flows for today, tomorrow, and all future time periods until the security ceases to exist. You don't need to hold the security to maturity to receive the actual cash flows: the price of the security will capture expectations (albeit noisily) of all future cash flows. Implicit in this last statement is an equivalence of cash flows that accrue over different time periods. Of course, there is a complicated discounting that is applied to expected future cash flows to arrive at a price. These statements are true for all financial assets, whether they be common stocks or bonds or any other contractual claim.

We can start with a simple general equation linking the price of a financial asset to its expected cash flow participation rights:

$$P = \frac{E[CF_1]}{(1+r)^1} + \frac{E[CF_2]}{(1+r)^2} + \frac{E[CF_3]}{(1+r)^3} + \cdots \frac{E[CF_{LT}]}{(1+r)^{LT}} \tag{1.1}$$

Equation 1.1 is a discrete time pricing formula generalizable to all financial assets. E[] captures expectations based on information today with respect to future cash flows, CF. These cash flows are discounted back to today, reflecting not just time value of money considerations but also perceived risk of associated cash flows. (We will have more to say on discount rates and its components throughout this book.) Fixed income securities are relatively unique, relative to equity securities, in two key respects. The key is in the name of the asset class: "fixed" income. First, the numerator is less important from a security valuation perspective (cash flows are "fixed"). Expected future cash flows for fixed income securities (the numerator) are typically known in advance, with almost complete certainty for truly risk-free securities. Uncertainty in the numerator (one-sided for fixed income and more two-sided for equity) is increasing in the risk that the issuer will be unable to deliver those future cash flows (e.g., a risky corporate issuer). Generally, fixed income security pricing is dominated by the denominator. In contrast, equity securities require detailed forecasting of both the numerator and denominator for any meaningful security valuation. Some might be tempted to say fixed income investing is easier as a result. Alas, it is not; it is just that your focus is shifted to the denominator. Second, fixed income securities have limited lives, and the life of the fixed income security is typically also "fixed." Of course, there are complexities with embedded options that can alter (usually shorten) the life of a fixed income security, but fixed income securities generally have a prespecified time to pay cash flows. This has very important implications for valuation of the cash flows. As time passes the value of the claim will change, absent any changing views of the expected cash flows. This gives rise to unique investment opportunities and challenges for fixed income securities (e.g., the importance of carry for identifying expected returns and the complications of modeling the deterministic time-varying risk profile of fixed income securities), all of which we will cover in detail later in this book.

So where do the fixed income securities come from? Entities of various forms require capital to finance their operating and investing activities. The most common entities that issue fixed income securities are (i) governments and quasi-government entities, and (ii) corporations. We will focus on fixed income securities from these two issuers in this book. Governments and corporations from all countries engage in debt financing across both developed and emerging markets. Our focus will be on developed markets, but there will be some discussion of the unique risks and investment opportunities in emerging market debt in Chapter 7. There is also a large set of asset-backed fixed income securities. These are largely repackaging of other fixed income securities into pools where the cash flow rights are reassigned to new fixed income securities. Perhaps the largest securitized market is the government sponsored mortgage-backed securities in the United States. But there are other large pools of securitized assets globally such as covered bonds issued by financial institutions (largely in Europe) and nonagency mortgages. We will have less to say on securitized assets in this book, outside of the prepayment risk premium to be discussed in Chapter 2. However, the security valuation frameworks and portfolio construction considerations we cover for the more common government and corporate fixed income securities can be tailored across the full breadth of fixed income securities.

1.2 HOW BIG ARE FIXED INCOME MARKETS?

Let's start broad when assessing the size of the potential investment opportunity set for the fixed income asset class. Although there are no universally accepted statistics for the true size of fixed income (or indeed equity) markets, the Bank for International Settlements is a commonly used reference for this purpose. Exhibit 1.1 shows the size of global fixed income markets as of December 31, 2020. Clearly, the global fixed income market is enormous, accounting for a little over $123 trillion USD. This estimate is an attempt to capture broadly investible fixed income markets. Ilmanen (2022) notes that the size of global fixed income markets could be closer to $200 trillion if all money market securities and all bank loans were included. Global equity markets, in contrast, were valued at $106 trillion USD as of December 31, 2020.[1] There is clearly a concentration in debt securities in developed markets, but there is an increasing presence of Chinese domiciled issuers over the past decade.

An alternative way to understand global fixed income markets is to assess the relative importance of issuer type. Exhibit 1.2 shows that

[1]SIFMA Capital markets Fact Book (https://www.sifma.org/wp-content/uploads/2021/07/CM-Fact-Book-2021-SIFMA.pdf).

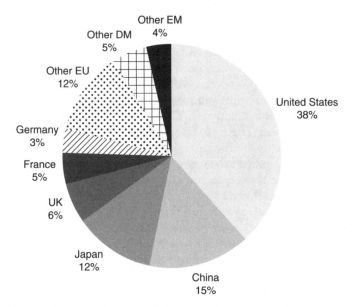

EXHIBIT 1.1   Market capitalization of global fixed income markets as of December 31, 2020. All securities are valued in USD. Fixed income securities are grouped into countries based on the domicile of the issuer and are dependent on source data availability at the country level.
Source: Data from Bank for International Settlements (www.bis.org/statistics).

government entities (includes supranationals and quasi-sovereign issuers) account for a little more than half of total fixed income securities outstanding. Financial institutions (inclusive of asset-backed securities and regular bonds) account for around a third of global fixed income securities, and nonfinancial corporations account for the remainder. This explains our focus on government and corporate fixed income securities, as these account for most global fixed income securities.

The debt securities included in Exhibits 1.1 and 1.2 include domestic debt securities (DDSs) and international debt securities (IDSs). The Bank for International Settlements (BIS) defines DDS as those instruments issued in the local market of the country where the borrower resides, regardless of the currency in which the security is denominated, and IDSs as those instruments outside the local market of the country where the borrower resides. Approximately 80 (20) percent of fixed income securities are DDSs (IDSs) as of December 31, 2020. Correspondingly, our focus will be on domestic fixed income securities, as this reflects the bulk of the fixed income investment opportunity set. This is not to say that international securities are not

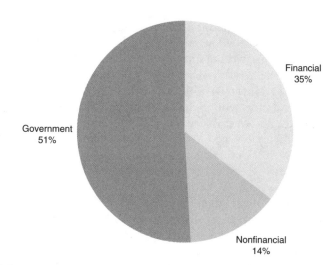

EXHIBIT 1.2 Market capitalization of global fixed income markets as of December 31, 2020. All securities are valued in US dollars. Fixed income securities are grouped into categories based on the nature of the issuing entity.
Source: Data from Bank for International Settlements (www.bis.org/statistics).

relevant. They are, and in Chapter 7 we will discuss hard currency emerging market debt specifically. It is important to remember that although the issuance of debt securities by an issuer in multiple countries (and multiple currencies) does expand the investment opportunity set, these additional securities, while not totally redundant, are usually highly correlated with the domestic security.

A final point to note about the size of the global fixed income market is that the BIS data is based on cash securities (i.e., bonds issued by governments and corporations). In addition to these cash securities, there is an extensive derivatives market covering fixed income. These include (i) interest rate derivatives (futures, options, and swaps) linked to the underlying cash bonds issued by governments (both developed and emerging markets), (ii) derivatives linked to specific securitized assets (e.g., the to be announced [TBA] market for mortgage pass-through securities in the United States), (iii) single-name credit derivatives (credit default swaps), and (iv) index-level credit derivatives (e.g., Markit and iTraxx indices). These markets are also very large, and a key benefit of these derivative markets is the concentration of liquidity into specific issuers and specific issues for a given issuer (although a company typically has only common equity claim outstanding, it may have many bonds outstanding). As we will see in greater detail later in this book (especially Chapter 9 on liquidity), there is oftentimes difficulty in sourcing inventory for a specific fixed income security.

A driver of the limited liquidity in fixed income, especially relative to equity markets, is the breadth of securities to select from for a given issuer. For example, as of November 30, 2021, there were 1,744 bonds in the Global Treasury subindex within the Bloomberg Global Aggregate Index. Of these 1,744 bonds, 267 were issued by the United States and 554 were issued by what is collectively referred to as the G-7 (excluding the United States): Japan (274), Italy (82), Germany (57), the UK (55), France (47), and Canada (39). There are many securities to choose from for each government issuer. A similar concentration in issuance is seen for corporate bonds where there are roughly seven bonds outstanding for each investment-grade-rated corporate issuer. As we'll see in detail in Chapters 5 (6) for government (corporate) fixed income securities, there is considerable redundancy across the multiple issues for a given issuer. Stated differently, bonds issued by the same issuer share a considerable amount of common variation. Investors are spoiled by breadth, and this leads to a bifurcation in liquidity across many redundant securities. Blackrock (2014) has noted the lack of standardization in the corporate bond market as a key driver of liquidity challenges. Although there are institutional reasons for the lack of standardization (e.g., issuance fees for intermediaries, cash flow maturity management from corporate treasury departments), there is limited need for so many securities from an investor perspective. A small number of securities (as few as two or three) can capture most of the return variation that is available to the investor. And this is where the derivative market can be very useful for the fixed income investor: liquidity can be concentrated in a small number of tenors for each issuer. Unfortunately, derivative markets are liquid for many but not all issuers and many but not all key tenors.

We can undertake a more detailed analysis of the investment opportunity set for fixed income investors by looking at the Bloomberg Global Aggregate Index. This is a very broad index commonly used as a policy benchmark by many large institutional asset owners. It contains investment-grade-rated bonds issued in multiple currencies that meet specific liquidity requirements (e.g., par value more than $300 million USD for USD-denominated debt). As of December 31, 2020, the Global Aggregate Index included 26,514 individual bonds amounting to $67.5 trillion USD outstanding. Exhibit 1.3 shows the breakdown of the market capitalization of the Global Aggregate Index. The $67.5 trillion USD is broken down into (i) $35.9 trillion USD for Global Treasury (TSY) securities (includes all investment-grade-rated debt issued by developed market sovereign entities),

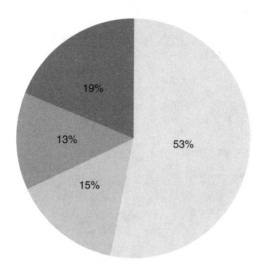

19%

13%

53%

15%

■ TSY ■ GREL ■ SEC ■ CORP

EXHIBIT 1.3 Market capitalization of Bloomberg Global Aggregate Index as of December 31, 2020.
Source: Data from Bloomberg Indices.

(ii) $10.0 trillion USD issued by government-related entities (GREL), (iii) $12.7 trillion USD issued by corporate (CORP) entities (includes all investment-grade-rated debt issued by corporations domiciled in developed markets), and (iv) $8.9 trillion USD of securitized (SEC) debt (the majority of which is mortgage-backed securities from the main US government agencies).

Exhibit 1.4 shows the breakdown of the number of issues contained within the Global Aggregate Index as at December 31, 2020. The 26,514 issues are comprised of (i) 1,681 bonds issued by developed sovereign entities, (ii) 5,828 bonds issued by government related entities, (iii) 13,831 bonds issued by corporate entities, and (iv) 5,174 bonds issued across agency and nonagency asset-backed securities, commercial mortgage-backed securities, and covered bonds. The proportional composition of the Global Aggregate Index looks very different when viewed through the lens of number of instruments; there are fewer government bonds outstanding, but they have a much larger market value per bond, and there are far more corporate bonds outstanding, but they have a much smaller market value per bond. The smaller issue size of corporate bonds is related to the liquidity challenges discussed earlier that we will return to in Chapter 9.

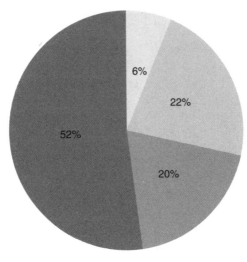

TSY GREL SEC CORP

EXHIBIT 1.4 Composition of Bloomberg Global Aggregate Index as of December 31, 2020.
Source: Data from Bloomberg Indices.

1.3 WHAT DOES IT MEAN TO BE SYSTEMATIC?

We are talking about *systematic* active investing in fixed income markets. Now that we have a handle on fixed income markets, we need to agree on what it means to be *systematic* in your investment approach. This is challenging. A systematic investor cannot be defined as an investor who has a quantitative approach. After all, as we will see later in this chapter, all investors in fixed income markets need to be able to understand (if not compute) derivatives (I mean duration and convexity, which we will cover in detail later in this chapter), which would seem to qualify most fixed income investors as quantitatively able. So, what then distinguishes a systematic investor? And if you are not a systematic investor, then what are you? These are related questions, and to help answer these questions I will make use of a simple visual (Exhibit 1.5) that is adapted from an AQR Alternative Thinking (2017) publication titled "Systematic vs Discretionary."

Exhibit 1.5 identifies both differences and similarities between systematic and discretionary approaches. While it can be natural to think of investment approaches as mutually exclusive, this would be a disservice to both approaches. So, let's first emphasize what is, and must be, common across the investment approaches. Both systematic and discretionary investors are

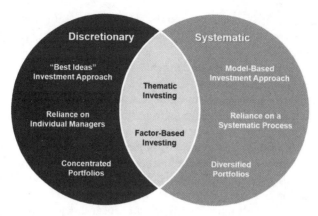

EXHIBIT 1.5 A comparison of systematic and discretionary investment approaches. *Source:* Data from AQR (2017). Systematic vs Discretionary. Alternative Thinking Quarterly, Q3 2017.

active investors. That means they are both willing to entertain that the market is not completely efficient with respect to certain value-relevant information, and that they have the investment acumen to identify that information and trade upon it profitably. It may also mean that they believe that markets are efficient but that there are opportunities to provide liquidity to the market to take advantage of price-taker traders (e.g., avoiding bad selling practices from rating downgrades or other index exclusions, and/or actively seeking out new issue concessions).

Both systematic and discretionary active investors must have a sound understanding of the sources of returns and risks within the fixed income market. Again, almost by definition, systematic and discretionary investors must share some common beliefs about the determinants of fixed income security returns. Indeed, I have often been told over the years that what we say and do, as systematic fixed investors, at a high level, sounds very familiar to a discretionary investment approach. A few years ago, I gave a presentation in front of a large internal team of fixed investment professionals at a large sovereign wealth fund, and I followed a senior investment professional from a large traditional (discretionary) fixed income asset manager. The head of the internal fixed income team spoke to me after the event and commented, "You sound very similar to the traditional (discretionary) manager, yet your final portfolios are quite different." It is that difference that this book seeks to identify and promote the diversifying potential of. A good systematic process should be trying to capture the best bits of a fundamentally driven discretionary approach and apply that in a highly diversified manner.

As we will see in Chapter 2, understanding risk-free yields and spreads is at the heart of fixed income investing. This is true for both the systematic and discretionary investor. A systematic investor does not have access to a secret sauce allowing them privileged access to the data-generating process that gives rise to asset returns. If only that were true! This book will lay out a fundamental framework to understand the risks and returns for the most common fixed income securities. Both discretionary and systematic fixed investors are likely to share common beliefs on this fundamental framework. The intersection of the Venn diagram in Exhibit 1.5 is a nod to this similarity in core investment beliefs, noting that the Venn diagram is not drawn to scale (if it were, the common area would be much larger, as I think the investment approaches are more similar to each other than they are different).

So, what then is the difference between systematic and discretionary investment approaches? I believe the primary differences are the reliance on individuals (discretionary) rather than a repeatable process (systematic), and the reliance on an investment narrative/story (discretionary), rather than an investment model (systematic). These differences may sound superficial at first glance, but they are what distinguishes a systematic process from a discretionary approach. The "narrative" in a systematic investment process is a set of measurable characteristics capturing fixed income assets that have the potential to generate higher excess returns. For fixed income this will include measures of value, quality, carry, and momentum (and other measures). These characteristics will be measured across a wide set of fixed income securities (the hundreds of government bonds and thousands of corporate bonds discussed earlier in this chapter). The "narrative" in a discretionary investment process will typically reflect a combination of top-down macro views (on inflation, growth, etc.) and detailed bottom-up credit analysis on specific issuers. The implicit belief is that this deeper contextual analysis is the source of investment value add. Both approaches have their merits (breadth for systematic and depth for discretionary).

The systematic approach does not rely on any one individual on a day-to-day basis to make trading decisions. Trade lists are generated as the result of a systematic process. That is not to say individuals do not look at the trade list. They do, just that the role of the individual is to confirm the integrity of the data and ensure that there are not any unmodeled news or risks that would negate the purpose of the intended trade (e.g., your systematically generated buy list includes a bond from a corporate issuer for which overnight, there was news of a leveraged buyout or some other corporate action). In those cases, there is a clear role for human intervention to take risk off the table in a controlled manner. Indeed, these interventions can also be built in a somewhat systematic manner. In contrast, the discretionary approach leans heavily and regularly on the lead portfolio manager. That individual is the holder of investment decision rights, and their narrative is inherently less objective than a prespecified systematic process. That approach has the potential benefit of responsiveness to changing market conditions and changing drivers of fixed income returns. However, it comes with the risk of individual biases that may be the root source of investment opportunities to start with. The investment approaches are different in their implementation of what I think are reasonably similar core investment beliefs/narratives.

The final portfolios are very different in expected ways. A more diversified portfolio typically means (i) more line items in the final portfolio (this characteristic is common for systematic portfolios), and (ii) lower tracking error as a direct consequence of the more diversified portfolio. This does mean that a discretionary fixed manager has the potential to generate higher excess returns, but that comes with additional risk. What ultimately matters for asset owners is the excess return generated per unit of active risk (a ratio of return to risk is called a Sharpe ratio or an information ratio, depending on the return that is examined: excess of cash returns is a Sharpe ratio, and excess of beta/benchmark returns is an information ratio). There is minimal evidence to suggest the information ratios are different across systematic or discretionary managers (for equity markets, AQR 2017, note that while the excess of benchmark returns are similar for systematic and discretionary managers, discretionary managers have a higher tracking error leading to slightly lower information ratios). We will discuss the Sharpe ratios and information ratios of incumbent active fixed income managers in detail in Chapter 4.

It is also important to remember that not all systematic fixed income managers will be the same. Just as not all discretionary managers are expected to hold similar portfolios, there is no reason that all systematic managers will hold the same portfolio. Indeed, research in equity markets has shown that the average pairwise correlation between excess returns for systematic active equity managers is as low as the average pairwise correlation between excess returns for discretionary active equity managers (see e.g., Lakonishok and Swaminathan 2010, and AQR 2017). As we work through the systematic fixed income framework developed in this book, hopefully the breadth of choices that must be made to build a final portfolio will become clear. Variations in those choices across asset managers will lead to meaningful differences in portfolio outcomes. At the end of the day, what matters most to an asset owner is a well-implemented (read liquidity and risk aware) portfolio that targets exposure to your investment hypothesis (read narrative for the discretionary manager or investment model for the systematic manager). It is those signals and implementation details that we will cover in detail in later chapters.

A word of caution is useful for the term *discretionary*. In a pure sense, all active investors are discretionary. A systematic investment approach requires many decisions to be made from everything to selecting data vendors to signal construction, signal weighting choices, various liquidity, and risk management choices, and so forth. All these decisions are discretionary in that a human (or group of humans) must make them. What is different is the stage of the investment process at which those decisions are made. A systematic investor is trying to make discretionary decisions at the start of the investment process. Think of these as strategic decisions that are then codified into a repeatable and scalable investment process.

A recipe for a systematic investment approach might look like the list that follows. I first heard this described when working at Barclays Global Investors (Richard Grinold was a key proponent) and I used this framework to summarize a broad literature on accounting-based anomalies in the equity market back in 2010 (see Richardson, Tuna, and Wysocki 2010):

a. Credible hypothesis: Does your investment idea pass a "sniff test"? What is it about your idea that would lead to future excess returns? Why does the market price not already reflect this information? What informational inefficiency or liquidity provision are you targeting? This is a subjective conceptual discussion. To the extent that there is discretion in the systematic investment process, this is the stage where it is most important.

b. Robust predictive power: Take your investment idea to the data and assess whether it robustly predicts future returns. This empirical exercise should look for as many possible markets to test the idea (developed and emerging markets, different time periods, other related asset classes, etc.).

c. Test the mechanism: Flesh out the implications of the investment hypothesis. If your measure is related to mispricing, then look for evidence beyond simple return correlations. If the investment idea is attributable to market participants failing to fully utilize information that is useful for forecasting fundamentals (e.g., inflation or growth for government bonds or free cash flows for corporate bonds) then test whether your "signal" can forecast future fundamentals in addition to future returns. Go one step further and assess whether capital market participants who are in the business of forecasting these fundamentals make systematic forecasting errors with respect to your information. These non-return-based tests add substantial conviction to the efficacy of your investment idea. In-sample fitting of returns (data mining) is a serious risk. Although many have criticized the lack of out-of-sample results in finance and advocate for multiple-testing adjusted test statistics, a simple protection for this risk is robust testing of the underlying economic mechanism.

d. Implementation: Test whether your investment idea survives the various implementation challenges. This would include expected transaction costs, potential market impact, inability to source inventory at time of trade, risk-based position limits, and so forth. Many ideas that look good on paper are too costly to implement in practice.

e. Additivity: Is your investment idea additive to what is already in the portfolio? Although there is a path dependency here to be handled (i.e., the first signal would seem to get a free pass by this criteria) this is critically important, as what matters is the active risk and return at the final portfolio level. If you keep adding highly correlated signals, you will end up with a very unbalanced portfolio.

There are clearly some necessary ingredients for a systematic investment approach to be adopted. Most notable is the need for reliable data. All the aforementioned testing procedures require data. That data needs to exist and needs to be point-in-time (i.e., available historically at the same time that market participants had access to it) and of reliable quality, so any hypothetical portfolio (back-test) is at least partially informative of what you may expect to experience in the future. One other key aspect for the success of systematic investing is liquidity in the markets in which the assets trade (both primary and secondary markets). There are fixed income markets (e.g., municipal bond markets and cash mortgage-backed securities) that are inherently ill suited for standard systematic investment processes. There is little point building an investment infrastructure to generate trade lists for assets that do not trade after issuance or that trade very infrequently. Trading as a liquidity taker in fixed income markets can be very costly, especially relative to the excess return potential, so liquidity in the market is almost a necessary condition to utilize a systematic investment approach. We will discuss the importance of liquidity provision for the successful implantation of systematic fixed income portfolios in Chapter 9.

How common are systematic investment approaches within the fixed income asset class? It is very difficult, if not impossible, to answer this question precisely. We can look at regular databases that store information about investment vehicles. Exhibit 1.6 shows the size and breakdown of institutional systematic fixed income investment vehicles as at December 31, 2020. To construct this chart various choices are made. Investment vehicles are long-only and fixed income benchmarked and the definition of *systematic* is made subjectively based on an understanding of which asset managers have described themselves as having a systematic approach to their investment philosophy. Using this subjective criteria and fund data from eVestment, the total size of the systematic fixed income investing universe is about $120

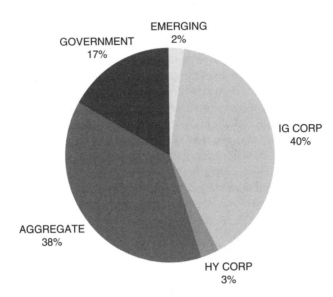

EXHIBIT 1.6   The size of the systematic fixed income investing universe.
Source: Data from eVestment.

billion USD. That is tiny relative to the size of the overall fixed income universe. But this total has grown significantly over recent years, adding more
than $50 billion in the past five years. Exhibit 1.6 obviously misses a con-
siderable portion of actively managed systematic fixed income assets. For
example, there could be internal pools of capital run systematically by asset
owners, and there could be internal systematic tools used to complement
traditional discretionary approaches. However, even including conservative
estimates for the potential additional systematic fixed income approaches,
systematic approaches are in the minority. Exhibit 1.6 notes that corporate
strategies (both investment-grade and high-yield) account for roughly half
of systematic fixed income assets and government bond or aggregate index
mandates account for the rest. As we will see throughout this book, government and corporate bonds are the two areas in which a systematic approach
is most likely to succeed: there is sufficient data access and market liquidity.
    What does the small size of actively managed systematic fixed income
funds mean? I am a firm believer in the notion of equilibrium. The fact that
something does not exist, or exists only at small scale, may speak to the
inefficiency of that practice. That is certainly a possible interpretation of the
small scale of active systematic fixed income investing. However, there is
another, more optimistic interpretation. It is difficult to successfully implement a systematic approach in fixed income, and it is challenging to convince

asset owners of the efficacy of this alternative investment approach. I am a firm believer in this optimistic interpretation. Indeed, one can view this book as a continued attempt to beat the drum of the legitimacy of systematic fixed income investing. This is a challenge to be embraced by asset managers and asset owners alike. Asset managers, and to some extent asset owners assessing whether, and how, to develop internal systematic capabilities, need to overcome inertia and cultural frictions. There is natural skepticism of new approaches, and incumbents are naturally averse to new things that threaten their existence. Of course, just because something is new does not mean it is better. Fixed income, and especially credit sensitive assets like corporate bonds, face considerable liquidity challenges and security idiosyncrasies that may make it too difficult to be successful as a systematic investor. So, a healthy dose of self-doubt is necessary, and we will cover these data and liquidity challenges in detail in Chapters 6 and 9. But, this introspection on investment challenges should be applied uniformly across all active fixed income investors. After all, concerns about liquidity, the ability to trade into and out of assets, and confidence in your ability to measure expected returns for idiosyncratic assets are ultimately a data challenge. And data is central to any investment process, whether it is systematic or discretionary.

1.4 WHICH FIXED INCOME MARKETS WILL THIS BOOK FOCUS ON?

The focus in this book will be on what I call public fixed income markets. This means constituents of the regular parent indices that most large asset owners use for their fixed income allocations. Versions of the Aggregate Index (Global, US, or European) will capture the breadth of investment-grade-rated fixed income assets that we will focus on. Section 1.2 of this chapter laid out the key components of the Global Aggregate Index, and our focus will be on the government and corporate sectors.

In addition, we will look at emerging market debt in Chapter 7. Our focus there will be mostly on hard currency (USD) debt issued by sovereign and quasi-sovereign entities. We will discuss the huge growth in local currency emerging market debt, but the return drivers of emerging government local currency debt is similar to that of developed government local currency debt, so we will focus our discussion of local currency debt on the differences across developed and emerging markets. We will have little to say about emerging market corporate debt, because the data quality and market liquidity is limited in this market, and consistent with the discussion in Section 1.3, a systematic approach in the emerging market corporate space is more challenging from an operational perspective.

High-yield corporate bonds are also important to cover. The distinction between investment-grade (IG) and high-yield (HY) rated corporate issuers is somewhat arbitrary. The returns data generating process for IG-rated corporate issuers is more similar than dissimilar to HY-rated corporate issuers. In Chapter 6, when we talk about investment frameworks for credit sensitive assets, we will emphasize the similarities across IG and HY corporates, and, where necessary, we note differences in return drivers. Similarly, in Chapter 9 when we discuss trading and liquidity considerations for fixed income securities, we will discuss trading differences in primary and secondary markets for IG- and HY-rated corporate bonds (for both North America and Europe) and the unique challenges and opportunities that liquidity provision creates for a systematic investor.

The leveraged loan market we will not cover in detail in this book. Leveraged loans are a type of syndicated loan issued by corporations that are high-yield-rated (often as part of corporate merger activity or buyout financing). These loans trade on secondary markets with extended settlement terms that make them less suitable for any investment vehicle that has frequent dealing. The leverage loan market is about $1.6 trillion USD as at December 31, 2020.[2] The return drivers of loans are similar to that of corporate bonds, so it is not any lack of understanding of return drivers that makes loans less suitable for a systematic investment process. It is a combination of extended settlement, limited secondary market liquidity, and challenges in sourcing reliable data for the private companies that issue loans that makes it challenging for systematic approaches to be used in the leveraged loan market. But these challenges also create opportunities as it less likely to be a crowded area.

Finally, this book will have little to say about the growing private debt markets. Global private debt markets have grown from essentially nothing in the early 2000s to nearly $1 trillion USD as of December 31, 2020 (see, e.g., JP Morgan 2021) covering mezzanine financing, direct lending, and distressed/special situations. Again, there is nothing structural about the return generating process of private markets that makes a systematic investment approach unsuitable. It is the data and operational challenges that make it difficult. Private markets are notorious for a lack of secondary market liquidity, and in the case of private debt it can be very difficult to source data that can be used in a consistent and reliable way across investment opportunities. As with leveraged loans, these challenges also present opportunities for those with data and liquidity access.

---

[2]SIFMA (https://www.sifma.org/wp-content/uploads/2019/03/Leverage-Loans-Fact-Sheet.pdf).

1.5 COMMONLY USED FIXED INCOME ANALYTICS

As discussed at the start of this chapter, fixed income security valuation focuses on the denominator. Let us work with a simple example to illustrate some of the key concepts related to the language of fixed income security pricing. We will work with a simple $100 par value 10-year maturity coupon bearing sovereign bond. The bond pays 2 percent annual coupon every six months (so effectively 1 percent compounded every six months). It is issued on January 1, 2022. Exhibit 1.7 illustrates the cash flow profile of this bond. We can write the price at time of issue for this bond as follows:

$$P = \frac{1}{(1+r)^1} + \frac{1}{(1+r)^2} + \frac{1}{(1+r)^3} + \ldots + \frac{101}{(1+r)^{20}} \quad (1.2)$$

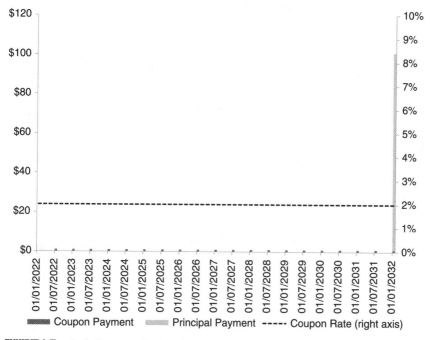

EXHIBIT 1.7 Cash flow profile of a $100 10-year coupon bond issued on January 1, 2022, with a 2 percent coupon rate paid semi-annually.

There is an inverse relation between price and discount rate, r. This is a highly nonlinear equation and captures the key element of fixed income investing: what is your view on r? Even working with an assumed flat term structure of discount rates (which we will loosen in Chapter 2 and beyond) it is easy to see that the impact of a change in r on price (P) will depend critically on the maturity profile of the cash flows.

Fixed income market participants tend to use the label *yield* to describe the discount rate for valuing fixed income securities. The prevailing yield can be thought of as an indicator of the expected return for a given fixed income security. It tells you the return an investor will receive for buying and holding the fixed income security to maturity, assuming no capital losses from forced selling or default prior to maturity and assuming the yield is the also the reinvestment rate for any coupons. So, what do yields look like for standard fixed income securities? Exhibit 1.8 shows the yield to worst (this is simply a measure of yield to maturity that adjusts for any embedded optionality or other contractual features that shortens the expected life of the fixed income security) for the Bloomberg Global Aggregate Index (bold line) as well as the four primary subindices (TSY, GREL, SEC, and CORP) over the 2001–2020 period.

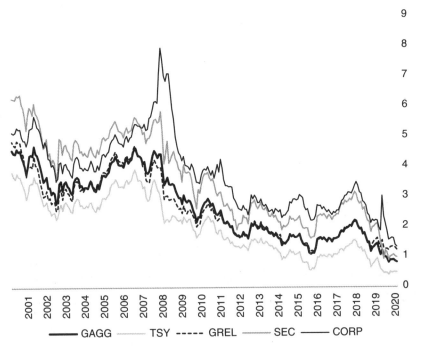

EXHIBIT 1.8   Yield to worst of Bloomberg Global Aggregate Index and subindices over the 20-year period ending December 31, 2020.
Source: Data from Bloomberg Indices.

There is a clear downward trend in yields, especially over the past decade. This downward trend is global in nature and yields are now at some of the lowest levels ever. That is a strong statement to make, but as can be seen in Exhibit 1.9, yields on government bonds today are at the lowest levels they have ever been (going back to the 1300s). The data for this exhibit comes from the Global Financial Database, and I have selected representative bonds through time as a proxy for the center of global financial markets. Over the past 700 years, the financial center of the world has passed from Italy to the Netherlands to England to the United States. Data includes the Consolidated Bonds of Genoa from 1304 to 1408, the Prestiti of Venice from 1408 to 1500, the Juros of Spain from 1504 to 1519, the Juros of Italy from 1520 to 1598, government bonds of the Netherlands from 1606 to 1699, English bonds, primarily the British Consol from 1700 to 1918 and United States 10-year Treasury bonds from 1918 to 2020. The most notable aspect of Exhibit 1.9 is the sharp decline in government bond yields over the most recent period. When market observers say interest rates are low, they aren't wrong! Of course, the data quality back in time, and any strict comparability through time, is questionable, but the pattern of historically low yields today is undeniable. Indeed, as at December 31, 2020, some 4,251 bonds out of the 26,514 bonds included in the Bloomberg Global Aggregate Index traded at negative yields. Collectively these bonds accounted for $16.1 trillion USD out of the total $67.5 trillion USD market capitalization of the entire index. These bonds were issued by sovereigns

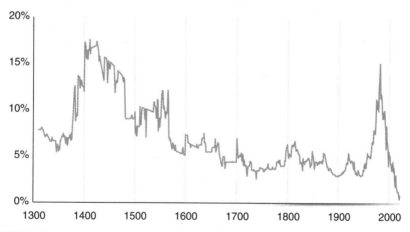

EXHIBIT 1.9 Proxy government bond yields from 1304 to 2020.
Source: Global Financial Database (https://globalfinancialdata.com/7-centuries-of-government-bond-yields).

(mostly) and corporates around the world (Japan, Germany, and France accounted for 30, 15, and 15 percent, respectively). Low, and negative, yields are a topic we will discuss in Chapters 2 and 3 about the strategic and tactical case for allocating to fixed income securities.

The concept of duration formalizes the relation between changes in prices and discount rates by taking the first-order derivative of Equation 1.2. Mathematically this can be written as $-\frac{dP(r)}{dr}\frac{1}{P}$. This simply means how does the price of the bond change when there is a change in the discount rate. The negative sign is convention: even though the relation between prices and discount rates is negative duration is typically quoted in positive units. The second multiplication, $\frac{1}{P}$, often causes confusion when you first see duration written mathematically. It just means that duration is measured for a bond at a given price (i.e., a given starting yield). The same set of cash flows will have a different duration depending on the starting yield. We will return to this point later in this chapter.

An equivalent way to capture the intuition of duration is a dollar weighting of the cash flows over the life of the fixed income security. All else equal, bonds with a longer time to maturity – and hence the more the cash flows are further into the future – have higher duration. This intuition is very powerful to quickly understand other deterministic differences in duration based on bond characteristics. Bonds with a higher coupon rate have a shorter duration (holding maturity fixed). Conversely, bonds with low coupons have a longer duration. There is a limit for the value of duration: a zero-coupon bond has a duration equal to its maturity.

Duration is a powerful summary statistic used to describe the properties of fixed income securities. It is worthwhile to understand exactly why. Duration can be close to a sufficient statistic for describing the first-order impact of changes in yields (interest rates) on prices of fixed income assets. Let us continue with our example of a 10-year coupon bond from earlier in this chapter. We can compute the duration of this bond when issued at par as 9.16 years. This duration of 9.16 means that for a 1 percent change in yields (discount rates) the price of the bond would change by 9.16 percent (or $9.16 if this change in yields was observed in the year after issuance at par). This implied change in price is, however, an approximation. While it is very useful for small changes in yields, duration's efficacy as a summary measure of interest rate sensitivity is lessened for bonds that exhibit greater convexity. Oh dear, we have another term to grapple with.

Convexity is another commonly used analytic to describe the sensitivity of fixed income security prices to interest rates. Mathematically, it can be written as $-\frac{d^2P(r)}{dr^2}\frac{1}{P}$. This is simply the second-order derivative reflecting how prices change for a given change in yields (discount rates). Duration was the first-order derivative, so you can think of convexity as the first-order derivative of how duration changes for a given a change in yields. This is perhaps easiest visualized. Exhibit 1.10 shows the relation between price and yield for our 10-year bond. The solid black line computes the precise value of our bond's cash flows for yield levels that vary from between 0 and 4 percent. The solid black point corresponds to a price of 100 and yield of 2 percent consistent with a 2 percent coupon bond issued at par. Using duration of 9.16 years we can approximate the value of our bond for all yield values between 0 to 4 percent. To do this we simply compute the price of the bond as the starting price ($100) plus the change in yield multiplied by −1 times duration (9.16). This is shown as the solid gray line in Exhibit 1.10. It should be readily clear that this is also a point of tangency on the curve capturing the relation between price and yield (this is exactly what a first derivative captures). It is also clear that for small changes in yields the

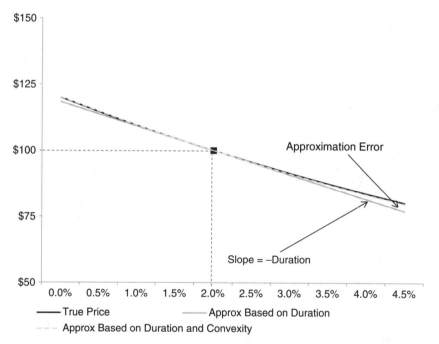

EXHIBIT 1.10 Relation between price and yield for a $100 10-year coupon bond issued on January 1, 2022, with a 2 percent coupon rate paid semi-annually. The solid black line reflects the actual price at all yield levels between 0 and 4 percent. The solid blue line reflects the approximation using duration alone. The dashed green line reflects the approximation using duration and convexity.

distance between the solid gray line and the solid black line are quite small. This is generally true for all fixed income securities. The quality of the approximation is lower for large changes in yields and for fixed income securities with greater convexity. We can easily repeat our approximation using knowledge of both duration and convexity. This is shown on Exhibit 1.10 as the dashed gray line and the approximation error is now very small across all possible values for yield. Again, this should not be surprising as that is exactly what a second derivative (convexity) is capturing. Convexity is not going to be the focus of this book as we will be considering primarily government bonds and corporate bonds that generally do not have substantial curvature in their relation between prices and yields.

We are now sufficiently well armed (and dangerous) to continue our exploration into fixed income investing. Before we go further, it is useful to be aware of the multiple ways in which duration measures are utilized. Fixed income securities embody at least two sources of risk: (i) time value of money considerations inclusive of refinancing/rollover risks, and (ii) spread risk reflecting the possibility that your contractually specified cash flows may not materialize (you may get paid sooner or later than you expected, or in some cases not at all). We can therefore generalize our fixed income pricing equation as follows:

$$P = \frac{1}{(1+y+s)^1} + \frac{1}{(1+y+s)^2} + \frac{1}{(1+y+s)^3} + \dots + \frac{101}{(1+y+s)^{20}} \quad (1.3)$$

We have now decomposed the discount rate to have two components: (i) y, reflecting the yield for a riskless security, and (ii) s, reflecting a spread for the additional risks of nonpayment. Equation (1.3) assumes no term structure associated with either yields or spreads. Our duration measures can therefore be either, $-\frac{dP(y,s)}{dy}\frac{1}{P}$, or $-\frac{dP(y,s)}{ds}\frac{1}{P}$. The first measure is typically called *effective (modified) duration* and captures the change in risk-free interest rates (yields) on fixed income prices. The second measure is typically called *spread duration* and captures the change in (credit) spreads on fixed income prices. Both are partial derivatives that consider how changes in y or s affect price independent of how the change in y or s may affect each other. To further complicate matters, there is a term structure for both y and s. Thus, there can be a multitude of duration measures (reflecting risk-free discount rates or spreads at different maturity points). We never said fixed income investing would be easy! But it is useful to note that for many of the government and corporate bonds that we examine in this book, we can go a long way in understanding return variation by utilizing a single yield or spread sensitivity.

Now that we have a basic understanding of duration it is useful to consider how duration has changed over time for the broad fixed income markets. Exhibit 1.11 shows the maturity profile of the Bloomberg Global Aggregate Index (bold line) as well as the four primary subindices (TSY, GREL, SEC, and CORP) over the 2001–2020 period. Except for securitized assets, there has been a consistent trend of longer dated bond issuance. This is partly attributable to the prevailing lower interest rates over the past decade. Combining that longer dated issuance with lower yields there is an even greater effect on duration (all else equal, lower yields imply a more negative relation between price and yield, and hence longer duration). Indeed, we see that clearly in Exhibit 1.12.

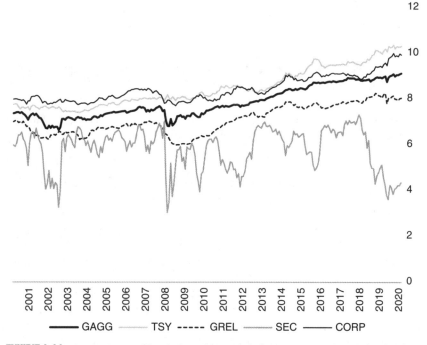

EXHIBIT 1.11 Maturity profile of Bloomberg Global Aggregate Index and subindices over the 20-year period ending December 31, 2020.
Source: Data from Bloomberg Indices.

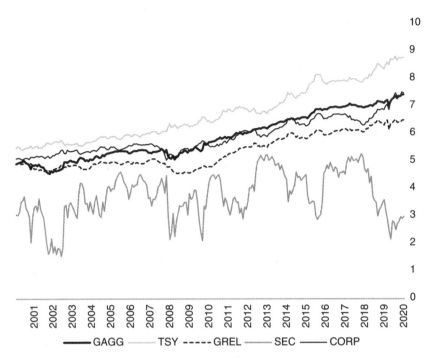

EXHIBIT 1.12   Duration profile of Bloomberg Global Aggregate Index and subindices over the 20-year period ending December 31, 2020.
Source: Data from Bloomberg Indices.

This evolution of the duration profile of fixed income securities is very important for asset owners. All else equal, any change in interest rates will have a greater effect on the prices of fixed income securities. In the current low yield environment, there is heightened concern about the prospect of rising interest rates and the impact of expected interest rate rises on longer-term yields and hence fixed income prices. Before rushing to any tactical asset allocations decisions at this point, Exhibit 1.12 is simply a cautionary reminder of how small changes in interest rates may have an outsized impact on the value of our fixed income allocation. In Chapter 2 we will discuss determinants of long-term yields, and we will then be in a better position to make strategic and tactical recommendations for the fixed income asset class.

1.6   OTHER FIXED INCOME CONSIDERATIONS

We have a few more ancillary topics to cover before we can move into the details of systematic fixed income investing.

1.6.1 Currency and Hedging

Most fixed income indices include bonds that are issued in multiple currencies. This can be due to an issuer opting to issue multiple bonds in different currencies or to the global nature of the index that includes issuers domiciled in different countries, who issue bonds in their local currencies. As with equity investment decisions, the asset owner needs to decide if they want the additional volatility of currency movements in their fixed income portfolio. The decision for fixed income investors is even more important, as the relative volatility of currency movements can dominate the volatility of the underlying fixed income asset. The perspective of this book is to operate with currency hedging in place. This ensures that active risk-taking decisions of fixed income securities are driven by investment views of the issuer and the specific issue without regard for the currency in which the bond is issued. A key benefit of this approach is delineating returns sources and allowing for specific investment views on (i) interest rates for country A relative to country B, and (ii) currency of country A relative to currency of country B. If you work with unhedged returns you are combining those views together and you are forced to have common views across the interest rate and currency portion of the fixed income security. It is better to separate them, and then you can take active currency views using currency forward contracts.

1.6.2 Home Bias

Over the years of managing fixed income portfolios, the extent of home bias in strategic fixed income allocations from asset owners I always found puzzling. Although asset owners make small allocations to emerging market debt and high-yield corporate debt from outside their local area, as a general rule, they have core fixed income policy benchmarks tied to their local geographies. For example, asset owners based in Australia will benchmark their core fixed income holdings to the Australian version of the Aggregate Index. Similar patterns are observed for North American- and European-based asset owners who benchmark their core fixed income holdings to the European and US versions of the Aggregate Index, respectively.

Exhibits 1.13 and 1.14 show this striking home bias. Using data from eVestment, the charts show the breakdown in the domicile of fund assets for two broad categories of core fixed income funds. First, in Exhibit 1.13 I show the breakdown in the approximately $1.9 trillion USD managed by nearly 300 individual funds benchmarked to the US Aggregate Index. Fully 96 percent of these funds are domiciled in the United States. Examination of the Core Plus category also reveals a similar extent of home bias (96 percent

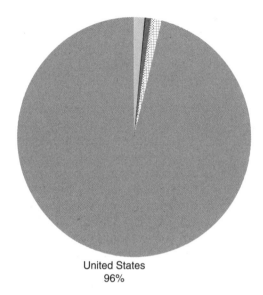

EXHIBIT 1.13   Domicile breakdown of institutional funds benchmarked to the US Aggregate Index.
Source: Data from eVestment.

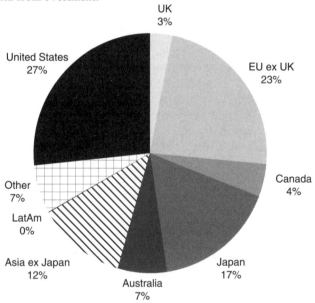

EXHIBIT 1.14   Domicile breakdown of institutional funds benchmarked to the Global Aggregate Index.
Source: Data from eVestment.

of Core Plus funds are also domiciled in the United States). Home bias is pervasive. In contrast, of the roughly $400 billion USD managed by slightly more than 100 funds benchmarked to the Global Aggregate Index, we see a far more diversified set of funds domicile. Global fixed income allocations are also less common.

There can be legitimate reasons for home bias. Core fixed income allocations are often an explicit liability hedge or economic hedge. In the case of a liability hedge, the cash flow profile inclusive of currency may be the preferred path. In that case, home bias is consistent with achieving that asset-liability match. If the purpose of the core fixed income allocation is an economic hedge, then ensuring the asset side of the asset owner's portfolio faces similar economic risks, thus it may also be optimal to exhibit some degree of home bias. What surprises me is the extent of the home bias. You see this in the data and across hundreds of client meetings over the years.

The key consideration for asset owners here is the potential loss of international diversification. It is true that the benefit of international diversification has waned over time as the financial system has become more interconnected (international supply chains connecting ever more larger corporations and deeply interlinked financial markets and capital flows connecting market participants globally), leading to increased correlations in government and corporate bonds across countries over time. However, it is still the case that international fixed income allocations across government and corporate bonds is diversifying, because shocks to economic growth and inflation are not perfectly correlated across markets. These diversification benefits are stronger when adding emerging markets into the mix and are stronger for corporate bonds than they are for government bonds. Home bias comes with the opportunity cost of lost diversification. Be sure to accept that home bias knowingly.

1.6.3 Active Share

A final point to close out Chapter 1 is the topic of Active Share. Active Share was first introduced by Cremers and Petajisto (2009); it measures the percentage of holdings in a manager's portfolio that differs from the benchmark. The claim is that portfolios that look very close to the benchmark are insufficiently active ("benchmark huggers"). There has been considerable debate on the usefulness of Active Share as a summary statistic for investors (see e.g., Frazzini, Friedman, and Pomorski 2016). I will not enter that debate, but rather make a simpler point that Active Share really is not relevant for corporate bond portfolios. Many corporate bonds do not have sufficient liquidity to be included in many portfolios. Indeed, standard exchange-traded funds (ETFs) that are designed to track IG or HY indices may contain only half the corporate bonds in the index been tracked. These ETFs can very closely track the index despite having what would be considered a very high Active Share. Corporate bonds are a good example of an asset class where there can be close substitutes (e.g., corporate issuers may issue multiple bonds) and hence simply counting differences in portfolio weights with no regard for the different risk contributions across bonds is quite naïve. Formal measures of tracking error are strictly superior to quantify the active risk taken in a portfolio. We will discuss measures of risk and tracking error for corporate bond portfolios in Chapter 8.

REFERENCES

AQR. (2017). Systematic vs. discretionary. *Alternative Thinking Quarterly* Q3.

BlackRock Investment Institute. (2014). The liquidity challenge (July 2).

Cremers, M. and A. Petajisto. (2009). How active is your fund manager? A new measure that predicts performance. *Review of Financial Studies*, 22, 3329–3365.

Frazinni, A., J. Friedman, and L. Pomorski. (2016). Deactivating active share. *Financial Analysts Journal*, 72, 1–8.

Ilmanen, I. (2022). *Investing Amid Low Expected Returns*. Wiley.

JP Morgan. (2021). Crisis Watch XLV: Private credit uncovered. Global Credit Research Note.

Lakonishok, J. and B. Swaminathan. (2010). Quantitative vs fundamental. *Canadian Investment Review*.

Richardson, S., I. Tuna, and P. Wysocki. (2010). Accounting anomalies and fundamental analysis: A review of recent research advances. *Journal of Accounting and Economics*, 50, 410–454.

CHAPTER 2

Fixed Income – Strategic Asset Allocation

OVERVIEW

This chapter undertakes a detailed examination of the return properties of fixed income securities. We start with an additive decomposition of total returns into "rates" and "spread" components. The influence of interest rates on fixed income securities is large and it pervades all fixed income securities. We will see the importance of rates declines when there is greater risk of nonpayment of the cash flows. This helps us structure our thinking for later chapters when we build a framework to forecast returns of fixed income securities: Exactly what component of returns should we focus on? We will then document the variety of betas (traditional market risk premia) that are commonly accessible in fixed income markets and show how they help diversify in the context of strategic asset allocation decisions. We will explain how and why fixed income allocations should be a core part of asset owner portfolios. This will involve a detailed discussion of yields and determinants of yields, setting up the stage for our next chapter on tactical allocations within fixed income.

2.1 WHAT ARE THE KEY DRIVERS OF FIXED INCOME SECURITY RETURNS?

In Chapter 1 we introduced the terms *yield* and *duration*. We will now turn to utilizing these measures to decompose the total returns to fixed income securities. We will start with the Bloomberg Global Aggregate Index and we will decompose the total returns of the Global Treasury, Global Government Related, Global Corporate, and Global Securitized subsectors within the Global Aggregate Index. We will also look at the total returns of the Bloomberg Global High Yield Index and the Bloomberg Emerging Market USD Aggregate Index. This will give us the opportunity to look at a broad set of fixed income securities where there is considerable variation in the credit risk (i.e., possibility of nonpayment of cash flows) of issuers. We will start with total returns for each category of issuers. Exhibit 2.1 shows the arithmetic annualized average returns and standard deviations for the six respective categories for the 2000–2020 period. The categories are sorted based on increasing credit risk, hence Global High Yield (GHY) is to the right. Return realizations are sample period dependent, so we are not going to emphasize the average returns too much for this single 20-year period. That said, risk-adjusted returns (as indicated by the Sharpe ratio, which is the ratio of the annualized average returns to the annualized standard deviation of returns) are very impressive. The purpose here is to understand the importance of components of returns.

EXHIBIT 2.1 Total returns (annualized averages and standard deviation) for Global Treasury, Global Government Related, Global Securitized, Global Corporates, Emerging Market USD Aggregate, and Global High Yield indices. Returns are excess of cash (US T-Bills).

	TSY	GREL	SEC	CORP	EM-USD	GHY
Average	4.59	4.71	4.47	5.52	6.94	7.06
Std. Dev.	6.49	5.41	3.33	6.49	9.02	10.14
Sharpe ratio	0.71	0.87	1.34	0.85	0.77	0.70

Source: Bloomberg Indices.

Our next step is to decompose total returns into a component attributable to movements in yields (let's call this the "rates" portion, $Return_{RATES}$) and a residual component that captures everything else such as liquidity risk and spread risk (let's call this the "spread" portion, $Return_{SPREAD}$). We will first quantify $Return_{RATES}$. An easy way to conceptualize the rates component of returns is to think of "duration." When yields move by a certain amount, multiplying that yield change by $-1 \times$ duration will give an approximation of the rates component of returns. As discussed in Chapter 1, this is an approximation, because it assumes a uniform change in yields (discount rates) across all bond cash flows that need to be discounted. More generally, duration can be measured at multiple tenor points. This gives rise to a term structure of duration measures also referred to as *key rate durations* (with the "key" reflecting standard tenor points such as six-month, one-year, two-years, etc.). Each bond will be assigned a set of key rate-duration exposures. For a given unit of time (e.g., a month) you can then observe yield changes at each key point and the sum product of the key rate durations, with the yield changes at each key point providing a measure of $Return_{RATES}$ (i.e., a duration-weighted average effect of yield changes). A given portfolio does *not* have the same rate return as a basket of government bonds; that is only true if their duration is the same. For example, the rates components of returns for the various fixed income asset classes in Exhibit 2.1 are not constant, in part due to differences in duration. The difference between total returns and the rates component is then the "spread" component of returns. As Asvanunt and Richardson (2017) note, simply subtracting treasury returns is incorrect, as it assumes duration is identical between the bonds in the portfolio whose returns are to be decomposed and the government bonds in the treasury portfolio. The simple additive total return decomposition is as follows:

$$Return_{TOTAL} = Return_{RATES} + Return_{SPREAD} \qquad (2.1)$$

An alternative, but conceptually equivalent, approach to decomposing returns is to match the cash flow profiles of a given risky bond with a riskless bond. The returns on the cash-flow-matched riskless bond is then $Return_{RATES}$, and as per Equation 2.1, the difference between the total return on the risky bond and $Return_{RATES}$ is $Return_{SPREAD}$. These measures are typically computed by index providers and are readily available to market participants.

Exhibit 2.2 reports the contribution of $Return_{RATES}$ and $Return_{SPREAD}$ for our six fixed income categories. To ease comparison of the relative contribution of return components across categories, total returns are standardized to 100 percent. Over this period, there has been a very attractive risk-adjusted return to riskless government bonds. Exhibit 2.1 showed a Sharpe ratio of 0.71 for global government bonds, and all of that return is attributable to "rates" (by definition). The tailwind of generally declining interest rates and yields over the 2000–2020 period is a key source of the strong positive returns to fixed income assets across the board. Across the other five categories we see that average returns over this period are dominated by the rates component and notably that the importance of the rates component declines as we move from left to right consistent with the increasing importance of credit, or default risk, as we move from safe developed sovereign issuers to risky corporate and emerging market issuers.

When we explore investment frameworks for government bonds, corporate bonds, and emerging market USD bonds later in this book, we will be focusing on the portion of return that is unique to that respective

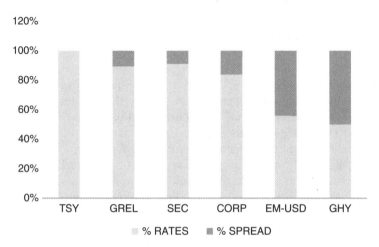

EXHIBIT 2.2 Total return decomposition into "rates" and "spread" components for Global Treasury, Global Government Related, Global Securitized, Global Corporates, Emerging Market USD Aggregate, and Global High Yield indices.
Source: Data from Bloomberg Indices.

fixed income category. For (developed market) government bonds the return source is completely attributable to yields (rates). Hence our investment focus needs to be centered on where yields are today and where they are likely to move to in the future. For corporate bonds, we will focus our investment effort on the potential for credit excess returns. Of course, corporate bonds inherit exposures to yields, but this is not why we trade corporate bonds. As we will see later, corporate bonds are a costly asset class to trade, so why pay a lot to express investment views on yields when you can do so far more cheaply with government bonds directly. For emerging market USD bonds, we will also focus our investment attention on the potential for spread returns unique to that market, again for the same reasons.

In addition to decomposing total returns, we can also decompose the variation of total returns for fixed income securities. A simple way to do this is to compute the standard deviation of $Return_{RATES}$ and $Return_{SPREAD}$ over the 2000–2020 period for each of our six fixed income categories. Exhibit 2.3 shows the relative contribution of the two sources of return standard deviation.

We see a similar pattern in the return variation decomposition as we saw with the return decomposition itself. The importance of the rates component

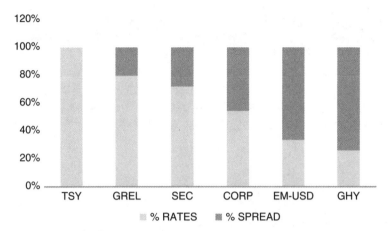

EXHIBIT 2.3 Standard deviation contribution of "rates" and "spread" return components for Global Treasury, Global Government Related, Global Securitized, Global Corporates, Emerging Market USD Aggregate, and Global High Yield indices. *Source:* Data from Bloomberg Indices.

declines as we move from left to right consistent with the increasing importance of credit, or default risk, as we move from safe developed sovereign issuers to risky corporate and emerging market issuers. Exhibit 2.3 is an imprecise method to show the relative importance of components of returns to explain the temporal variation in returns. The imprecision is due to correlation. The components of returns, $Return_{RATES}$ and $Return_{SPREAD}$, are correlated, and over the 2000–2020 period they are typically negatively correlated, especially for those fixed income securities with heightened credit risk. This is related to the topic of stock–bond correlation that we will cover later in this chapter. The correlation of the spread component and rates component of returns for the Global Securitized and Global Corporate subindices are –0.10 and –0.07, respectively. In contrast, the correlation of the spread component and rates component of returns for the Emerging Market USD Aggregate and Global High Yield indices are –0.37 and –0.35, respectively. This is a direct manifestation of the strong negative association between stocks and bonds that has been seen over the past two decades. Fixed income securities with significant credit risk share a very high positive correlation with equity securities.

To account for the correlation across return subcomponents, we need to introduce some terminology for variance and covariance. We can rewrite

Equation 2.1 using symbols for the various types of returns we have discussed so far: (i) r_t for total returns, (ii) r_r for the rates component of returns, and (iii) r_s for the spread component of returns.

$$r_t = r_r + r_s \tag{2.2}$$

Using the variance operator (σ_X is the standard deviation of X, and $\rho_{X,Y}$ is the correlation between X and Y), we have:

$$\sigma_t^2 = \sigma_r^2 + \sigma_s^2 + 2\rho_{r,s}\sigma_r\sigma_s \tag{2.3}$$

If we divide this expression by total return variance, σ_t^2, we arrive at an additive decomposition of return variation:

$$1 = \frac{\sigma_r^2 + \sigma_s^2 + 2\rho_{r,s}\sigma_r\sigma_s}{\sigma_t^2} \tag{2.4}$$

$$1 = \frac{\sigma_r^2 + \rho_{r,s}\sigma_r\sigma_s}{\sigma_t^2} + \frac{\sigma_s^2 + \rho_{r,s}\sigma_r\sigma_s}{\sigma_t^2} \tag{2.5}$$

How correlation affects return variation decomposition should now be clear(er). The covariance between the rate and spread portion of returns is explicitly accounted for. These components are not perfectly correlated with each other and, as mentioned earlier, can be negatively correlated to each other. This results in a meaningful lower variation for total returns than the simple sum of return variation across the two components. That's diversification for you.

Although you could estimate volatilities and correlations of the various components of returns, there is a simpler approach that makes use of linear algebra. We can run the following simple regressions, and the regression coefficients provide our answer.

$$r_r = \alpha_r + \beta_r r_t + \varepsilon_r \tag{2.6}$$

$$r_s = \alpha_s + \beta_s r_t + \varepsilon_s \tag{2.7}$$

The regression coefficients contain the relevant information:

$$\beta_r = \frac{\text{COV}(r_r, r_t)}{\text{VAR}(r_t)} \tag{2.8}$$

$$\beta_s = \frac{\text{COV}(r_s, r_t)}{\text{VAR}(r_t)} \tag{2.9}$$

We can combine Equation (2.2) with Equation (2.8) and expand some terms:

$$\beta_r = \frac{\mathrm{COV}(r_r, r_r + r_s)}{\mathrm{VAR}(r_t)} \tag{2.10}$$

$$\beta_r = \frac{\mathrm{COV}(r_r, r_r) + \mathrm{COV}(r_r, r_s)}{\mathrm{VAR}(r_t)} \tag{2.11}$$

$$\beta_r = \frac{\sigma_r^2 + \rho_{r,s}\sigma_r\sigma_s}{\sigma_t^2} \tag{2.12}$$

And similarly, for the spread portion of returns:

$$\beta_s = \frac{\sigma_s^2 + \rho_{r,s}\sigma_r\sigma_s}{\sigma_t^2} \tag{2.13}$$

Now it is easy to see that $\beta_r + \beta_s = 1$, and the respective betas are the exact same calculations as in Equation (2.5). Exhibit 2.4 shows the total return variance decomposition using this approach.

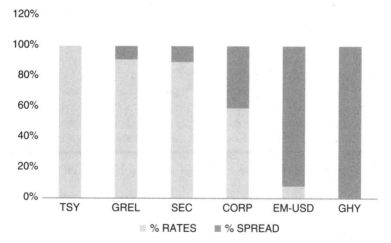

EXHIBIT 2.4 Total return variance decomposition into "rates" and "spread" component for Global Treasury, Global Government Related, Global Securitized, Global Corporates, Emerging Market USD Aggregate, and Global High Yield indices. *Source:* Data from Bloomberg Indices.

The difference between Exhibit 2.3 and Exhibit 2.4 is simply the correlation between return components. For those fixed income assets with greater risk, and hence greater correlation to equity securities, the importance of rates is greatly reduced. This is the effect of the greater negative correlation between the rate and spread component of returns for those types of assets.

2.2   WHAT TRADITIONAL RISK PREMIA CAN BE HARVESTED IN FIXED INCOME?

Now that we have an appreciation of the source of returns from fixed income securities, let's ask a fundamental question: What unique return sources are available to asset owners in fixed income? We will answer that question looking at a broad set of fixed income returns across the following categories: (i) Global Treasury (same index as previously), (ii) Emerging Market Local Currency Government, (iii) US Mortgage Backed Securities (a subset of the Global Securitized subindex examined previously), (iv) Corporate (global Investment-Grade corporate bonds), (v) Emerging Market USD Aggregate, (vi), US High Yield (as subset of the Global High Yield we examined previously), and (vii) US Leveraged Loans (using Credit Suisse Leveraged Loan Total Return). We will also look at global equity market returns (MSCI World Index). Returns data for categories (i)–(vi) are sourced from Bloomberg Indices. All return series are measured monthly and reported in USD.

Exhibit 2.5 reports the correlations across these return series using the longest possible time series for each category available. The first row in Exhibit 2.5 lists the first year data is available for each series. These correlations are all based on total returns, which we now know share a large common rates component across the fixed income categories. Therefore, it is not surprising to see reasonably high correlations across the various categories using total returns (inclusive of cash returns). And these correlations are computed over the longest time series possible for each pair, so these averages will mask any temporal variation.

There are a couple of notable patterns. The riskier fixed income securities have higher correlations to each other (e.g., Emerging Market bonds, corporate bonds, and loans), and to equity markets. A cleaner way to assess the potential uniqueness for each source of returns is to look at *excess* returns. For the credit sensitive assets (corporate bonds, loans, and emerging market debt) we remove the rates component of returns as discussed earlier (i.e., accounting for the duration exposure to interest rates). For government bonds and equities, we subtract one-month US Treasury Bill returns (cash returns) to compute excess returns for those categories. Exhibit 2.6 reports the correlations across monthly excess returns for the

EXHIBIT 2.5 Correlations of USD monthly total returns across Global Treasury, Emerging Market Local Currency, US Mortgage-Backed Securities, Investment Grade Corporates, Emerging Market USD debt, Corporate High Yield Bonds, Leveraged Loans, and MSCI World Equity.

	1987	2008	1976	1973	2001	1983	1992	1970
	GL TSY	EM LOCAL	US MBS	CORP IG	EM USD	CORP HY	LOANS	WORLD EQ
GL TSY	1.00	0.66	0.52	0.55	0.48	0.13	−0.04	0.20
EM LOCAL		1.00	0.18	0.57	0.78	0.67	0.42	0.70
US MBS			1.00	0.83	0.33	0.21	−0.13	0.14
CORP IG				1.00	0.72	0.55	0.37	0.34
EM USD					1.00	0.77	0.57	0.65
CORP HY						1.00	0.77	0.61
LOANS							1.00	0.50
WORLD EQ								1.00

Sources: Data from Bloomberg Indices, Credit Suisse, MSCI.

same categories (the time periods are shorter for some categories due to the requirement of analytics for subtracting the rate component of returns).

The correlation between the credit-sensitive assets and the correlation of credit-sensitive assets to equity markets increases when looking at excess returns. This is an important fact that will become a common theme in the book. There are categories of securities within the fixed income landscape that are strongly positive correlated with equity markets, and there are other categories of fixed income assets that have low, or even negative, correlation with stocks (e.g., government bonds over the past couple of decades). I have chosen the longest period for completeness in Exhibit 2.6 but note that more recent periods, during which the stock–bond correlation has become more negative, show even stronger positive correlations of excess returns across credit sensitive assets.

To appreciate the considerable temporal variation in the risk-adjusted returns across fixed income sectors, Exhibit 2.7 plots rolling 36-month Sharpe ratios, using the same measure of excess returns from Exhibit 2.6 (the astute reader will note I am a little loose with my use of the Sharpe ratio here as the excess returns are excess of cash for some return series and excess of duration for return series; a pure labeling might use the information ratio for the excess of duration return series). Although there is a clear common component across fixed income sectors (the full sample correlations in Exhibit 2.6 suggest this), there are periods when different

EXHIBIT 2.6 Correlations of USD monthly *excess* returns across Global Treasury, Emerging Market Local Currency, US Mortgage-Backed Securities, Investment Grade Corporates, Emerging Market USD debt, Corporate High Yield Bonds, Leveraged Loans, and MSCI World Equity.

| | 1987 | 2008 | 1988 | 1988 | 2001 | 1988 | 1992 | 1988 |
	GL TSY	EM LOCAL	US MBS	CORP IG	EM USD	CORP HY	LOANS	WORLD EQ
GL TSY	1.00	0.66	−0.08	0.01	0.09	−0.10	−0.03	0.19
EM LOCAL		1.00	0.32	0.55	0.68	0.60	0.43	0.71
US MBS			1.00	0.38	0.52	0.42	0.36	0.32
CORP IG				1.00	0.81	0.82	0.80	0.63
EM USD					1.00	0.85	0.73	0.75
CORP HY						1.00	0.79	0.67
LOANS							1.00	0.51
WORLD EQ								1.00

Sources: Data from Bloomberg Indices, Credit-Suisse, MSCI.

subsectors perform better or worse than others. Let's examine what the source of this return variation might be.

But first, one caveat for the analysis in Exhibit 2.7: stale/smooth data. Certain subsectors in fixed income are notorious for their lack of liquidity, pre- and post-trade price transparency, and quality of marks used in index pricing. Of the categories we have examined, corporate bonds and, especially, leveraged loans are most guilty. The Sharpe ratios are therefore overstated for these fixed-income subcategories, because any resulting smoothing in prices and returns will dampen the empirically estimated volatilities used when computing Sharpe ratios. Yes, there are approaches to correct for staleness in pricing, but at this stage our purpose is simply to note temporal variation in performance across fixed income subsectors. This sets up our discussion on the diversifying potential of risk premia embedded in fixed income markets.

Broadly speaking we can categorize the types of fixed income risk premia as follows.

2.2.1 Term Premium (and Yields)

The term premium is the additional return an investor expects to receive from holding to maturity a long-term risk-free government bond relative to the return generated from rolling a series of shorter-dated risk-free government bonds. The risks that the longer-term bondholder faces are not

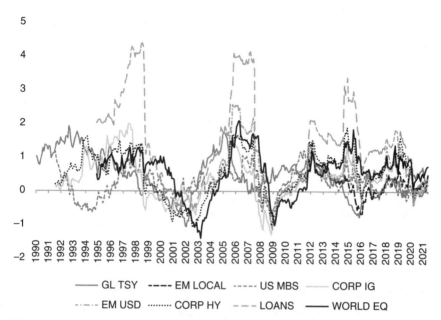

EXHIBIT 2.7   Rolling 36-month Sharpe ratios of USD monthly *excess* returns across Global Treasury, Emerging Market Local Currency, US Mortgage-Backed Securities, Investment Grade Corporates, Emerging Market USD debt, Corporate HighYield Bonds, Leveraged Loans, and MSCI World Equity.
Sources: Bloomberg Indices, Credit Suisse, MSCI.

credit risk in the sense of nonpayment of coupons by the government. The risk is that price, or alternatively yield, of the long-term government bond will change over the investment holding period, resulting in mark to market gains/losses along the way to maturity. (In contrast, the investor rolling positions across a series of shorter-term government bonds is able to reinvest at the then-prevailing interest rate.)

Before we look at the returns of long-term government bonds, let's first ensure we understand the determinants of yields on long-term government bonds. Brooks (2021) describes a simple framework that we will lean on for our discussion. This framework is helpful to make links between yields, an indicator of return potential, and what we are talking about here: (ex-ante) term premia.

Equation 2.14 summarizes the simple framework in Brooks (2021):

$$Yield = i_r + E[i_r] + Term\ Premium \qquad (2.14)$$

In words, the yield on a long-term government bond is equal to the prevailing short-term interest rates, i_r, expectations of those same short-term interest rates over the life of the long-term government bond, $E[i_r]$, and a residual component that we will call *term premium*. Central banks in all developed markets (our current focus) are responsible for the setting of short-term interest rates. Although the precise mechanism can vary across countries, the idea is that the central banks influence key short-term interest rates used by financial institutions. For example, the US Federal Reserve uses the Federal Funds Rate as its key short-term interest rate. This is the interest rate that financial institutions charge each other for overnight lending. Although there is some disagreement about the precise role/mandate of central banks in the developed world, most market participants agree that it includes a focus on price stability and full employment. If this is the objective of the central bank, then why focus on short-term interest rates? Central banks can control short-term interest rates, and these rates ultimately affect the cost of borrowing for businesses and customers, leading to aggregate effects on credit and broad economic activity. This will impact employment and inflation, which are the ultimate objectives of the central bank. This is the mechanism by which modern monetary policy works (or is believed to work).

So with central bank objectives to target stable price and full employment, what tools do they have available to deliver on these objectives via the interest-rate channel? Although central banks are challenged in their ability to directly control long-term government bond yields directly (perhaps via direct market purchases), they focus on what they can influence, and here they have several options. First, as discussed earlier, they can set short-term interest rates directly. Second, they can influence expectations of future short-term interest rates. Via credible implementation of monetary policy over the past few decades, central banks have built up considerable trust with capital markets and are able, to a point, to signal their intentions with respect to future monetary policy decisions. Setting expectations of future short-term interest rates is a key component of modern monetary policy. Third, central banks can directly influence the prices of financial assets by purchasing, or expressing intent to purchase, these assets in secondary markets. Central banks do not have to purchase financial assets, nor in large amounts to influence prices in large amounts; the mere expectation that they might intervene can have significant effects on prices (see e.g., Gilchrist, Wei, Yue and Zakrajsek 2021). It is this third policy tool that can influence the term premium directly.

The determinants of term premium extend far beyond central banks, because they are not the only force acting on longer-term interest rates. There are a variety of other capital market participants and basic economic forces at work. Macroeconomic theory suggests that long-term interest rates should be anchored to the natural real interest rate, an equilibrium concept consistent with stable inflation absent any demand and supply shocks, and long-term inflation expectations. The role of central banks is to adjust interest rates around the natural rate based on their views of economic activity and inflation (the well-known Taylor Rule). If central banks believe economic activity is below (above) potential, they will lower (raise) short-term interest rates, and if they believe inflation is below (above) their target level, they will also lower (raise) interest rates. There is a risk of overemphasizing the influence of central banks on long-term yields, as central banks respond to economic growth "gaps" and inflation "gaps." In a free market, the long-term anchors of yields are set by economic forces: underlying real economic growth (per capita) is the primary driver of the real rate of interest, and no central bank can wave a wand to directly change economic growth. They are responding to signals about deviations from potential growth.

Other determinants of longer-term government bond yields that fall within the residual "term premium" include (i) uncertainty about the path of future inflation expectations (e.g., inflation uncertainty), (ii) general business cycle uncertainty can influence longer-term government bond yields (e.g., general risk aversion), and (iii) behaviors of capital market participants such as large pools of capital (e.g., pension plans and sovereign states) whose net demand for "safe" assets can directly influence their price. Heightened concerns about inflation uncertainty would increase the term premium; heightened risk aversion in the economy would also increase the term premium. In contrast, actions from large asset owners to seek safe assets (sovereign reserve managers) or seek hedges for longer-dated liabilities (pension funds, but perhaps their demand is more in longer-dated corporate bonds as opposed to longer-dated government bonds) will reduce the term premium.

In summary, there is a lot going on that influence yields on longer-term government bonds. A component of that yield is the term premium. From an asset owner perspective, it is that term premium you are looking to capture with your allocation to government bonds. So, what does the data look like for the term premium? Rather than attempting to extract the ex-ante term premium from yields, which is noisy at best (see e.g., Laubach and Williams 2003 and Holston, Laubach, and Williams 2017), we are going to look at ex-post returns.

Using an updated data series from Asvanunt and Richardson (2017) covering the 1926–2020 period, we can examine the long-run evidence from investing in long-term government bonds relative to the alternative of short-term government bills. The source data for this time series is Ibbotson's U.S. Long-Term Government Bond Total Return minus Ibbotson's

U.S. Treasury Bill Total Return from 1926 to 1972 and Bloomberg US Treasury index since 1973. Over the 1926–2020 period, the full sample Sharpe ratio is 0.34. This compares favorably with the Sharpe ratio on US equity markets of 0.44 for the same period. There is considerable variation in the performance of long-term government bonds through time, and Exhibit 2.8 shows the cumulative and rolling three-year average returns.

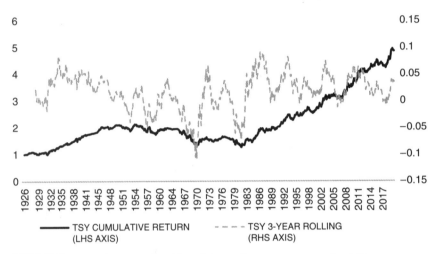

EXHIBIT 2.8   Cumulative and rolling 36-month excess returns for US government bonds.
Source: Ibbotson's US Long-Term Government Bond Total Return minus Ibbotson's US Treasury Bill Total Return from 1926 to 1972 and Bloomberg US Treasury index since 1973.

Although there have been very attractive risk-adjusted returns for holding long-term government bonds over the past century, there have been extended periods of underperformance. Long-term government bonds have experienced a couple of lean decades in the middle of the past century, but experienced stellar returns over the last few decades with the secular decline in interest rates and yields. Combining Exhibit 2.8 with the declining and low yields seen in Chapter 1, it is natural to ask whether investing in government bonds (core fixed income) is still worthwhile.

All investors would agree that if your investment view were that yields will increase going forward, then tactically you would reduce allocations to core fixed income. However, simply noting that yields are low, and therefore yields must rise, is too naïve. Equation 2.14 notes that yields are expected to be low if current short-term interest rates are low, expected future short-term interest rates are low and the term premium is low. At the time of this writing (the end of 2021), yields are low because the determinants of yields suggest so. We will revisit tactical investment decisions for fixed income in Chapter 3. Our purpose here is to make the strategic case for investing in long-term government bonds to harvest the term premium. There is a century of evidence to support this on a stand-alone basis. In the next section we will see how fixed income diversifies alongside equity to provide a more balanced overall portfolio.

2.2.2 Credit Premium

The credit premium is the additional return an investor expects to receive from holding a risky bond relative to the return from holding a similar riskless bond. The risky and riskless bonds are similar in their cash flow profiles; they differ in terms of the probability of getting paid your coupons. A riskless government bond has zero probability of nonpayment, whereas for riskier corporate issuers there is a nonzero probability of nonpayment. The greater the risk of nonpayment, the greater the need for the expected return to compensate the investor.

It is possible to quantify the extent of this risk ex ante. In Chapter 1 we talked about a "spread" and this is a market-implied view of the credit risk of the issuer. The spread can be computed by taking the difference in yields between the riskless and risky bonds with identical cash flows. If we extend our example of a 10-year coupon-bearing bond from Chapter 1, we can price that bond assuming the issuer is riskless, as in Equation (2.15), or risky, as in Equation (2.16):

$$P_{riskless} = \frac{1}{(1+y)^1} + \frac{1}{(1+y)^2} + \frac{1}{(1+y)^3} + \ldots + \frac{101}{(1+y)^{20}} \quad (2.15)$$

$$P_{risky} = \frac{1}{(1+y^*)^1} + \frac{1}{(1+y^*)^2} + \frac{1}{(1+y^*)^3} + \ldots + \frac{101}{(1+y^*)^{20}} \quad (2.16)$$

The only difference across Equations 2.15 and 2.16 is the discount rate. For the riskless bond we use a risk-free discount rate, y, such as a government bond yield. For the risky bond we use a different discount rate, y^*, such as a corporate bond yield. Generally speaking, $y^* > y$, and the difference is the spread, that is, $s = y^* - y$, and, because spreads are positive, $s > 0$, the price of the risky bond will be below that of the similar riskless bond, $P_{risky} < P_{riskless}$.

The credit spread is an ex-ante measure of the return potential from exposure to credit risk, analogous to yield as an ex-ante measure of the return potential from exposure to the term premium. We will have much to say on the determinants of credit risk, and hence credit spreads, later in Chapter 6 when we examine the default process in greater detail. Now, let's look at the data to see whether investors have been compensated for bearing credit risk.

Using an updated data series from Asvanunt and Richardson (2017) covering the 1926–2020 period, we can examine the long-run evidence from investing in long-term corporate bonds. There are a variety of corporate bonds to select from for this exercise. To ensure consistency with the data historically, we will focus on investment-grade-rated corporate bonds (the high-yield market did not really develop until the 1980s). The source data for this time series is Ibbotson's US Long-Term Corporate Bond Total Return for the 1926–1988 period and Bloomberg Indices (LUAC) for 1988–2020. Estimates of credit excess returns prior to 1988 require empirically estimating interest rate sensitivities. Asvanunt and Richardson (2017) describe the details, but the basic idea flows from an understanding of what duration is. If we have access to corporate bond returns (we do, Ibbotson data goes back to 1926), and we can observe contemporaneous changes in government bond yields (we do, bond yield data also goes back at least as far as 1926), you can then approximate duration. A simple regression of the total returns of corporate bonds onto changes in government bond yields will produce a regression coefficient. That regression coefficient tells you the change in corporate bond prices (i.e., returns) for a given change in yield. And that is duration! Asvanunt and Richardson (2017) applied this approach to a century of corporate bond data and found reliable evidence of a credit risk premium. Using updated data through to 2020, Exhibit 2.9 shows the cumulative and rolling three-year average returns for US corporate bonds. Over the 1926–2020 period, the full sample Sharpe ratio is 0.48, again favorable to the 0.34 for the term premium and 0.44 for the equity risk premium over the same period. There is considerable variation in the performance of corporate bonds through time. It is also worth noting that this series only covers investment-grade corporate bonds issued in the United States. There is a broader set of corporate issuers in many other countries, and for the last few decades there has been a large, and growing, set of high-yield corporate bonds. The century of evidence in Exhibit 2.9 may understate the magnitude of the credit risk premium.

Some additional caveats are necessary for Exhibit 2.9. The quality of the data back in time is lower, and of particular concern is the completeness of the data with respect to default events. If defaults or other large negative return realizations are missing, this will lead to an overstatement of the credit premium. Although care has been taken to obtain the highest-quality data possible, there are still limitations with older corporate bond return data. Indeed, Kizer, Grover, and Hendershot (2019) suggest that removing the first

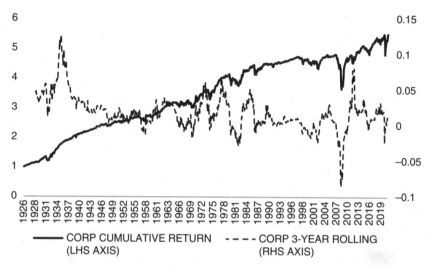

EXHIBIT 2.9 Cumulative and rolling 36-month excess returns for US corporate bonds.

Source: Ibbotson's US Long-Term Corporate Bond Total Return minus empirical-duration-matched long-term government bonds from Ibbotson's US Long-Term Government Bond Total Return. From 1926–1935, durations are estimated using in-sample regressions. From 1936–1998, they are estimated using rolling 10-year regressions. Full details in Asvanunt and Richardson (2017). Excess returns post 1988 are from Bloomberg Indices (LUAC).

couple of decades reduces the size of the credit risk premium. Although in a strict sense that is correct, the pervasiveness of the credit-risk premium across geographies, rating categories, and its existence in both cash and index derivative markets makes its existence noncontroversial. A fun exercise for the reader is to use the century of data and find periods where there is no credit risk premium or select random periods and see how frequently you find a positive risk-adjusted return (the same can be done for the equity risk premium and term premium). I find this helpful to remind students what a risk premium means: over a long period the average return is positive, but in any one period it is not guaranteed to be positive. This also starts to get students thinking about what causes temporal variation in risk premium, setting up tactical investment decisions that we will cover in Chapter 3.

2.2.3 Prepayment/Complexity/Volatility Premium

One other large set of fixed income securities is the "securitized" market. This includes a wide variety of bonds whose cash flows are linked to cash flows from other obligations. They are a repackaging of existing contractual commitments. There are sound economic reasons for these repackaged bonds: they allow for improved risk sharing among capital market participants. Of course, that efficient risk sharing only works if those market participants understand the risks that they are sharing in. Some would say that the Great Financial Crisis is the poster child for a lack of such understanding. In any event, the securitized market is here to stay. As we noted in Chapter 1, the Global Securitized subcategory accounted for approximately $9 trillion USD, out of the $68 trillion USD outstanding bonds in the Global Aggregate. The securitized market is very large. Within this category, however, there are many different types of securitized bonds.

The Bloomberg Global Securitized index includes securitized bonds from four broad categories: (i) agency mortgage-backed passthrough securities, (ii) asset-backed securities, (iii) commercial mortgage-backed securities, and (iv) covered bonds. Agency MBS includes the passthrough bonds issued by government agencies including GNMA (Ginnie Mae, or the Government National Mortgage Association), FHLMC (Freddie Mac, or the Federal Home Loan Mortgage Corporation), and FNMA (Fannie Mae, the Federal National Mortgage Association). This category accounts for 75 percent of the total global securitized market (Bloomberg indices) as at December 31, 2020, and the majority of these are 30-year conventional fixed rate mortgages. These three entities are all government sponsored, whose purpose is to provide backing and security to a vast array of home mortgage loans facilitating home ownership in the United States. The passthrough securities are pools of underlying mortgages backed by each respective entity. New bonds are issued backed by the cash flows of the pool and they are guaranteed by the respective agency that takes a fee for that guarantee and associated mortgage servicing activities. If these bonds are guaranteed, one may ask what is the risk that would require compensation? It is the risk of payment at different times than initially contracted. The underlying mortgage holders may refinance for a variety of reasons and hence pay early. This prepayment risk is a unique source of risk underlying mortgage-backed securities.

Asset-backed securities within the Bloomberg Global Securitized Index accounted for a little over $100 billion USD as of December 31, 2020, and they typically cover credit card, automobile, and business-related loans. These bonds contain their own issuer-specific credit risk and associated prepayment risks. Commercial mortgage-backed securities (CMBSs) within the Bloomberg Global Securitized Index accounted for approximately $570 billion USD as of December 31, 2020. These CMBSs cover a wide range of securitized bonds including guaranteed bonds linked to multifamily residential properties, small businesses, and project loans. These bonds can be single-tranche or multitranche facilities, which adds a further layer of complexity to the securitization. The covered-bonds category within the Bloomberg Global Securitized Index accounted for around $1.4 trillion USD as at December 31, 2020, and is almost exclusively related to mortgage loans issued outside the United States (typically by European financial institutions).

What all the securitized bonds share is a risk associated with early pre-payment. That risk commands a premium in the form of a spread over cash-flow-matched riskless government bonds. In some cases, there will also be credit risk associated with the underlying entity creating and servicing the securitized debt. Estimating the duration profile of these securitized bonds, so as to measure spreads, can be very challenging, as the future cash flows are dependent on current interest rates and expected paths of future interest rates. The behavior of the underlying mortgage holders may also need to be modeled in response to your forecasted future path of interest rates. This is no easy task, and different smart people trying to estimate the same interest rate sensitivities may end up with very different answers.

Diep, Eisfelt, and Richardson (2021) examined the prepayment risk pre-mium embedded in the US securitized market using 30-year fixed-rate bonds backed by Fannie Mae. This involved assessing the return profile across the "coupon stack." At a point in time there will be outstanding pooled mort-gages from various points in time, so while new fixed-rate mortgages all have a similar rate, over time, as interest rates change, there will be hetero-geneity in the coupon rate across different mortgage pools. Some pools will have a coupon rate above (below) the prevailing market mortgage rate and they are called premium (discount) bonds. This variation in coupon rates across mortgage pools gives rise to prepayment risk. Mortgages that have a coupon rate higher than prevailing interest rates are at risk of having the underlying mortgages repaid earlier, leaving the holder of the MBS at risk of having to reinvest those proceeds at a lower rate. You thus expect to see spreads on mortgage-backed securities to be larger when deviating further from "par"; that is, mortgage bonds with an underlying coupon rate higher than prevailing rates are at greater risk of prepayment, so they are worth less and hence carry a higher spread. Consistent with this, Diep, Eisfelt, and Richardson (2021) find an upward-sloping pattern of spreads and coupon rates (i.e., spreads are higher for premium MBS), but that pattern is concen-trated when there are more premium coupon bonds outstanding (and the risk bearing capacity of capital-constrained participants in securitized mar-kets is lower, so capital-constrained market participants therefore command a greater premium). In markets in which there are more mortgage pools with

coupon rates below prevailing market rates (i.e., the supply of MBS is dominated by discount MBS) the opposite is true: discount coupons attract higher
spreads. The market price of prepayment risk is time varying.

Why all this seemingly technical discussion? This will be clear when we
look at the return profile of excess returns for securitized bonds. Exhibit 2.10
shows the cumulative and rolling three-year average returns for US MBS.
Over the 1988–2020 period the full sample Sharpe ratio is 0.26, which is
only slightly smaller than the risk premia observed for the term premium
and credit premium. This Sharpe ratio of 0.26 is considerably lower than the
1.34 reported in Exhibit 2.1 because we are now talking about the nonrate
component of returns (i.e., excess returns over duration marched government bonds, not excess returns over cash). Over this time period, the rate
component of returns for all fixed income assets was strongly positive. Still, a
Sharpe ratio of 0.26 is economically meaningful, but it does mask an exceptionally low average excess return (about three basis points annualized over
this period). What is causing this? It could be measurement error in the
estimates of duration used to measure spreads. This is likely not the cul-
prit, as similar patterns of tiny excess returns are observed using estimates
of duration across different index providers or using empirical estimates of
duration. The source of the small average excess return is that the MBS index
has most of its securities outstanding at close to par (prevailing mortgage
rates). This means that most securitized bonds included in the index are not

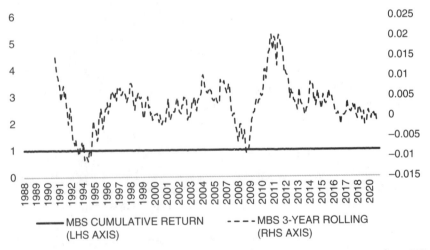

EXHIBIT 2.10 Cumulative and rolling 36-month excess returns for US
mortgage-backed securities.
Source: Data from Bloomberg Indices (LUMS). Data is for the period 1988–2020.

sensitive to prepayment shocks ($100 notional will return $100). They will be sensitive to volatility in interest rates because there may be future prepayment risk for these bonds, but that effect is small. Attempts to capture the prepayment risk premium need to focus on securities that are distant from par (i.e., premium and discount securities in the "wings" of the coupon stack) and ideally condition exposure to discount and premium bonds based on the prevailing market price of prepayment risk. The greatest excess return potential for securitized assets resides in the less liquid corners of this market (e.g., nonagency securitized bonds and far out of the money mortgage pools).

We could add further categories of fixed income risk premia. The two most obvious categories would be for emerging and private markets. An emerging market fixed income risk premium would reflect the combination of return opportunities across emerging market local currency bonds, emerging market hard currency bonds, and emerging currency returns. The emerging market corporate risk is very similar in spirit to the developed market credit premia already discussed, and the emerging market local currency (mostly government bonds) is like the developed market term premium already discussed. Extending the cross-section of government and corporate bond issuers beyond developed markets will provide additional diversification benefits as the risks underlying term premium (inflation and growth shocks) and credit premium (growth shocks) can be diversified internationally. Finally, emerging market hard currency bonds share some similarity to the general credit risk premium, and we will discuss this market in detail in Chapter 7.

Private credit markets are a growing segment of the fixed income market. Interest from asset owners has ballooned over the last five years. Although data for this market is hard to identify, there are some index providers. A commonly used benchmark is the Cliffwater Direct Lending Index. It seeks to measure the unlevered, gross of fee performance of US middle-market corporate loans, as represented by the asset-weighted performance of the underlying assets of Business Development Companies (a BDC is an organization that invests in small- and medium-sized companies as well as distressed companies). This total return index includes income return, and realized and unrealized gains and losses. As with all private markets, there is concern about the quality of marks giving rise to unrealized gains and losses. That said, the annualized return for private markets over the 2004–2020 period is 9.1 percent with an associated Sharpe ratio of 2.47. This is amazing. Part of this return may be attributable to operating and investing efficiency from direct lending activities and excellent security selection. But part of this is attributable to the smoothing benefit of private markets (i.e., the stale data issue mentioned in Chapter 1). To corroborate this assertion, the annualized total return of the Bloomberg High Yield Index (LF98) over the 2004–2020 period was 7.6 percent and an associated Sharpe ratio of 0.83. This is a lot smaller than the 2.47 Sharpe ratio for private markets over the same period, but the difference is primarily attributable to return volatility, not to the level of returns. Private markets are another way to capture the credit risk premium, but it is not clear how diversifying they really are. And for some direct-lending activities that have short track records, there is concern about security selection around default risk. Private credit markets have the potential to add to credit risk premium, but more data analysis is needed.

2.3   THE STRATEGIC DIVERSIFICATION BENEFIT OF FIXED INCOME

We can now put what we have learned together to think about broader asset allocation decisions. Why do we allocate to fixed income markets, and subcategories within fixed income markets? Section 2.2 illustrated stand-alone evidence supporting (i) investments into government bonds to harvest the term premium, (ii) investments into corporate bonds (and other credit-sensitive assets) to harvest the credit premium, and (iii) investments into securitized markets to harvest the prepayment premium. But are these risk premia additive in the context of the asset owner's overall portfolio? This is particularly important in the context of investments into the less liquid, and hence more costly to trade, corners of the fixed income markets like corporate and securitized bonds. Don't incur transaction costs and introduce liquidity risk to your portfolio unless you are compensated for doing so.

Let's start with the empirical fact that equity markets (public and private) are represented in most, if not all, asset owner portfolios. The equity risk premium has long been the base building block of asset allocation. Government bonds are added to equities in the classic 60/40 portfolio (60 percent capital allocated to equities and 40 percent allocated to bonds). The ubiquitous nature of the 60/40 portfolio reflects the fundamental strategic diversification benefit of fixed income relative to equities. Indeed, there are now many risk parity variants (e.g., Bridgewater, PanAgora, AQR etc.) that prudently utilize leverage to allocate across stocks and bonds (and other diversifying asset classes) to balance the risk contribution across different types of risk premia and still deliver equity-like returns. Our focus here will be simpler and just noting how and why it is that fixed income diversifies equity.

Exhibit 2.11 shows the annualized return of US government bonds and US stocks over the 1926–2020 period using rolling 10-year periods to estimate annualized returns. The exhibit also shows the correlation between US bonds and US stocks over the past 120 months. The correlation between stocks and bonds has varied enormously over this period, but it has only been reliably negative for the past couple of decades. A 60/40 combination of US bonds and US stocks generates a full sample Sharpe ratio of 0.49 that exceeds the 0.44 (0.35) Sharpe ratio for US stocks (bonds) over the same period. This higher risk-adjusted return is due to the less than one correlation between stocks and bonds and the fact that they both have a similar return per unit of risk. Of course, the unlevered 60/40 portfolio generates a total return that is lower than that of equities (5.6 percent annualized return for 60/40 vs. 8.2 percent annualized returns for US stocks), but leverage can increase the return of the 60.40 portfolio to 9.1 percent and yield the same overall volatility of the US stocks only portfolio.

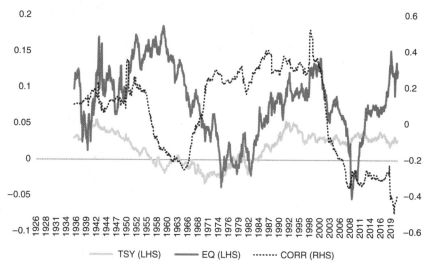

EXHIBIT 2.11   Annualized returns and rolling 10-year correlation for US bonds and US stocks.

Sources: Combination of Ibbotson's Long-Term Government Bond Total Return, Barclays US Treasury total returns, and Standard & Poor's Indices. Data is for the period 1926–2020.

US bonds help diversify a US stock-only portfolio. Similar results can be found looking at global bond and global stock portfolios. Why is this the case? Stocks as the residual claim against free cash flows generated by corporations are exposed to underlying macroeconomic variables: growth and inflation. Stocks have a positive exposure to economic growth shocks (stock prices rise and fall with changing expectations of the business cycle). Stocks have a relation to inflation shocks (generally they fare better in lower inflationary environments, but this relation is more subtle – see e.g., Ilmanen, Maloney, and Ross 2014). Government bonds, as we discussed in Section 2.2, are also exposed to growth and inflation. Improving business cycle outlook or increasing inflation leads to more cautionary monetary policy and higher yields (hence lower returns), whereas worsening business cycle outlook or falling inflation leads to more accommodative monetary policy and lower yields (hence higher returns). It should therefore be clear that stocks and bonds structurally have a different sign on their sensitivity to growth shocks (growth shocks are good for stocks and bad for bonds), but a similar sign on their sensitivity to inflation shocks (inflation shocks are bad for stocks but even worse for bonds). It is this difference in sensitivities to underlying macroeconomic state variables that creates the diversification benefit across stocks and bonds. Of course, there are other drivers of stock and bond returns including (i) aggregate risk aversion that would increase the common component of stock and bond returns, and (ii) sentiment or net demand factors from capital market participants seeking safe-haven assets that decrease the common component of stock and bond returns. Indeed, the temporal variation in the strength of the correlation between stocks and bonds in Exhibit 2.11 shows how these economic forces are varying through time and affecting stocks and bonds differently throughout time.

Another way to see the diversification benefit of stocks and bonds is to examine similarities in their downside risk based on drawdown profiles (i.e., peak to trough decline). Exhibit 2.12 computes the drawdown profile of US stocks and US bonds over the 1926–2020 period. The return series are converted to a price index, and each month is then identified as having a price that is below (or at or above) the prior maximum price level. If the current price index is below a prior maximum, then a drawdown is identified. Exhibit 2.12 shows the cumulative return profile of drawdown periods over the last century. US stocks have larger drawdowns (stock returns are more volatile). The fact that the drawdowns (either in length or severity) do not perfectly align is evidence of diversification in the left-tail of return realizations.

Statistically, we can do even better. Utilizing the data for the past century, we can simultaneously solve for the optimal set of portfolio weights across government bonds, corporate bonds, and stocks that would have yielded the highest Sharpe ratio. This procedure is described in detail in Asvanunt and Richardson (2017), and I note the relevant material here. We need to solve for the ex-post optimal allocation weights for a portfolio consisting of

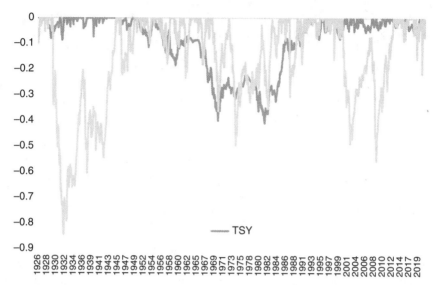

EXHIBIT 2.12 Drawdowns for US bonds and US stocks over the 1926–2020 period. *Sources:* Ibbotson's US Long-Term Government Bond Total Return minus Ibbotson's US Treasury Bill Total Return from 1926 to 1972 and Bloomberg US Treasury index since 1973. Standard & Poor's data for US stocks.

corporate bonds, government bonds, and stocks subject to no shorting and leverage constraints, namely

$$\max_w \frac{w'R}{\sqrt{(w'\Sigma w)}} \tag{2.17}$$

$$\text{subject to} \quad w'\mathbf{1} \leq 1 \tag{2.18}$$

$$w_i \geq 0, \quad \forall i \tag{2.19}$$

R is a vector of average corporate bond, government bond, and stock excess returns; **w** is the vector of portfolio weights to be solved for; and **Σ** is the corresponding excess return covariance matrix. The optimal portfolio solution is mean-variant efficient. An important caveat for the large asset owner is that this analysis does not incorporate information on the expected transaction costs or capacity of each asset, and as such the results here should be interpreted with caution for large asset allocation decisions. Capacity considerations would reduce the importance of less liquid assets (e.g., corporate bonds and/or credit index derivatives) in the overall portfolio.

For the 1926–2020 period, the optimal weights are 55 percent for corporate bonds, 36 percent for government bonds, and 9 percent for stocks. Of course, this analysis can be run for different time periods with very different optimal weights. For the period 1973–2020 (which is the period after the original Lehman indices that pre-date the Bloomberg Indices started) the optimal weights are 23 percent for corporate bonds, 63 percent for government bonds, and 14 percent for stocks.

A potential limitation of this optimal weight analysis is that it is based on a mean-variant analysis of returns, which may be less relevant when the underlying distribution of returns is not normal. Asvanunt and Richardson (2017) assess whether the inference that the credit risk premium is additive to both the term and equity risk premium is robust to return nonnormality. That analysis uses the Sortino ratio (e.g., Sortino and Price 1994):

$$\text{Sortino Ratio} = \frac{R - T}{Downside\ Deviation} \qquad (2.20)$$

where T is the target or required rate of return (for simplicity, we set the target return to 0 percent), and

$$\text{Downside Deviation} = \sqrt{\frac{1}{N}\sum_{t=1}^{N}\min(R_t - T, 0)^2} \qquad (2.21)$$

Given our choice of a 0% target return, the numerator of our Sortino ratio will be the same as that for the Sharpe ratio. The difference is in the denominator, where the Sortino ratio only "penalizes" return realizations that are below the target return. Both the frequency and magnitude of below-target returns are penalized. For the period 1926–2020 the optimal weights that maximize the Sortino ratio are as follows: 51 percent for corporate bonds, 39 percent for government bonds, and 10 percent for stocks. There is consistent evidence that fixed income allocations are important for overall portfolio diversification.

2.4   IS THE STRATEGIC DIVERSIFICATION BENEFIT OF FIXED INCOME THREATENED IN A LOW-INTEREST-RATE ENVIRONMENT?

We have seen that fixed income as an asset class diversifies equity risk for asset-owner portfolios. And we have an understanding about why that diversification exists. Yet, the last decade has seen many question the role of fixed income in their overall portfolio. This skepticism is typically anchored in a strong belief in mean reversion. If government bond yields are low, they must revert to a higher level. And if the fear is that mean reversion will happen soon, that fear leads to an investment decision: reduce allocations to the asset class with near-term expected losses. Although rising yields do not automatically lead to negative returns, because carry still has a positive expected return (i.e., the change in the yield multiplied by duration needs to exceed the initial yield), directionally rising yields mean lower future returns.

Is that fear of rising yields rational? The discussion of term premium in Section 2.2 tells us that long-term government bond yields are determined by current short-term interest rates, expected short-term interest rates in the future, and the term premium (a catch-all for risk aversion, sentiment, and general macroeconomic uncertainty). The low yields today might be justified if we look at the economic backdrop (low levels of inflation, low levels of economic growth, and central banks universally consistent in their use of monetary policy to help stimulate the real economy). Although inflation and growth expectations remain low, government bond yields may remain low for the foreseeable future. What does this mean for fixed income investors? There is still the potential for positive returns by allocating to long-term government bonds. And this is especially true for the investor who can make use of derivatives to maintain a constant-maturity exposure to a long-dated government bond (e.g., 10-year Treasury Note Future). Although the shape of the yield curve remains upward sloping, the positive yield at the 10-year point (at least true in the United States) combined with attractive roll-down properties makes for attractive positive returns from exposure to the term premium. Investors do, however, need to keep in mind that yields are much lower today than they have been over the last century. This means lower levels of returns and, for the investor who is unable to utilize leverage, fixed income is less attractive today than it has been historically. For the investor who can utilize leverage, fixed income may still be as attractive as it ever was. It does not mean fixed income allocations should go to zero! Just because fixed income markets may look relatively expensive compared to history (that's what a low yield means), it is not the case that other asset classes, such as stocks, are any less expensive. Fixed income still preserves its diversification benefit.

REFERENCES

Asvanunt, A., and S. Richardson. (2017). The credit risk premium. *Journal of Fixed Income*, 26, 6–24.

Brooks, J. (2021). What drives bond yields. AQR working paper.

Diep, P., A. Eisfelt, and S. Richardson. (2021). The cross-section of MBS returns. *Journal of Finance*, 76, 2093–2151.

Gilchrist, S., B. Wei, V. Yue, and E. Zakrajsek. (2021). The Fed takes on corporate credit risk: An analysis of the efficacy of the SMCCF. NBER working paper.

Holston, K., T. Laubach, and J. Williams. (2017). Measuring the natural rate of interest: International trends and determinants. *Journal of International Economics*, 108, S39–S75.

Ilmanen, I., T. Maloney, and A. Ross. (2014). Exploring macroeconomic sensitivities: How investments respond to different economic environments. *Journal of Portfolio Management*, 40, 87–99.

Kizer, J., S. Grover, and C. Hendershot. (2019). Re-examining the credit premium. Buckingham Strategic Wealth, working paper.

Laubach, T., and J. Williams. (2003). Measuring the natural rate of interest. *Review of Economics and Statistics*, 85, 1063–1070.

Sortino, F. A. and L. N. Price (1994). Performance measurement in a downside risk framework. *Journal of Investing*, 3, 59–64.

CHAPTER 3

Fixed Income – Tactical Asset Allocation

OVERVIEW

This chapter lays out a framework for timing the two primary traditional risk premia in fixed income markets: the term premium and the credit premium. Building on our understanding of the sources of these risk premia discussed in Chapter 2, we will start to think about forecasting when those risk premia are expected to out (under) perform. The framework is designed to be general to identify the relevant inputs for timing models. We are not designing the "best" possible timing models. That arduous task is for the fixed-income investor. That said, the simple timing models introduced in this chapter show some promise for out-of-sample forecasts of risk premia. Data mining concerns are especially important with timing models, as there is a very limited dataset to work with (one history for one asset), so we will discuss the importance of point-in-time timing models and unconscious bias that creeps into reworked timing models.

3.1   MARKET TIMING – TERM PREMIUM

3.1.1   Framework for Timing

In Chapter 2 we saw that long-term US government bonds generated an attractive risk-adjusted excess (of cash) return over the past century. This is known as the term premium. Obviously, although the term premium has a positive average excess return, there was considerable temporal variation. Indeed, the annualized average excess return was 1.8 percent and the average annualized volatility was 5.1 percent over the past century. The asset owner then asks: Is it possible to vary my exposure to the term premium through time to try and capture more than just the average 1.8 percent return? That is the purpose of this section.

A simple way to think of fixed income return potential is to start with our pricing equations introduced in Chapter 1, which I reproduce here with a discount-rate term structure (i.e., discount rates vary based on the maturity of the cash flow that is to be discounted). I am using the label y for the discount rate to be used for (risk-free) government bonds (this captures the rates component of bond returns as described in Chapter 2).

$$P = \frac{E[CF_1]}{(1+y_1)^1} + \frac{E[CF_2]}{(1+y_2)^2} + \frac{E[CF_3]}{(1+y_3)^3} + \dots \frac{E[CF_{LT}]}{(1+y_{LT})^{LT}} \tag{3.1}$$

In the case of a government bond, the numerator values are fixed. So, let's rewrite that with fixed coupon, C, and par payments, P, with no possibility of early or no repayment:

$$P = \frac{C_1}{(1+E[y_1])^1} + \frac{C_2}{(1+E[y_2])^2} + \frac{C_3}{(1+E[y_3])^3} + \dots \frac{C_{LT}+PL_T}{(1+E[y_{LT}])^{LT}} \tag{3.2}$$

Returns for a government bond are then simply given by the cum-coupon change in price over the period. We can think of the return potential as driven by changes in prices through time. Looking at Equation (3.2), the uncertainty stems from the expectations operator in the denominator. How yields are expected to change over time will determine government bond returns. We can write an approximation for returns as follows:

$$\begin{aligned} Returns \approx \Delta P = &\frac{C_1}{(1+\Delta E[y_1])^1} + \frac{C_2}{(1+\Delta E[y_2])^2} \\ &+ \frac{C_3}{(1+\Delta E[y_3])^3} + \dots \frac{C_{LT}+PL_T}{(1+\Delta E[y_{LT}])^{LT}} \end{aligned} \tag{3.3}$$

To be clear, this is an approximation simply to illustrate that changing expectations about the discount rate will determine the change in government bond prices and hence the return. The other component of the return is governed by the initial yield: ownership of the bond carries participation rights in the expected, and in this case known, coupons and principal payments. As discussed in Chapter 1, at the time of purchase of the bond the price of the bond implies a yield to maturity. So our expected return has two broad components:

$$E[Returns] \approx Initial\ Yield + E[Changes\ in\ Yields] \tag{3.4}$$

We now have our simple framework. Our timing model for the term premium will focus on these two components of expected excess returns (i.e., in excess of cash to be consistent with our definition of term premium at the start of the chapter). First, we have the initial yield. More generally, this can be thought of as the "carry" associated with the government bond position. Second, we have the expected change in yields over the investor's holding period. Technically, this change in yield needs to be multiplied by duration to convert the expected change in yield to an expected return.

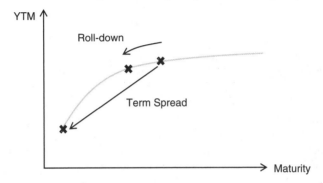

EXHIBIT 3.1   Visual representation of the expected return for a risk-free bond from "carry."

Exhibit 3.1 provides a simple representation of what "carry" is. If nothing happens but the passage of time, carry is the return you will receive. In the case of our risk-free government bond from Equation (3.4), this means that the return we get from carry is the price change for our bond when the discount-rate term structure remains unchanged, but, we are now discounting the fixed set of coupon and principal payments after rolling the cash flows forward (i.e., we are repricing the bond cash flows with the same discount rates, but because the cash flows are shifted forward they are discounted at different rates). We can write the approximate expected excess return (here the excess of cash is explicit) assuming the discount rate structure remains unchanged as:

$$E[Returns] - y_t^{ST\ Bond} \approx y_t^{LT\ Bond} - Duration$$
$$* E[y_{t+1}^{LT\ Bond} - y_t^{LT\ Bond}] - y_t^{ST\ Bond} \tag{3.5}$$

$$E[Returns] - y_t^{ST\ Bond} \approx y_t^{LT\ Bond} - y_t^{ST\ Bond} - Duration$$
$$* E[y_{t+1}^{LT\ Bond} - y_t^{LT\ Bond}] \tag{3.6}$$

Equation (3.6) is approximate, because we have made use of duration and are working with a linear, first-order approximation of expected returns. We are ignoring higher-order moments of yield curve changes. This simply says that a measure of carry should reflect the current yield to maturity and expected changes in yields from the passage of time (i.e., yield curve does not change its shape).

For our measure of carry we will use what is called the term spread, $y_t^{LT\ Bond} - y_t^{ST\ Bond}$, the difference in the nominal long-term government bond yield and the nominal short-term government yield (labeled by the thick black arrow in Exhibit 3.1). This is simply the first portion of Equation (3.6). We are making this choice for data expediency. As we will discuss in Section 3.1.b, our data access for the last century does not include rich data of the entire yield curve, so this approximation is out of necessity. As depicted in Exhibit 3.1, this simple measure will miss curvature in the yield curve and the associated "roll-down" component (labeled by the thin black arrow in Exhibit 3.1). This "roll-down" captures the expected change in yield from the passage of time. This gives a better measure of "carry," but still leaves open the possibility of other expected changes in yields (and hence returns).

The second component of expected excess returns in Equation (3.4) is the expected change in yields. For this, we will lean heavily on recent research (e.g., Asness, Moskowitz, and Pedersen 2013, and Asness, Ilmanen, and Maloney 2017) and group our timing models into two broad categories: value and momentum. Both measures are designed to forecast changes in yields. In the case of momentum, that is for continuation in recent yield changes. In the case of value, that is for expected reversal of current yields to a "normal" level of yields.

How should we think about measuring momentum and value for a government bond timing model? We will use the same approach as in Asness, Ilmanen, and Maloney (2017) and extend the time series to the end of 2020. The measure of momentum will be the 12-month arithmetic average of government bond excess (of cash) returns. The measure of value will be real bond yields computed as the nominal yield on long-term government bonds less a survey-based forecast of long-term inflation.

3.1.2 Data (Some Details)

Our term premium timing model will be assessed on data sourced from Global Financial Data. This data vendor is selected because they maintain very long time series of market data across many asset classes and geographies. We limit our analysis of timing term premium to the period 1920–2020 primarily due to Treasury Bill data. Although Treasury bills (one-month) were only formally introduced in 1929, Global Financial Data can source Treasury instruments with a slightly longer maturity (three to six months) to complete the series back to 1920. Treasury bill secondary market prices and yields are computed as the averages of the bid rates quoted by a sample of primary dealers who report to the Federal Reserve Bank of New York. We use prices and yields as of the close of the last trading day each month to compute (i) T-bill yield (used as a component of our carry measure), and (ii) T-bill returns (used as our measure of cash returns).

Data for the yields and returns of long-term government bonds are also from Global Financial Data. Over our 1920–2020 period, long-term government bond yield and return data are linked to the Federal Reserve Board's 10–15 Treasury Bond Index for the 1920–1941 period, and specific 10-year bonds are used from 1941 onward. This data is used to compute (i) US government bond nominal yield (used as part of the real bond yield value measure), and (ii) US government bond total returns (used to compute US government bond excess returns, our primary variable of interest to forecast).

Data for long-term inflation expectations comes from multiple sources (thank you to Antti Ilmanen for graciously sharing this data). From 1920 to 1955, statistical estimates based on a weighted average of past 10-year inflation rates are used. From 1955–1978 statistical estimates of long-term inflation expectations from Kozicki-Tinsley (2006) are used (their statistical estimates use a different weighting function that also makes use of near-term survey forecasts of inflation). From 1978–1989 an average across multiple surveys is used (e.g., Survey of Professional Investors, Livingston, Blue Chip Economic Indicators, and Consensus Economics). Finally, for the 1990–2020 period, the average annual inflation forecasted for the next decade (Consensus Economics) is used. This data series is used directly in the construction of real bond yield, the value measure.

3.1.3 Converting Raw Data to Signals

We can now assess whether, and how, our return forecasting framework works. To do this we need to create a time series of "signals" that indicate our willingness to increase or decrease our exposure to long-term government bonds (term premium). We will assess our skill from the perspective of a real money investor who needs to remain invested in the fixed income markets, but is able to dial up or down the amount of capital invested into the market at any specific point in time.

We have three investment signals: (i) value (measured as real bond yield, the difference between nominal long-term government bond yields and long-term inflation forecasts), (ii) momentum (measured as the most recent 12-month arithmetic average of long-term government bond excess returns, and (iii) carry (measured as the term spread, or difference between long-term government bond nominal yields and short-term government bill nominal yields).

For each of these three measures we need to convert them to a "signal." It is important that we do not make use of any future information when constructing these signals (that would be cheating). For each measure we will conduct the following transformations: (i) extreme value treatment (to help reduce the influence of extreme values we will cap and floor each signal based on the expanding 95th and 5th percentile values, respectively), (ii) benchmarking (we will subtract from the current realization of the unprocessed signal the expanding median value of its value), (iii) volatility scaling (we will divide that benchmark adjusted value by a measure of volatility, we will use a nonparametric method computed as an expanding window of the difference between the 95th and 5th percentile value of the respective signal), and (iv) timing curves (our effectively Z-scored signal is converted to a value that can be applied to the capital invested in long-term government bonds, we will use a simple linear capped and floored transformation that is restricted to be between 50 and 150 percent invested in bonds). These choices mirror those made in Asness, Ilmanen, and Maloney (2017).

3.1.4 Scatter Plots

It is easiest to see how these various transformations affect the raw values of signals visually. Exhibit 3.2 consists of four panels that illustrate the impact of each transformation on our real bond yield value signal. Panel A is a scatter plot reflecting the impact of treatment of extreme values. At first glance this may look surprising, as there is not a concentration of data points at a global extreme value. This is because the capping and flooring is done each month using all data available up until that point. Consequently, what is extreme is an evolving concept over time. The correlation between the original and capped/floored values is 0.96.

Panel B is a scatter plot reflecting the impact of benchmarking and volatility scaling. This transformation is changing the information contained in real bond yields over the full period. What is going on? This is because our analysis needs to be at a point in time. For each month we can only make use of the information that was available at that point in time. Thus, the benchmarking is based on a median of real bond yield using all data up to the month of interest, and the nonparametric volatility scaling is also only using information on the distribution of real bond yields up to the month of interest. The correlation between the capped/floored real bond yield and the fully transformed value signal is 0.86. In contrast, if we had

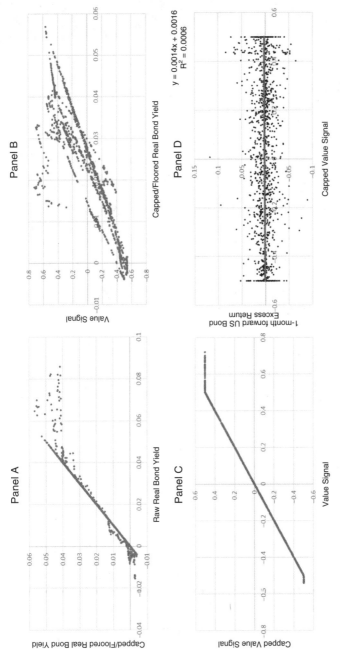

EXHIBIT 3.2 Value signals – term premium. Panel A shows the effect of capping and flooring values at the 95th and 5th percentile (expanding window). Panel B shows the effect of benchmarking and volatility scaling (nonparametric Z-scoring of the capped signal). Panel C shows the final signal timing curve. Panel D shows the link between value timing and one-month-ahead long-term government bond excess returns.

Sources: Described in text, period 1920–2020.

used a full-sample median and full sample 95th less 5th percentile deflator we would have a correlation of 1. This is not a loss of information from a tactical asset allocation perspective. You can only use information that is available to you at the relevant time.

Panel C then shows the impact of our selected timing curve. This has the expected shape as all values more than 0.5 in absolute value are floored and capped at −0.5 and +0.5, respectively. This monotone transformation is one way to scale the strength of your convictions in the signal. There is a lot of choice here. Our choice is linear in the transformed real bond yield signal between −0.5 and +0.5. We are choosing not to tactically vary our positions in government bonds too much. Alternative choices could be placing even less weight on central values and only taking active positions when your signal is sufficiently large in either direction.

Finally, we are now able to assess whether our simple value measure has any out-of-sample success in timing exposure to the term premium. Panel D shows the data. The vertical axis is the one-month forward excess return of long-term government bonds, and the horizontal axis is the fully trans-formed value signal. The line of best fit is shown on the exhibit and it has an R^2 of 0.0006, which corresponds to a correlation (information coefficient) of 0.024. This is a small correlation coefficient and suggests value signals, at least as we have chosen to measure them, have only limited success in timing exposure to the term premium.

Exhibit 3.3 and Exhibit 3.4 show scatter plots for momentum and carry, respectively. Capping and flooring extreme values has minimal impact on the information content of each signal (Panel A). There is a similar less-than-perfect correlation between the capped signals and the bench-marked and volatility scaled transformed signal (Panel B) with a correlation of 0.90 and 0.95 for momentum and carry, respectively. Again, this is attributable to the point-in-time nature of our forecasting exercise. Both momentum and carry have the same timing curve applied (Panel C). Finally, the investment efficacy of momentum and carry are superior to value (Panel D). Specifically, the correlation of the fully transformed momentum (carry) signal and one-month forward excess return of long-term government bonds is 0.061 (0.107), respectively.

A natural question to then ask is, how do these investment signals work individually and in combination? Our investment decision was to decide whether to invest $1 into long-term government bonds each month or some other allocation of between $0.50 and $1.50, based on the respective invest-ment signal. The active return is then the excess of cash return of the out-performance attributable to that investment signal. Exhibit 3.5 provides a summary of the active investment return potential for the various signal combinations.

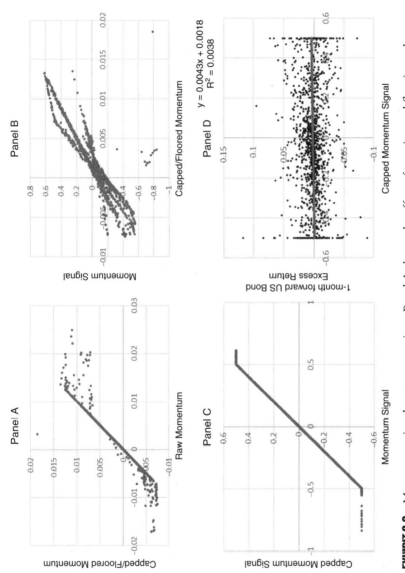

EXHIBIT 3.3 Momentum signals – term premium. Panel A shows the effect of capping and flooring values at the 95th and 5th percentile (expanding window). Panel B shows the effect of benchmarking and volatility scaling (nonparametric Z-scoring of the capped signal). Panel C shows the final signal timing curve. Panel D shows the link between momentum timing and one-month-ahead long-term government bond excess returns.

Sources: Described in text, period 1920–2020.

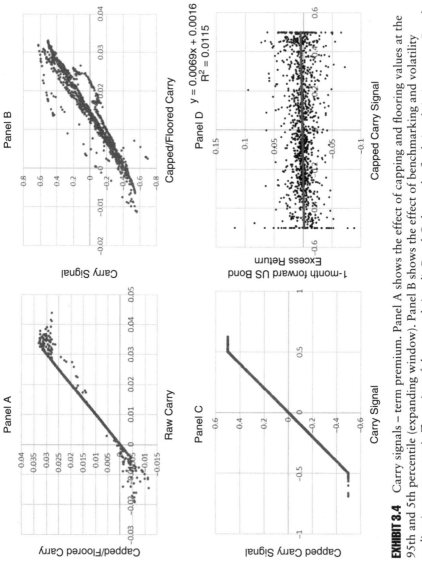

EXHIBIT 3.4 Carry signals – term premium. Panel A shows the effect of capping and flooring values at the 95th and 5th percentile (expanding window). Panel B shows the effect of benchmarking and volatility scaling (non-parametric Z-scoring of the capped signal). Panel C shows the final signal timing curve. Panel D shows the link between carry timing and one-month-ahead long-term government bond excess returns. *Sources:* Described in text, period 1920–2020.

EXHIBIT 3.5 Active returns from tactically timing term premium.

	Value	Momentum	Carry	Value + Momentum	Value + Momentum + Carry
Average	0.16%	0.35%	0.76%	0.27%	0.42%
Std. Dev.	0.0222	0.0228	0.0242	0.0150	0.0148
Sharpe	0.07	0.15	0.31	0.18	0.29
Alpha (ann.)	−0.02%	0.37%	0.68%	0.18%	0.35%

Sources: Described in text, period 1920–2020.

The correlation across the active return series is informative to help understand the return profile of the combinations of signals. Value and momentum have a modest negative correlation of −0.17, value and carry have a very low correlation of 0.01, and momentum and carry have a positive correlation of 0.48 (part of this higher correlation is due to the use of total returns as the measure of momentum that includes the realization of carry). The combination of value and momentum, and value and momentum and carry, are formed by simple averages of the underlying fully transformed individual signals. Given their low pairwise correlations, it is not surprising to see improved risk-adjusted returns from the combinations. This is diversification at work.

Although the Sharpe ratios are all positive, the magnitude is small compared to the full sample Sharpe ratio for the term premium (0.35). The astute reader will notice that this Sharpe ratio is slightly different than the 0.34 quoted in Chapter 2 (this is due to a slightly longer time period and different data source used here). The average excess return for long-term government bonds is around 2 percent for the 1920–2020 period. Except for carry, the "alphas" in Exhibit 3.5 are small relative to the term premium itself (of course, leverage can be applied to a long/short implementation of the various timing signals to increase the level of returns). Furthermore, these active investment decisions all require active trading, which would incur additional trading costs. The returns that we have looked at are all before accounting for implementation costs. In summary, the small timing returns are the basis for the working title of the paper on which this analysis was based: "Sin a Little" (Asness, Ilmanen, and Maloney 2017).

3.1.5 Skill in Timing

Another way to visualize the investment return potential from tactically timing exposure to the term premium is to track cumulative excess return performance and the associated outperformance for each of the signals individually. This can help place the relative scale of returns into context. Exhibit 3.6 shows the cumulative excess returns to a buy-and-hold position in long-term government bonds (solid black line). This is what a Sharpe ratio of 0.35 looks like (over the long run, your wealth is a lot more than where it started from, $1 in this chart, but there are some ugly periods along the way, the middle decades of the 1900s). The full tactical timing model that made equal use of value, momentum, and carry signals has an even more attractive cumulate excess return profile (solid gray line). This is the net benefit of our investment insights outlined in the prior section. When we strip out the outperformance of each individual signal (dashed lines), the return potential here is small relative to the passive exposure to the term premium. Therefore, people say, "sin a little" (there is some evidence of out-of-sample return predictability for timing exposure to the term premium, but the magnitude of that return is small relative to the amount of risk taken).

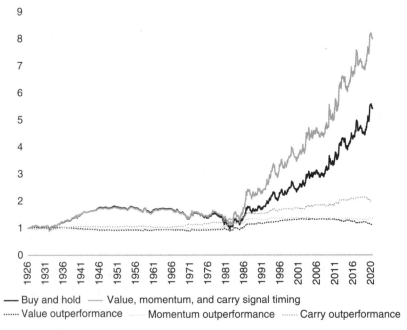

EXHIBIT 3.6   Cumulative excess returns from long-term government bonds and associated tactical exposures.
Sources: Described in text, period 1920–2020.

3.1.6 Extensions

Everything we have explored for tactical investment decisions is based on sound economic principles. However, the precision and breadth of information we have looked at to measure carry and forecast expected changes in yields was deliberately limited. Our purpose was to lay out a framework. A user is then free to improve the specific investment insights to make better tactical investment decisions. Later, I discuss various avenues that asset owners and investors may wish to consider for their tactical investment decisions for term premium.

Our carry measure only captured the term spread. This makes only limited use of information in the shape of the yield curve. In developed markets like the United States there are many bonds trading in secondary markets (and associated interest rate derivatives). From these secondary market prices, it is possible to build a zero-coupon bond yield curve. With this granular zero curve, you can then re-price a given bond on a roll-forward basis (e.g., 6 or 12 months later). Comparing the two prices of the bond, cum-coupon, will provide a more comprehensive measure of carry that makes complete use of yield curve information.

Our momentum measure only made use of the most recent 12 months of bond excess returns. Although there is a lot that could be done by altering the look-back period and weighting schema used for momentum, I think that is an exercise prone to in-sample data mining. Careful thought should be given to the measure of price momentum. Do you want to use total or excess return momentum? Return momentum includes the realization of carry, which you may not want to include, leaving carry as a separate signal. Additionally, asset owners and investors should give thought to what are the determinants of yields (see Chapter 2) and use those insights to broaden measures of momentum. For example, we saw in Chapter 2 that risk-free government bond yields are intrinsically linked to economic growth and inflation expectations. Thus, measures of the real economy (industrial production, GDP, aggregate employment, capacity utilization) and inflation expectations can be used directly as additional measures of momentum. Government bonds have a negative sensitivity to both economic growth and inflation, so momentum in growth and inflation would be a negative signal for the term premium. Brooks (2017) provides a useful summary of the types of approaches that could be used to capture non-price-based measures of momentum relevant for the fixed income market.

Finally, our value measure was very crude. Chapter 2 made it clear that long-term inflation expectations are but one of the determinants of yields. If we are trying to build a forecast of where yields are likely to move to, we should explore what macroeconomic models have to offer. There are many such models to choose from, but they generally provide structure (i) linking how current short-term interest rates will evolve over the life of the long-term government bond (e.g., a statistical or economically motivated path of future interest rates), and (ii) anchoring longer-term interest rates (e.g., to economic growth and productivity and long-term inflation expectations). Armed with information on the structural determinants of yields, you can then estimate the distance between actual yields and model yields. This gap can be thought of as a "term premium" but, depending on construction, may also be your forecast of expected yield changes.

There are clearly a lot of potential extensions of the term premium tactical timing model that we have discussed. One important caveat should be kept in mind though. Despite all the effort that could be expended on improving the tactical investment decision, this is an inherently low-breadth investment choice (see e.g., Grinold and Kahn 2000). You can either over- or underweight your exposure to long-term government bonds (long-only investor) or long or short interest rate derivatives (unconstrained long/short investor). For both investor types the low breadth implies that the amount of risk allocated to these tactical decisions should be moderate. Remember the adage "sin a little."

3.2 MARKET TIMING – CREDIT PREMIUM

3.2.1 Framework for Timing

We will use a similar framework for thinking about tactical investment decisions for corporate bonds, with one key exception. As Chapter 2 demonstrated, the unique source of return potential for corporate bonds is the return over and above risk-free yields. Our focus now is on credit-excess returns.

We can extend Equation (3.3) to allow for both risk-free and risky components of discount rates (y reflects the risk-free portion and s the risky portion). Using the language from Chapter 2, y captures the rates component of corporate bond returns, and s captures the spread component of corporate bond returns. The return approximation in Equation (3.7) notes that changing expectations of both the risk-free and risky components of discount rates will generate returns. We will ignore the risk-free portion here (that was covered in the previous section). In practice, this means that we are looking at interest-rate hedged portfolios of corporate bonds or credit index derivatives.

$$Returns \approx \Delta P = \frac{C_1}{(1 + \Delta E[y_1] + \Delta E[s_1])^1} + \frac{C_2}{(1 + \Delta E[y_2] + \Delta E[s_2])^2} +$$
$$\frac{C_3}{(1 + \Delta E[y_3] + \Delta E[s_3])^3} + \cdots \frac{C_{LT} + P_{LT}}{(1 + \Delta E[y_{LT}] + \Delta E[s_{LT}])^{LT}}$$
$$(3.7)$$

This approximation helps to identify the importance of changes in credit spreads, s, and how they affect corporate bond prices. Credit spreads and, more specifically, the term structure of credit spreads imply an initial expected credit-excess return. The discussion for carry in the context of government bonds applies here too, except that the curve we are talking about is for credit spreads, not risk-free yields. So, our expected credit excess return has two broad components:

$$E[Credit\ Excess\ Returns] \approx Initial\ Spread + E[Changes\ in\ Spreads] \quad (3.8)$$

We have our framework. First, there is the "carry" component of credit excess returns. This is the expected return if the shape of the credit-term structure remains unchanged. Estimating the carry component of corporate bonds can be quite challenging, but the idea is to re-price a given corporate bond, or a portfolio of corporate bonds, using the same credit curve but rolling forward all associated cash flows.

Second, we have a catchall component of returns for the changes in credit spreads. For this, we will lean on research examining cross-sectional predictability of credit spreads and credit excess returns (e.g., Houweling and van Zundert 2017 and Israel, Palhares, and Richardson 2018). Value and momentum are common investment themes in these papers, and both are designed to forecast changes in credit spreads. In the case of momentum, that is for continuation in recent changes in credit spreads. In the case of value, that is for expected reversal of credit spreads to a "normal" level.

We will use a simple price-based measure of momentum: the 12-month arithmetic average of index level corporate bond excess returns. Our measure of value is based on an expanding window regression as follows:

$$Spread = \alpha + \beta_{LEV}Leverage + \beta_{PROF}Profitabilty + \beta_{VOL}Volatility + \varepsilon \quad (3.9)$$

Spread is the index-level option-adjusted spread (this is the credit spread adjusted for the expected exercise of any embedded options in the underlying corporate bonds that would affect the duration profile and hence yield of the corporate bond). Leverage is the average market leverage of US firms (approximated by Russell 1000 index constituents) measured as the market value of equity plus the book value of all net debt (including minority interest and preferred stock) divided by the market value of equity. Profitability is the average profitability of US firms (using gross profits divided by total assets). Volatility is the average total return volatility for US large capitalization firms using BARRA risk model (USE3). The three explanatory variables are measured monthly using trailing 12-month data. As expected, the regression coefficients on leverage and volatility are strongly positive (for US investment-grade (IG) corporate bonds β_{LEV} is 1.63 with a test statistic of 23.5, β_{VOL} is 2.81 with a test statistic if 9.89; for US high yield (HY) corporate bonds β_{LEV} is 4.43 with a test statistic of 22.4, β_{VOL} is 11.97 with a test statistic if 14.88) and the regression coefficient for profitability is strongly negative (for US IG corporate bonds β_{PROF} is −8.07 with a test statistic of −11.07; for US HY corporate bonds β_{PROF} is −12.91 with a test statistic of −5.49).

We estimate Equation (3.9) separately for the US IG corporate and US HY corporate markets. We use an expanding window regression starting in 1990 for US IG and 1994 for US HY. Thus, our value measures cover a shorter period than what is available for momentum (starts in 1988 for US IG and 1989 for US HY) and carry (starts in 1989 for US IG and 1994 for US HY).

3.2.2 Data (Some Details)

Our credit-premium timing model will be assessed on data sourced from Bloomberg Indices. We will examine both IG and HY corporate bond indices. A benefit of the IG index is that it had a longer time series, whereas the benefit of the HY index, as we saw in Chapter 2, is that there is more credit premium and variability in credit excess returns in the HY market. And the magnitude and variability of the credit premium is a necessary condition for tactical investment decisions to be economically meaningful. Our data will be from 1989–2020 for the US IG index and 1994–2020 for the US HY index. Although we can measure momentum (using excess returns) in the HY markets back to 1990, option adjusted spreads (necessary for both carry and value measures) are only available from 1994 onward.

3.2.3 Converting Raw Data to Signals

We can now assess whether, and how, our return forecasting framework works. We need to create a time series of "signals" that indicate the relative attractiveness of corporate bonds (credit premium). Consistent with our analysis of the term premium, we will assess our skill from the perspective of a real money investor who needs to remain invested in the fixed income markets, but is able to dial up or down the amount of capital invested into the market at any specific point in time.

We have three investment signals: (i) value (measured as the regression residual from an expanding window regression of index-level credit spreads projected onto measures of average profitability, leverage, and volatility for a typical US firm), (ii) momentum (measured as the most recent 12-month arithmetic average of corporate bond excess returns), and (iii) carry (measured as the credit spread).

For each of these three measures we need to convert them to a "signal." We use the same transformation procedure as we did for the term premium. Please refer to Section 3.1.3 for a reminder.

3.2.4 Scatter Plots

Let's start with an examination of the three signals individually. Exhibits 3.7, 3.8, and 3.9 show scatter plots for value, momentum, and carry for the US IG corporate bond market, respectively. Exhibits 3.10, 3.11, and 3.12 show scatter plots for value, momentum, and carry for the US HY corporate bond market, respectively. The structure of these exhibits is like what was shown previously for analysis of the term premium. Across all signals and both corporate bond markets the impact of capping and flooring extreme values is small (and behaves exactly as expected), and the benchmarked and volatility scaled transformed signal preserves a lot of the information of the raw signals (the correlations between the capped signals and the transformed signal vary between 0.82 and 0.93 for US HY and between 0.82 and 0.84 for US IG). Again, the lack of perfect correlation is attributable to the point-in-time nature of our forecasting exercise. All measures use the same timing curve. Finally, the investment efficacy of value, momentum, and carry are shown in the bottom right (Panel D) of each exhibit. Credit-premium timing in the US IG markets over the 1989–2020 period has been less successful than the US HY markets. Specifically, the correlations of value, momentum, and carry timing with one-month forward US IG corporate bond index credit excess returns are 0.01, −0.01, and 0.06, respectively. In contrast, the correlations of value, momentum, and carry timing with 1-month-forward US HY corporate bond index credit-excess returns are 0.09, 0.08, and 0.03, respectively.

There are striking differences in the timing-model performance across IG and HY markets. First, there is lower predictability in IG markets, perhaps due to the lower magnitude and variability of credit-excess returns (there is just less credit premium to be tactically timed). Second, there are differences in the relative performance of the signals. Momentum works better in HY markets, and carry works better in IG markets. The finding of momentum working less well in safer corporate bonds is evident in the cross-section of corporate bond returns, so it is not surprising to see that result translate to the index level (e.g., Israel, Palhares, and Richardson 2018).

A natural question to then ask is how do these investment signals work individually and in combination. Exhibits 3.13 (US IG) and 3.14 (US HY) provide a summary of the active returns from the respective timing signals,

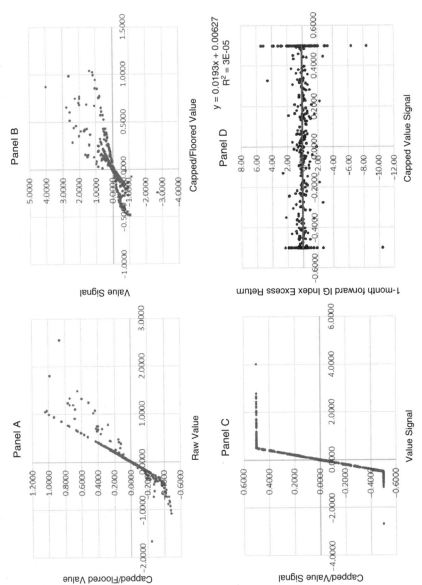

EXHIBIT 3.7 Value signals – Credit Premium (US IG). Panel A shows the effect of capping and flooring values at the 95th and 5th percentile (expanding window). Panel B shows the effect of benchmarking and volatility scaling (nonparametric Z-scoring of the capped signal). Panel C shows the final signal-timing curve. Panel D shows the link between value timing and one-month-ahead IG corporate bond index excess returns. Sources: Described in text, period 1989–2020.

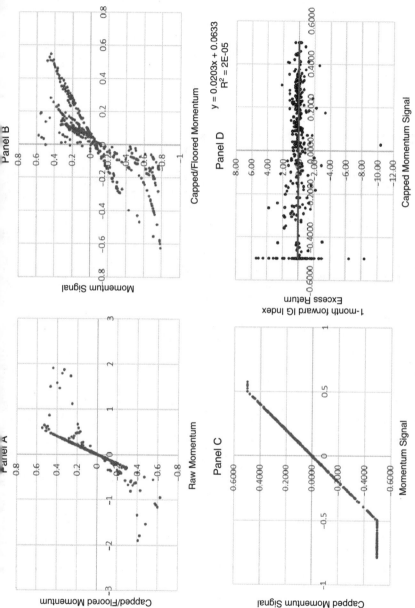

EXHIBIT 3.8 Momentum signals – Credit Premium (US IG). Panel A shows the effect of capping and flooring values at the 95th and 5th percentile (expanding window). Panel B shows the effect of benchmarking and volatility scaling (nonparametric Z-scoring of the capped signal). Panel C shows the final signal-timing curve. Panel D shows the link between momentum timing and one-month-ahead IG corporate bond index excess returns.
Sources: Described in text, period 1989–2020.

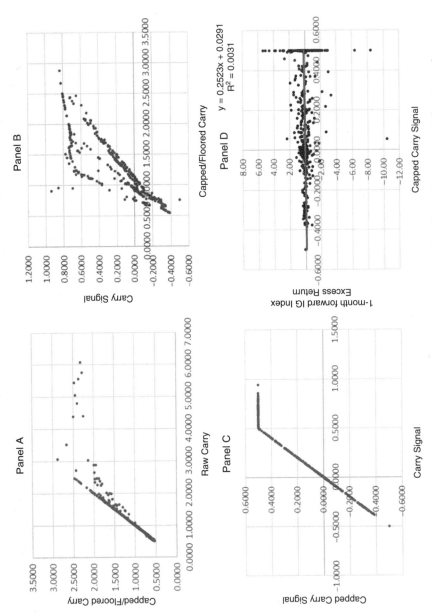

EXHIBIT 3.9 Carry signals – Credit Premium (US IG). Panel A shows the effect of capping and flooring values at the 95th and 5th percentile (expanding window). Panel B shows the effect of benchmarking and volatility scaling (nonparametric Z-scoring of the capped signal). Panel C shows the final signal-timing curve. Panel D shows the link between carry timing and one-month-ahead IG corporate bond index excess returns.

Sources: Described in text, period 1989–2020.

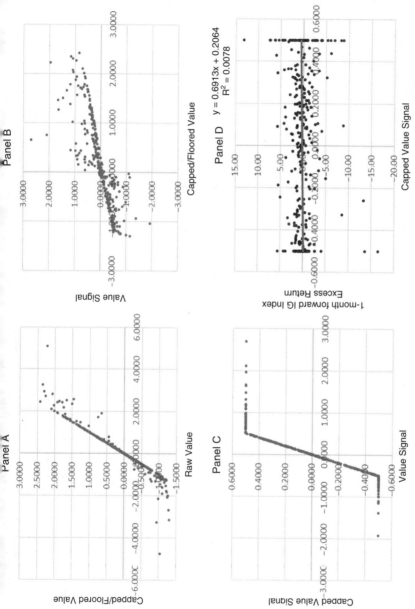

EXHIBIT 3.10 Value signals – Credit Premium (US HY). Panel A shows the effect of capping and flooring values at the 95th and 5th percentile (expanding window). Panel B shows the effect of benchmarking and volatility scaling (nonparametric Z-scoring of the capped signal). Panel C shows the final signal-timing curve. Panel D shows the link between value timing and one-month-ahead HY corporate bond index excess returns.

Sources: Described in text, period 1994–2020.

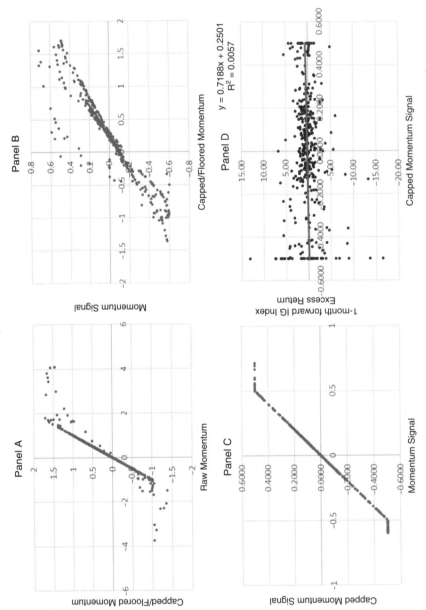

EXHIBIT 3.11 Momentum signals – Credit Premium (US HY). Panel A shows the effect of capping and flooring values at the 95th and 5th percentile (expanding window). Panel B shows the effect of benchmarking and volatility scaling (nonparametric Z-scoring of the capped signal). Panel C shows the final signal-timing curve. Panel D shows the link between momentum timing and one-month-ahead HY corporate bond index excess returns.

Sources: Described in text, period 1994–2020.

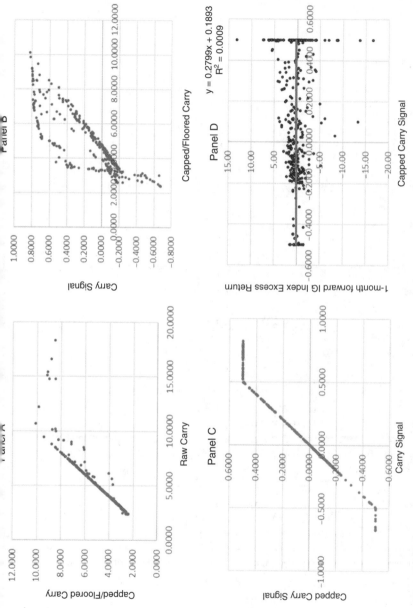

EXHIBIT 3.12 Carry signals – Credit Premium (US HY). Panel A shows the effect of capping and flooring values at the 95th and 5th percentile (expanding window). Panel B shows the effect of benchmarking and volatility scaling (non-parametric Z-scoring of the capped signal). Panel C shows the final signal-timing curve. Panel D shows the link between carry timing and one-month-ahead HY corporate bond index excess returns.

Sources: Described in text, period 1994–2020.

EXHIBIT 3.13   Active returns from tactically timing credit premium (US IG Corporate Bonds).

	Momentum	Carry	Value	Value + Momentum	Value + Momentum + Carry
Average	0.02%	0.27%	0.01%	0.01%	0.10%
Std. Dev.	0.0169	0.0179	0.0210	0.0081	0.0078
Sharpe	0.01	0.15	0.01	0.02	0.13
Alpha (ann.)	0.22%	0.00%	−0.10%	0.06%	0.04%

Sources: Described in text, period 1989–2020.

EXHIBIT 3.14   Active returns from tactically timing credit premium (US HY Corporate Bonds).

	Momentum	Carry	Value	Value + Momentum	Value + Momentum + Carry
Average	0.94%	0.19%	0.93%	1.03%	0.82%
Std. Dev.	0.0387	0.0394	0.0398	0.0284	0.0169
Sharpe	0.24	0.05	0.23	0.36	0.48
Alpha (ann.)	1.73%	−0.79%	0.83%	1.37%	0.71%

Sources: Described in text, period 1994–2020.

both individually and in combination. The active return is then the excess of cash return of the outperformance attributable to that investment insight (in excess of the return from the credit market itself).

The correlation across the active return series is informative to help understand the return profile of the combinations of signals. Value and momentum have a modest negative correlation of −0.33 (IG) and −0.02 (HY), value and carry have a modest positive correlation of 0.31 (IG) and 0.02 (HY), whereas momentum and carry have a very negative correlation of −0.85 (IG) and −0.86 (HY). This latter negative correlation is not surprising, because momentum tends to be positive when credit spreads have tightened relative to history (tightening spreads means positive credit excess returns), and carry is positive when credit spreads have widened relative to history. Of course, such a strong negative correlation raises questions about the efficacy of the selected measures. Indeed, more complete measures of carry that cover the entire shape of the credit curve, and broader measures of momentum, generate lower, but still negative correlations.

As with the term-premium timing exercise, the combination of value and momentum, and value and momentum and carry, are formed by simple averages of the underlying fully transformed individual signals. Given their low pairwise correlations it is not surprising to see improved risk-adjusted returns from the combinations. Again, this is diversification at work.

Although the Sharpe ratios are all positive, the magnitude is small especially for the IG market. The "alphas" are all very small in the IG market except for carry, but are much larger for the HY markets, especially for value and momentum. The caveat we stressed earlier about implementation costs and challenges is even more important for this market. Anyone planning to engage in timing the credit premium should understand the liquidity and trading costs. Credit index derivatives have become increasingly popular over the last 10 years, but the trading volumes are still small relative to equity index derivatives.

3.2.5 Skill in Timing

Exhibits 3.15 (IG) and 3.16 (HY) show the cumulative excess returns to a buy-and-hold position in corporate bonds (solid black line in each respective graph). The full tactical timing model that made equal use of value, momentum, and carry signals provides a useful addition, but only for HY markets

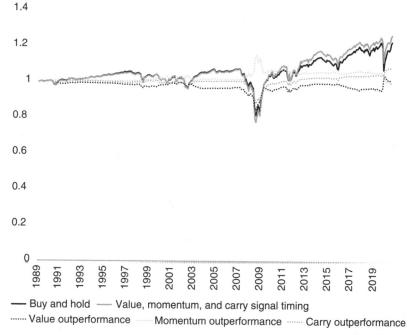

— Buy and hold — Value, momentum, and carry signal timing
······ Value outperformance ···· Momentum outperformance ···· Carry outperformance

EXHIBIT 3.15 Cumulative excess returns from US IG corporate bonds and associated tactical exposures.
Sources: Described in text, period 1994–2020.

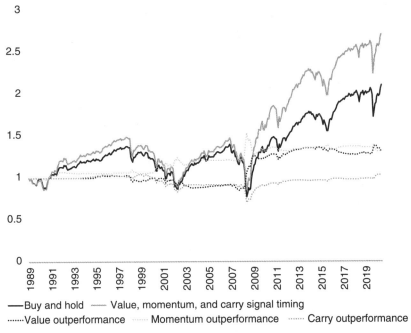

—Buy and hold ⸺ Value, momentum, and carry signal timing
⋯⋯Value outperformance ⋯⋯ Momentum outperformance ⋯⋯ Carry outperformance

EXHIBIT 3.16 Cumulative excess returns from US HY corporate bonds and associated tactical exposures.
Sources: Described in text, period 1994–2020.

(solid gray line). As with term premium timing, when we strip out the outperformance of each individual signal (dashed lines), the return potential is small relative to the passive exposure to the credit premium. Remember, "sin a little."

3.2.6   Extensions

Next, I discuss various avenues that asset owners and investors may wish to consider for their tactical investment decisions for the credit premium. The model developed in this chapter is far from exhaustive; there are many profitable extensions to explore. Carry measures can be enhanced by making full use of the credit term structure. Momentum can span price and fundamental measures. Our timing model only utilized price-based momentum for the credit index itself, but price-based measures of related assets (e.g., equity-index returns) can also be examined. Fundamental measures can include changing expectations of firm level data (e.g., cash flows, operating profits, margins, etc.), and changing expectations of firm level defaults. This firm level data can be aggregated across companies in the index to form an index level view. Similarly, fundamental data can be sourced at the economy level directly. Corporate bond spreads are directly linked to economic growth expectations. Thus, measures of the real economy (industrial production, GDP, and aggregate employment) can be used as additional measures of momentum. Corporate bonds have a positive sensitivity to economic growth, so momentum in growth would be a positive signal for the credit premium.

Indeed, Asvanunt and Richardson (2017; AR), document that the credit risk premium varies with aspects of the business cycle. Using a growth composite based on the Chicago Fed National Activity Index and the "surprise" in the US industrial production growth, AR find that index-level credit-excess returns are higher in periods of economic growth. This is expected as companies benefit from overall economic growth, it will increase their ability to generate free cash flow that will, in turn, increase their asset value, thereby making them 'safer'. Credit spreads naturally fall during periods of rising economic growth giving rise to positive credit-excess returns. Using Moody's annual global default rates for investment grade bonds, AR construct a credit default composite of the year-on-year change in aggregate default rates and a measure of the surprise in aggregate default rates. Their surprise measure is the difference between the realized default rate over the 12-month period relative to the Moody's Baa-Aaa spread at the beginning of the period. AR find that credit excess returns are significantly higher during periods of lower default intensity. It is important to note that the analysis in AR is purely descriptive, because they were looking at measures of changing expectations of economic growth and default rates that are measured contemporaneously with credit-excess returns. Investors looking to expand on their credit-timing models should focus on business cycle forecasts and default intensity. We will have a lot to say about default modeling in Chapter 6.

Finally, on potential improvements to value metrics, a book could be written on the different approaches taken to explain credit spreads. As we will see in Chapter 6, the key determinant of credit spreads is expected loss given default (apologies for jumping ahead). Improved value metrics will focus on forecasting that directly: improved forecasts of default or credit migration and associated recovery rates.

3.3 OTHER CONSIDERATIONS

3.3.1 Dangers of Data Mining

Although the dangers of data mining and in-sample fitting are relevant for all investors, and especially for systematic investors who rely on data for their investment decision-making process, this risk is particularly important for timing models. As we saw in Sections 3.1 and 3.2, there is only one data series that is utilized to test the efficacy of a timing model. In the case of timing the term premium, we were fortunate to have nearly a century of data to work with. For timing the credit premium, we had less than three decades of data. This is a problem.

Although systematic investors may pride themselves on not explicitly engaging in data mining (i.e., not running hundreds of specifications to try and find the specification that worked best in sample) there are at least two areas where implicit data mining creeps into the analysis. First, there are many choices that need to be made once you chose a raw data attribute to be utilized in a model. For example, we used the real bond yield as a value signal for timing exposure to the term premium. This measure is the difference between the yield on the asset to be timed and a maturity matched inflation forecast. There are choices about where the data for inflation forecasts are sourced. If you use survey data, which survey provider do you use? Do you use the mean or median value across the forecasters covered by that provider? Do you want to equally weight forecasters (i.e., those who have more skill or whose forecasts are likely to contain newer information might be up weighted)? There are choices about how to convert a real bond yield at a point in time to a signal. In most cases, you subtract an historical benchmark value of your signal to identify the sign of your signal. But how is this done? Do you use rolling look-back periods or expanding look-back periods? Mean or median values to identify the benchmark? Equal weighting for all prior time periods or place more weight on the more recent history? Often, a signal is also scaled by a measure of volatility to identify the strength of the signal (e.g., you expect to see larger changes in values for your signal in more volatile time periods). Do you want to volatility scale your signal? If so, do you use a parametric or nonparametric method? How do you convert your transformed signal to a trading decision (i.e., what is the shape of your timing curve)? Although we consistently used a capped/floored linear curve, there are many other possibilities.

All these choices were made for both timing models in Sections 3.1 and 3.2. Were these the best choices or most easily defensible choices? Although they may not have been obvious at the time, you now know there is considerable room for different choices to be made across each dimension for each signal. Similar choices need to be made for each signal and further choices as to how to aggregate across signals. If you were to map this out, there would be a very large number of combinations. The impact of these choices individually is not likely to matter too much, but the choices can quickly compound differences. Indeed, in a recent paper, Kessler, Scherer, and Harries (2020) examine 3,168 alternative implementations of equity value strategies in the S&P 500 universe and find full-sample Sharpe ratios vary between −0.10 and 0.78. Therein lies the data-mining risk: out of a large set of feasible design choices, there is a risk of "fitting" to maximize an in-sample result. This concern is relevant not only for timing models covered in this chapter, but also for the cross-sectional relative-value models that we will cover in Chapters 5–7. A potential remedy for this type of data-mining risk is to ensure consistency in choices across the research effort. If choices are made on data sources that are relevant across different geographies or asset classes, use the same data source. If choices are made for timing models in different asset classes (e.g., lookback periods, volatility scaling, demeaning, etc.) ensure similar choices are made across individuals. This helps mitigate data-mining risks.

Second, there is a somewhat unique data-mining risk that comes with timing models – namely, memory. This is especially true for those who have been investing for a while. Such individuals will have a good memory of mistakes that were made in the past and/or data attributes that they wished they had access to back in time. The risk here is that attempts to improve timing models over time add elements into the model that were either not available back in time (e.g., new data were collected once people realized they were relevant and that data are then back-filled) or if the data were available investors were not aware of them or utilizing them correctly. Back-filling is a serious risk, because, arguably, the model is "cheating" with respect to knowledge of that data and their efficacy should be tested only after the data are genuinely available to an investor. Newfound awareness is also a risk, but perhaps that reflects your ability to identify useful information, albeit after the fact, and the risk is that the model tweak is only beneficial for one data point in the time series.

Another approach that is often used by systematic investors where there may be a concern about data quality is to build your model using data from one provider (e.g., you may use yields, spread, and historical return information from ICE/BAML) and then test the return performance using data from a different provider (e.g., you may use future excess returns from Bloomberg). This is a prudent way to help mitigate finding false positives.

3.3.2 Adding Breadth

Our analyses in Sections 3.1 and 3.2 were limited to considering one market – namely, the United States. This was a deliberate choice, as we have the longest series of data to test the efficacy of tactical models. Asset owners do not need to limit themselves to timing decisions in just the United States, nor for limiting the investment decision to just one asset (10-year bonds in the case of term premium and US IG corporate bond index in the case of credit premium). There is a wide set of risk-free assets across developed markets from which it is possible to express timing views on the relative attractiveness of the term premium. Similarly, there are multiple corporate bond indices from which it is possible to express timing views on the relative attractiveness of the credit premium. These tactical models could be extended to emerging markets as well. Although this can enhance the breadth of tactical allocation models, it is important to keep in mind that these are not independent bets, because there is a large common component in yield moves across countries and aggregate credit spreads across geographies and rating categories. Careful risk budgeting is needed to account for the correlated positions.

Expanding breadth for tactical investment decisions on term and credit premium also opens the choice of delta-adjusting your investment views. For example, in the cross-section of credit sensitive securities, there is natural variation in the sensitivity of the credit and equity claims for an issuer (see e.g., Lok and Richardson 2011). As the riskiness of the borrower increases (think of increased leverage and/or increased volatility), the credit claim starts to resemble the equity claim more closely (Schaefer and Strebulaev 2008). In options-pricing language, the debt claim is more in the money and the value of that claim is more sensitive to the underlying asset value of the corporate issuer. Exhibit 3.17 shows this relation for a company that has both debt and equity outstanding. For simplicity, we assume that the risk-free rate is zero, the firm does not pay dividends, asset volatility is 40 percent, and the outstanding debt has a value of $100. The hockey-stick shaped lines capture the intrinsic value of the respective claim (i.e., the equity claim has an intrinsic value of zero when the value of assets is less than the amount

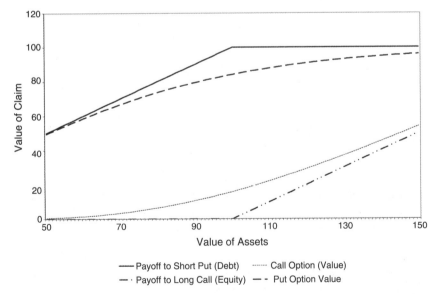

EXHIBIT 3.17   Relation between credit and equity values and underlying asset value.

that needs to be paid to creditors). The dashed and dotted curves reflect the market value of the debt and equity claims, respectively, using standard option pricing formulae.

What can we learn from Exhibit 3.17? As you start at the far right of Exhibit 3.17, the asset value of the firm is far more than the outstanding debt. Thus, any change in the expected asset value has very minimal impact on the credit value (i.e., the slope of the upper dashed line is relatively flat, so the debt claim is out of the money). But as you move from right to left, the asset value decreases relative to the value of the outstanding debt (the "distance to default" decreases) and the sensitivity of the credit claim to underlying asset value increases. At the point where the asset value approaches the value of outstanding debt, the sensitivity of the credit claim to changes in asset value approaches the sensitivity of the equity claim to changes in asset value (i.e., the slope of the two dashed lines become more similar as you move toward the middle). This is the key take-away: the credit and equity are expected to co-move more strongly when there is more underlying credit risk (up to a point, of course, because in distressed situations the equity claim becomes insensitive to changes in asset values because it is too far out of the money).

What is the relevance to our tactical timing discussion? Investment decisions around aggregate credit markets might include views on (i) North American vs European corporate indices, (ii) IG vs. HY corporate indices, and (iii) developed vs. emerging market corporate indices. The set of issuers in the respective indices vary based on their underlying credit risk and, as such, the relevance of equity market information may be differentially important.

A similar line of reasoning can be applied to tactical investment decisions around the term premium. There are multiple liquid points across the yield curve in most developed markets. This provides additional breadth to capture attractive term premium at different points on risk-free curves. Although the yield curve shares common exposure to current short-term interest rates and the expected path of future short-term interest rates, the sensitivity of longer-term yields to expected central bank monetary policy actions, and recent news related to real economic growth (e.g., employment, GDP, industrial production, etc.) is less, so there is scope in tailoring investment decisions by utilizing differential sensitivity to fundamental information. This is true for both risk-free and risky bonds.

3.3.3 Remaining Fully Invested

Let's finish this chapter with an important reminder of the bigger picture. All the analysis in this chapter was about varying your capital (or risk) allocation to fixed income assets based on forecasts of the conditional attractiveness of the term premium or credit premium. Therefore, at certain times you will be overinvested in government or corporate bonds and at other times you will be underinvested in government or corporate bonds. The determination of conditional attractiveness was made in a partial equilibrium framework with no direct awareness of what else was happening in the asset owner's overall portfolio.

Similar approaches for tactical timing can be applied to other asset classes, especially stocks. An asset owner needs to appreciate the consequences of tactical timing decisions in one asset class. How are these investment decisions to be funded? If the tactical insights are implemented via a derivative overlay, that may simply mean allowing risk levels to vary through time around a long-term target. By itself, that may not be too challenging, but when there are multiple tactical timing decisions across asset classes (and even within asset classes as we have examined here with term and credit premia), what happens if tactical investment views across the board are suggesting to take more or less risk? As of writing in 2021, with interest rates low and elevated asset prices across most markets (public and private), this is a daunting challenge for asset owners. Although it might be easy to say government bonds look expensive, what else looks cheap where you may reallocate your capital (risk)?

REFERENCES

Asness, C., A. Ilmanen, and T. Maloney. (2017). Market timing: Sin a little resolving the valuation timing puzzle. *Journal of Investment Management*, 15, 23–40.

Asness, C., T. Moskowitz, and L. Pedersen. (2013). Value and momentum everywhere. *Journal of Finance*, 68, 929–985.

Asvanunt, A., and S. Richardson. (2017). The credit risk premium. *Journal of Fixed Income*, 26, 6–24.

Brooks, J. (2017). A half century of macro momentum. AQR working paper.

Grinold, R., and R. Kahn. (2000). *Active Portfolio Management*. McGraw-Hill.

Houweling, P., and J. van Zundert. (2017). Factor investing in the corporate bond market. *Financial Analysts Journal*, 73, 100–115.

Israel, R., D. Palhares, and S. Richardson. (2018). Common factors in corporate bond returns. *Journal of Investment Management*, 16, 17–46.

Kessler, S., B. Scherer, and J. Harries. (2020). Value by design? *Journal of Portfolio Management*, 46, 25–43.

Kozicki, S., and P. Tinsley. (2006). Survey-based estimates of the term structure of expected US inflation. Bank of Canada, working paper.

Lok, S., and S. Richardson. (2011). Credit markets and financial information. *Review of Accounting Studies*, 16, 487–500.

Schaefer, S. M., and I. A. Strebulaev. (2008). Structural models of credit risk are useful: Evidence from hedge ratios on corporate bonds. *Journal of Financial Economics*, 90, 1–19.

CHAPTER 4

Incumbent Active Fixed Income Managers

OVERVIEW

This chapter starts with a high-level overview of the types of investment approaches that are commonly used by fixed income managers. Active fixed income investment strategies include (i) avoidance of bad-selling practices (e.g., avoiding simple reliance on index inclusion rules), (ii) duration timing and yield curve management generally (e.g., variants of the tactical timing strategies discussed in Chapter 3), (iii) rotation across the broad sectors within aggregate indices (e.g., moving from developed to emerging markets or switching from duration to spread risk), (iv) seeking additional sources of return beyond the benchmark (e.g., private credit, bank loans and emerging markets), and (v) security selection, the primary focus of this book. Most of the active fixed income returns in excess of benchmark can be explained by passive beta, particularly an overreliance on the credit premium. We will see this pervasive pattern of reaching for yield via credit exposures across a wide set of active fixed managers including (i) US aggregate benchmarked managers (Core Plus), (ii) Global aggregate benchmarked managers, (iii) unconstrained bond managers, (iv) emerging market managers, and (v) credit long/short managers.

4.1 FRAMEWORK FOR ACTIVE FIXED INCOME MANAGEMENT

Let's start with a summary of the different types of investments an active fixed income manager can make. As outlined in Chapter 1 there is a huge investment opportunity set available in fixed income markets: (i) bonds issued by sovereign entities in developed and emerging markets, (ii) bonds issued by quasi-government entities across developed and emerging markets, (iii) asset-backed securities issued by government agencies (developed markets) and other nonagency asset-backed securities, (iv) bonds, and loans, issued by corporations across developed and emerging markets. There is no shortage of fixed income securities to choose from.

Although each active fixed income manager will describe what they do in their own idiosyncratic language, there is a lot of commonality in the types of investment choices made. The following list is an attempt to categorize these investment choices:

a. Avoidance of bad selling practices: This covers a wide set of active investment choices designed to avoid forced trading decisions because of index inclusion rules. Investment guidelines used by many large asset owners that force adherence to fixed income policy benchmarks can give rise to investment opportunities for those who are less constrained with respect to these guidelines. There are many examples. First, bonds are continually issued over time as the entities issuing them are going concerns and they need a regular source of financing for their operating and investment decisions. When bonds are newly issued, they do not enter bond indices until the month after their issuance. This creates a liquidity provision opportunity for asset owners who can participate in the primary market and collect what is known as the "new issue concession" (see e.g., Chapter 7 in Ben Dor, Desclee, Dynkin, Hyman, and Polbennikov 2021). Second, corporate bond parent indices continue to be demarcated by investment grade (IG) and high-yield (HY) ratings. Investor guidelines, especially for large insurance and pension entities, can limit or even preclude noninvestment grade rated securities. As, and when, corporate bonds are downgraded from IG to HY, this creates another liquidity provision opportunity for asset owners who are less rating constrained. This tolerance for rating downgrades can avoid the losses that get realized by selling around the time of the downgrade, because prices are depressed at this point from a net supply–demand imbalance (see e.g., Chapter 2 in Ben Dor, Desclee, Dynkin, Hyman, and Polbennikov 2021). Third, bonds are continually naturally dying as they mature, and most bond indices have inclusion rules that require a bond to have at least one year of maturity remaining. Again, avoiding selling bonds as they become shorter dated is another potential liquidity provision return source for the patient asset owner. As we will see later in Chapters 5 and 6, holding shorter-dated bonds may be preferred, because they have historically generated a higher return per unit of risk (see e.g., Ilmanen 2011), and if you already hold such securities, why remove them?

b. Asset allocation decisions: This covers the type of tactical investment decisions discussed in detail in Chapter 3 and related extensions. For example, tilting toward asset-backed securities relative to standard government bonds or corporate bonds, or tilting toward nonagency asset-backed securities relative to agency asset-backed securities, or tilting exposures across different geographies or rating or maturity buckets. This also includes general duration timing and yield curve management. As a gentle reminder of the difficulty in making profitable tactical asset allocation decisions (if Chapter 3 was insufficient to dissuade you from market timing), Exhibit 4.1 is useful.

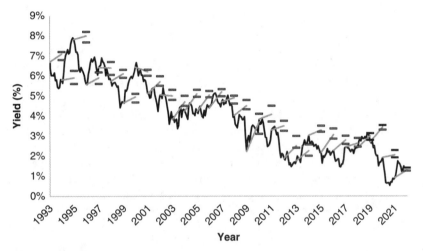

EXHIBIT 4.1   Forecasting 10-year US nominal yields.
Source: Consensus Economics for yield forecasts and Bloomberg Indices for 10-year government bond yields. Graph design originated by AQR.

The solid black line in Exhibit 4.1 is the time series of the US 10-year nominal bond yield over the 1993–2021 period. The short gray lines capture the forecast at the start of each calendar year for what the yield will be at the end of that calendar year. Nominal yield forecasts are the average across participants in the Consensus Economics dataset (results are similar if the median is used instead). The short dark pairs of horizontal lines that straddle the end of the gray lines capture the lower and upper quartile of yield forecasts across the forecasters covered by Consensus Economics. It should be very clear that professional forecasters are not successful in their forecasts of one-year forward long-term US bond yields. If these forecasters were investors, the average absolute error in their forecasts is 1 percent. Given the duration for US 10-year government bonds is about 8, this translates to an average –8 percent annualized return from duration timing or yield curve management if you relied on professional yield forecasts. Humbling.

   c. Out-of-benchmark tilts: This covers a wide variety of fixed income securities that are either excluded or only thinly represented in standard fixed income policy benchmarks (e.g., Aggregate Indices). Examples include riskier HY corporate bonds, corporate loans, collateralized debt obligations, inflation-linked securities, and various forms of emerging market debt. Although the number of these out-of-benchmark sectors suggests a substantial increase in the investment opportunity set, it is useful to see how correlated the returns are across these sectors. Exhibit 4.2 reports the correlation of returns over the 1992–2020 for the main out-of-benchmark sectors. Although each sector has a low correlation with the term premium, and hence is potentially diversifying, it is important to note the very high correlation among these out-of-benchmark sectors. They do not appear to be diversifying beyond the credit premium. This will be a common theme for the rest of the chapter.

d. Liquidity provision: This can cover some of the avoidance of bad selling practices discussed earlier, but it also reflects the return potential from efficient portfolio construction and trading execution. This is true especially for corporate bonds, where liquidity can be hard to source, and even when it is found it can be very expensive to be a liquidity taker in corporate bond markets. So asset owners who have the scale and wherewithal to position themselves as regular liquidity providers can reap the benefits of very cheap trading. We will have more to say on this in Chapter 9 when we focus on trading.

e. Security selection: This covers a wide variety of investment decisions based on the relative attractiveness of specific bonds at a particular point in time, including security selection within government bonds, securitized assets, and corporate bonds included in the benchmark. Security

EXHIBIT 4.2   Correlation of rolling three-month returns across out-of-benchmark sectors.

	TSY	LOANS	EM DEBT	US HY	EQ
TSY	1	−0.016	0.065	−0.076	0.065
LOANS		1	0.800	0.863	0.679
EM DEBT			1	0.853	0.669
US HY				1	0.753
EQ					1

Source: Global Treasuries (TSY) total returns are from the Bloomberg Indices. Bank loan (LOAN) total returns are from the Credit Suisse Leveraged Loan Index. Emerging Debt (EM DEBT) excess returns are from the JP Morgan EMBI Global Diversified Index. US High Yield (US HY) excess returns are from the Bloomberg Indices. Equity (EQ) total returns are from the MSCI World Index.

selection defined in this way means active risk taking that focuses on attractive idiosyncratic returns, and portfolio positions that are built to isolate this idiosyncratic return potential without capturing the beta of the asset class to which a bond belongs. This type of security selection is the focus of Chapter 5 for government bonds, Chapter 6 for corporate bonds, and Chapter 7 for emerging market bonds.

So active fixed income investment decisions cover a vast opportunity set. Let us examine how successful incumbent active fixed managers are. Does the typical active fixed income manager beat the benchmark? If so, how are they beating the benchmark? Fixed income markets have idiosyncrasies (e.g., constantly evolving market with regular new issuance, option exercises, tenders, bifurcated liquidity pools, etc.) that may make it easier to beat the fixed income benchmark (see e.g., Baz, Mattu, Moore, and Guo 2017).

What follows is an updated analysis of the excess of benchmark returns for a broad set of active fixed income managers. For full details of the original research, I refer readers to the following papers: (i) Brooks, Gould, and Richardson (2020) for the analysis on US Aggregate, Global Aggregate, and Unconstrained Bond funds, (ii) Brooks, Richardson, and Xu (2020) for the analysis of emerging market bond funds, and (iii) Palhares and Richardson (2020) for the analysis of credit long/short managers.

In all cases, the empirical analysis will focus on returns. This has the benefit of consistent comparability across a very large number of active fixed income funds, allowing for greater generalizability of the results. It does, however, have the limitation of unobservability of holdings in the respective fixed income funds. We can only infer the exposures of each fixed income manager based on the observed correlation of their returns with what we call traditional market risk premia. For the sake of parsimony, we will use the main risk premia discussed in Chapter 3 (term premium and credit premium) and we will add to them measures of the excess returns for emerging markets and emerging currency returns. A full list of the traditional market risk premia used to explain the excess of benchmark returns across the various active fixed income fund categories is contained in Exhibit 4.3.

We should also note the active return analysis that follows uses the explanatory variables listed in Exhibit 4.3, most of which are directly tradable assets (e.g., the corporate credit excess returns for the credit premium can be invested in via a swap on a corporate bond index or via a credit index derivative; the emerging market credit excess returns could also be invested via a swap or other index derivative). However, our analysis assumes that these are all costless to access. Although this is reasonable for some of the very liquid traditional risk premia we examine (e.g., interest rate derivatives in developed markets for the term premium, or currency forward to capture

EXHIBIT 4.3   Traditional risk premia proxies.

Risk Premium	Measure	Detail
Term	US Term (USTP)	Bloomberg Indices US Treasury excess of cash returns
Term	Global Term (GTP)	Bloomberg Indices Global Treasury excess of cash (USD hedged) returns
Term	Global Aggregate (GAGG)	Bloomberg Indices Global Aggregate excess of cash (USD hedged) returns
Term	Inflation Linked Securities (INF)	Bloomberg Indices Global Aggregate Inflation Linked Securities excess of cash (USD hedged) returns
Credit	Corporate Debt (CP)	50%/50% Barclays U.S. High Yield Corporate Bond Index return in excess of Duration-Matched Treasuries/ S&P Leverage Loan Index in excess of three-month Libor
Credit	Emerging Debt (EMD)	Bloomberg Indices Emerging Market Debt duration-adjusted excess returns
Credit	Emerging Corporate (EMCORP)	Bloomberg Emerging Markets Corporate Index duration-adjusted excess returns
Credit	Emerging Currency (EMFX)	Equal-weighted basket of emerging currency returns
Volatility	Treasury Implied Volatility (VOL)	Delta-hedged straddles on 10-year US Treasury futures

Source: Bloomberg Indices, JP Morgan indices, and Standard & Poor's indices.

emerging currency risk), it is arguably less appropriate for the riskier end of the spectrum of traditional risk premia such as the credit premium. So an alternative interpretation of excess of benchmark returns might be that it is a cost-effective way to obtain exposure to traditional risk premia. The asset owner will need to make that determination: Is the fee paid for the active fixed income management service too much for traditional market risk premium exposure?

4.2   US AGGREGATE (CORE PLUS) BENCHMARKED FIXED INCOME MANAGERS

For our analysis of Core Plus US aggregate benchmarked managers, we use the full universe of 154 active funds covered in the eVestment database under the "US Core Plus" category as of the start of 2021. All active funds are retained for the analysis, and funds with less than 24 months of returns data are excluded. This leaves a final sample of 142 funds for the returns analysis that follows, and this reduced sample of funds covers 97 percent of the $1.7 trillion USD covered in this category. All returns are gross of fees.

We run the following regression specification for each individual fund as well as for an equally weighted average across all funds. The period starts in January 1993 and runs through the end of 2020, and we use the full period available for each fund.

$$R_{CorePlus} = \alpha + \beta_{USTP} USTP + \beta_{CP} CP + \beta_{EMD} EMD$$
$$+ \beta_{EMFX} EMFX + \beta_{VOL} VOL + \varepsilon \tag{4.1}$$

$R_{CorePlus}$ is the monthly gross of fee return for the Core Plus fund (or average across all Core Plus funds in a month). The right-hand variables are all as defined in Exhibit 4.3. Exhibit 4.4 summarizes the regression analysis.

EXHIBIT 4.4 Regression analysis for US Core Plus funds.

	Active Return	Sharpe Ratio	β_{USTP}	β_{CP}	β_{EMD}	β_{EMFX}	β_{VOL}	α	IR	ρ_{CP}
Q1	0.73%	0.37	−0.07	0.11	−0.01	−0.02	−0.01	0.00%	0.01	0.62
AVG	1.18%	0.54	−0.04	0.19	0.02	0.01	0.02	0.41%	0.36	0.72
Q2	1.09%	0.49	−0.02	0.17	0.01	0.01	0.02	0.36%	0.30	0.78
Q3	1.43%	0.63	0.01	0.24	0.06	0.04	0.04	0.69%	0.63	0.87
EW portfolio	1.82%	0.66	−0.01	0.18	0.01	0.02	0.02	0.36%	0.60	0.92

Source: Bloomberg Indices, JP Morgan indices, and eVestment. Q1 (3) is first (third) quartile. AVG is average. Q2 is median. EW portfolio is the equally weighted average across all funds with nonmissing data cach month. 1993–2020 period examined.

The average active (excess of benchmark) return is 1.18 percent (annualized) across all 142 funds. The average realized tracking error is 2.4 percent (annualized), leading to an average Sharpe ratio of 0.54. Impressive. For this analysis we have forced all funds to have the same benchmark: Bloomberg US Aggregate. The regression coefficients suggest meaningful positive exposure to the credit premium. The strength of that positive correlation is emphasized in the last column that shows the average correlation of active returns to credit premium, ρ_{CP}, is 0.72. Exhibit 4.5 shows a frequency histogram of this correlation coefficient across the 142 funds and Exhibit 4.6 shows a scatter plot of the monthly returns to the EW portfolio and credit premium. The strength of this passive beta capture is striking.

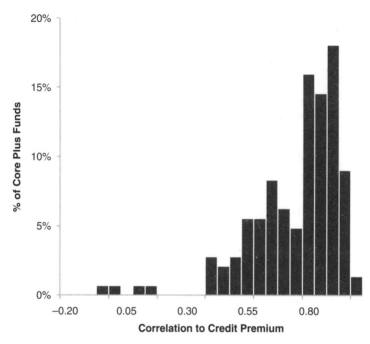

EXHIBIT 4.5 Relative frequency histogram of correlation between excess of benchmark (active) returns and credit premium returns (ρ_{CP}) for US Core Plus Funds.
Source: Bloomberg Indices, JP Morgan indices, and eVestment.

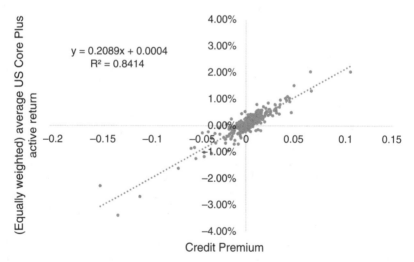

EXHIBIT 4.6 Scatter plot of equally weighted average US Core Plus fund excess of benchmark (active) returns and credit premium returns.
Source: Bloomberg Indices, JP Morgan indices, and eVestment.

Removing the effects of passive exposure to traditional market risk premia reduces the average active return of 1.18 percent to an "alpha" return of 0.41 percent, a reduction of 65 percent. To emphasize the broad-based impact of how great an influence traditional market risk premia exposures have on the impressive active returns reported earlier, Exhibit 4.7 shows the relative frequency histograms of the annualized active returns and annualized alphas. The superimposed bell-shaped curves are normal distributions with a zero average return and standard deviation equal to the sample return standard deviation. This easily allows the reader to see both the economic and statistical impact of passive beta exposure on estimated alphas. The bars are clearly far to the right of zero for active returns and much less so for alphas.

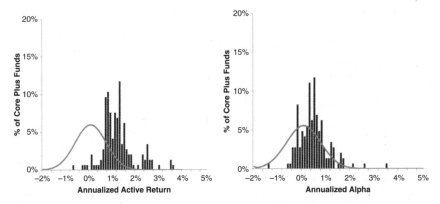

EXHIBIT 4.7   Relative frequency histograms of annualized active returns and annualized alphas for US Core Plus Funds.
Source: Bloomberg Indices, JP Morgan indices, and eVestment.

4.3 GLOBAL AGGREGATE BENCHMARKED FIXED INCOME MANAGERS

For our analysis of Global Aggregate benchmarked managers, we use the full universe of 108 active funds covered in the eVestment database under the "Global Aggregate" category as of the start of 2021. All active funds are retained for the analysis, and funds with less than 24 months of returns data are excluded. This leaves a final sample of 94 funds for the returns analysis that follows, and this reduced sample of funds covers 90 percent of the $355 billion USD covered in this category. All returns are gross of fees.

We run the following regression specification for each individual fund as well as for an equally weighted average across all funds. The period starts in

January 1993 and runs through the end of 2020, and we use the full period available for each fund.

$$R_{GAGG} = \alpha + \beta_{GTP}GTP + \beta_{CP}CP + \beta_{EMD}EMD$$
$$+ \beta_{EMFX}EMFX + \beta_{VOL}VOL + \varepsilon \tag{4.2}$$

R_{GAGG} is the monthly gross of fee return for the Global Aggregate benchmarked fund (or average across all Global Aggregate funds in a month). The right-hand variables are all as defined in Exhibit 4.3. Exhibit 4.8 summarizes the regression analysis.

EXHIBIT 4.8   Regression analysis for Global Aggregate Funds.

	Active Return	Sharpe Ratio	β_{GTP}	β_{CP}	β_{EMD}	β_{EMFX}	β_{VOL}	α	IR	ρ_{CP}
Q1	0.16%	0.07	−0.19	−0.01	−0.01	−0.26	−0.01	−0.10%	−0.07	0.00
AVG	0.77%	0.26	−0.13	0.07	0.07	0.01	0.05	0.57%	0.26	0.29
Q2	0.77%	0.27	−0.04	0.07	0.05	0.03	0.04	0.52%	0.19	0.38
Q3	1.40%	0.46	0.04	0.14	0.16	0.15	0.09	1.69%	0.56	0.59
EW portfolio	0.93%	0.42	−0.06	0.06	0.07	0.03	0.02	0.23%	0.19	0.60

Source: Bloomberg Indices, JP Morgan indices, and eVestment. Q1 (3) is first (third) quartile. AVG is average. Q2 is median. EW portfolio is the equally weighted average across all funds with nonmissing data each month. 1993–2020 period examined.

The average active (excess of benchmark) return is 0.77 percent (annualized) across all 94 funds. The average realized tracking error is 3.8 percent (annualized), leading to an average Sharpe ratio (excess of benchmark returns) of 0.26. For this analysis we have forced all funds to have the same benchmark: Bloomberg Global Aggregate. The regression coefficients suggest positive exposures to the credit premium, emerging market premium, and volatility premium. The average correlation of active returns to the credit premium, ρ_{CP}, is 0.29, considerably lower than what was seen for the Core Plus category. Exhibit 4.9 shows a scatter plot of the monthly returns to the equally weighted (EW) portfolio and credit premium, and we can again see a pervasive passive credit beta capture.

Removing the effects of passive exposure to traditional market risk premia reduces the average active return of 0.77 percent to an "alpha" return of 0.57 percent, a reduction of 25 percent. Exhibit 4.10 shows the relative frequency histograms of the annualized active returns and annualized alphas. Again, it is easy to see the economic and statistical impact of

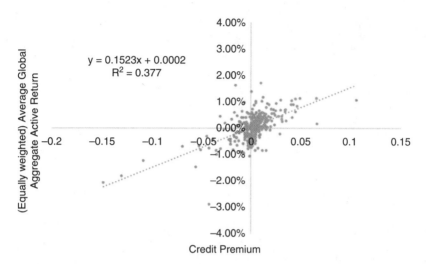

EXHIBIT 4.9 Scatter plot of equally weighted (EW) average Global Aggregate fund excess of benchmark (active) returns and credit premium returns.
Source: Bloomberg Indices, JP Morgan indices, and eVestment.

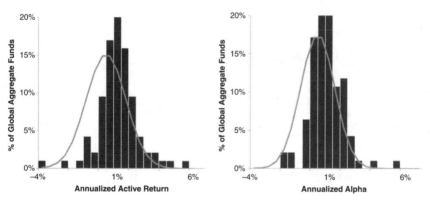

EXHIBIT 4.10 Relative frequency histograms of annualized active returns and annualized alphas for US Core Plus Funds.
Source: Bloomberg Indices, JP Morgan indices, and eVestment.

passive beta exposure on estimated alphas. The bars shift to the left as you move from active returns to alphas, but the alphas for this category are still significant. The astute reader will notice that the reduction of alpha for the Global Aggregate category is less than shown in the original research of Brooks, Gould, and Richardson (2020). The analysis here covers a slightly longer period and uses monthly returns, whereas the original research had examined nonoverlapping three-month periods. The purpose is not to replicate the original research, simply to note the pervasiveness of beta capture across fixed income categories.

4.4 UNCONSTRAINED BOND FUNDS

For our analysis of Global Unconstrained Bond funds, we use the full universe of 113 active funds covered in the eVestment database under the "'Global Aggregate" category as of the start of 2021. All active funds are retained for the analysis, and funds with less than 24 months of returns data are excluded. This leaves a final sample of 103 funds for the returns analysis that follows, and this reduced sample of funds covers 90 percent of the $450 billion USD covered in this category. All returns are gross of fees.

We run the following regression specification for each individual fund as well as for an equally weighted average across all funds. The period starts in November 1997 and runs through the end of 2020, and we use the full period available for each fund. The inclusion of the inflation risk premium shortens the sample by four years (Bloomberg Indices for inflation-linked securities started in 1997).

$$R_{Unconstrained} = \alpha + \beta_{GAGG}GAGG + \beta_{INF}INF + \beta_{CP}CP + \beta_{EMD}EMD$$
$$+ \beta_{EMFX}EMFX + \beta_{VOL}VOL + \varepsilon \tag{4.3}$$

$R_{Unconstrained}$ is the monthly gross of fee return for the Global Unconstrained Bond fund (or average across all Global Unconstrained Bond funds in a month). The right-hand variables are all as defined in Exhibit 4.3. Exhibit 4.11 summarizes the regression analysis.

EXHIBIT 4.11   Regression analysis for Unconstrained Bond Funds.

	Active Return	Sharpe Ratio	β_{GAGG}	β_{INF}	β_{CP}	β_{EMD}	β_{EMFX}	β_{VOL}	α	IR	ρ_{CP}
Q1	2.14%	0.34	0.27	−0.23	0.13	−0.20	0.03	−0.05	−0.58%	−0.17	0.54
AVG	4.09%	0.74	0.65	−0.21	0.39	−0.01	0.40	0.07	0.57%	0.34	0.63
Q2	3.76%	0.70	0.47	−0.06	0.34	0.02	0.13	0.03	0.47%	0.18	0.68
Q3	4.99%	1.03	0.86	0.02	0.61	0.15	0.71	0.11	1.61%	0.55	0.80
EW port.	5.29%	1.03	0.68	−0.05	0.37	0.01	0.36	0.04	−0.06%	−0.03	0.72

Source: Bloomberg Indices, JP Morgan indices, and eVestment. Q1 (3) is first (third) quartile. AVG is average. Q2 is median. EW portfolio is the equally weighted average across all funds with nonmissing data each month. 1997–2020 period examined.

The average active (excess of benchmark) return is 4.09 percent (annualized) across all 103 funds. The average realized tracking error is 6.9 percent (annualized), leading to an impressive average Sharpe ratio (excess of benchmark returns) of 0.74. For this analysis we have forced all funds to have the same benchmark: US cash rates (T-bill returns). The regression coefficients suggest strong positive exposures to the term premium, credit premium, and emerging market currency premium. The average correlation of active returns to credit premium, ρ_{CP}, is 0.63. Exhibit 4.12 shows a scatter plot of the monthly returns to the EW portfolio and credit premium, and we can again see a pervasive passive credit beta capture.

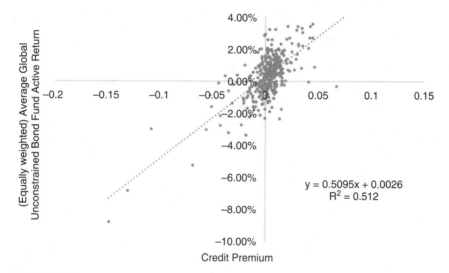

EXHIBIT 4.12 Scatter plot of equally weighted average Global Unconstrained Bond fund excess of benchmark (active) returns and credit premium returns.
Source: Bloomberg Indices, JP Morgan indices, and eVestment.

Removing the effects of passive exposure to traditional market risk premia reduces the average active return of 4.09 percent to an "alpha" return of 0.57 percent, a reduction of 85 percent. Exhibit 4.13 shows the relative frequency histograms of the annualized active returns and annualized alphas. Again, it is very easy to see the economic and statistical impact of passive beta exposure on estimated alphas. The bars shift to the left as you move from active returns to alphas, and in this case the "alphas" are very small compared to reported active returns. This is one category of active fixed income management in which the repacking of beta as alpha is both very large and very pervasive.

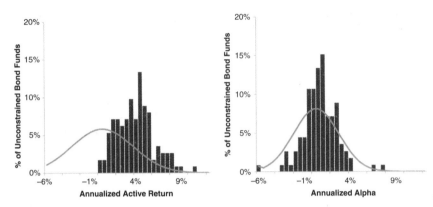

EXHIBIT 4.13   Relative frequency histograms of annualized active returns and annualized alphas for Global Unconstrained Bond Funds.
Source: Bloomberg Indices, JP Morgan indices, and eVestment.

4.5   EMERGING MARKET FIXED INCOME MANAGERS

For our analysis of emerging market bond funds, we use the full universe of 131 active funds covered in the eVestment database under the "'Global Aggregate" category as of the start of 2021. All active funds are retained for the analysis and funds with less than 24 months of returns data are excluded. This leaves a final sample of 117 funds for the returns analysis that follows, and this reduced sample of funds covers 98 percent of the $355 billion USD covered in this category. All returns are gross of fees.

We run the following regression specification for each individual fund as well as for an equally weighted average across all funds. The period starts in February 2003 and runs through the end of 2020, and we use the full period available for each fund. The inclusion of the emerging corporate risk premium shortens the sample by a further six years (Bloomberg Indices for emerging corporate securities started in 2003).

$$R_{EM} = \alpha + \beta_{USTP} USTP + \beta_{EMD} EMD$$
$$+ \beta_{EMCORP} EMCORP + \beta_{EMFX} EMFX + \varepsilon \tag{4.4}$$

R_{EM} is the monthly gross of fee return for the emerging market bond fund (or average across all emerging market bond funds in a month). The right-hand variables are all as defined in Exhibit 4.3. Exhibit 4.14 summarizes the regression analysis.

The average active (excess of benchmark) return is 1.04 percent (annualized) across all 117 funds. The average realized tracking error is

EXHIBIT 4.14   Regression analysis for Global Aggregate Funds.

	Active Return	Sharpe Ratio	β_{USTP}	β_{EMD}	β_{EMCORP}	β_{EMFX}	α	IR	ρ_{CP}
Q1	0.25%	0.09	−0.25	0.00	−0.10	−0.07	−0.23%	−0.11	−0.03
AVG	1.04%	0.29	−0.12	0.11	0.04	0.07	0.54%	0.23	0.26
Q2	0.95%	0.29	−0.12	0.15	0.03	0.07	0.49%	0.20	0.33
Q3	1.65%	0.48	0.02	0.25	0.16	0.18	1.17%	0.53	0.55
EW portfolio	4.01%	0.87	−0.15	0.11	−0.05	0.13	0.87%	0.65	0.21

Source: Bloomberg Indices, JP Morgan indices, and eVestment. Q1 (3) is first (third) quartile. AVG is average. Q2 is median. EW portfolio is the equally weighted average across all funds with nonmissing data each month. 2003–2020 period examined.

3.66 percent (annualized), leading to an average Sharpe ratio (excess of benchmark returns) of 0.29. For this analysis we have forced all funds to have the same benchmark: the Bloomberg Emerging Market USD Aggregate Index. The regression coefficients suggest positive exposures to the emerging market premium and to a lesser extent the volatility premium. The average correlation of active returns to credit premium, ρ_{CP}, is 0.26, lower than what was seen for the core-plus and unconstrained categories.

Removing the effects of passive exposure to traditional market risk premia reduces the average active return of 1.04 percent to an "alpha" return of 0.54 percent, a reduction of just over 50 percent. Exhibit 4.15 shows the relative frequency histograms of the annualized active returns and

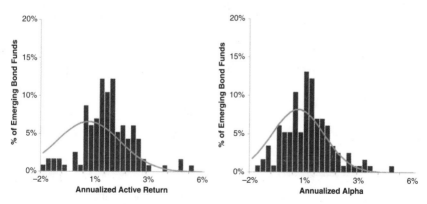

EXHIBIT 4.15   Relative frequency histograms of annualized active returns and annualized alphas for Emerging Market bond funds.
Source: Bloomberg Indices, JP Morgan indices, and eVestment.

annualized alphas. Again, it is easy to see the economic and statistical impact of passive beta exposure on estimated alphas, with the bars shifting to the left as you move from active returns to alphas.

4.6 CREDIT LONG/SHORT MANAGERS

For an analysis of credit hedge funds, we need to use a different data source. We will use the same data source as Palhares and Richardson (2020) – namely, Hedge Fund Research Indices (HFRI) (HFR database). For the time-series analysis examining the beta and systematic exposures of actively managed credit hedge funds, we use the HFRI Relative Value: Fixed Income: Corporate Index. The data analysis spans the 1996–2020 period. We limit ourselves to individual funds within this HFR category that are current constituents of the index as of 2021. This leaves a sample of 51 live credit hedge funds. This sample size is smaller than the 219 credit hedge funds examined in Palhares and Richardson (2020), as they also looked at the "graveyard" funds. So although we have a smaller set of funds here, any evidence of positive risk-adjusted returns will be positively biased due to survivorship (they are all live funds). That bias is fine for our purposes, as we wish to explore the extent to which passive beta exposure can explain credit hedge funds returns. All the returns data examined in this section are net of fee (so any excess of benchmark return for this category should be viewed as more impressive than the previous categories that were all gross of fee).

We run the following regression specification for each individual fund, as well as for an equally weighted average across all funds. The period starts in 1996 and runs through the end of 2020, and we use the full period available for each fund.

$$R_{CLS} = \alpha + \beta_{USTP} USTP + \beta_{CP} CP + \beta_{EP} EP + \varepsilon \qquad (4.5)$$

R_{CLS} is the monthly net-of-fee return for the credit long/short hedge fund (or average across all credit long/short hedge funds in a month). The right-hand variables are based on those included in Palhares and Richardson (2020): (i) term premium (USTP), (ii) credit premium (CP), and (iii) equity risk premium (EP). The return analysis here, and for the regressions that follow, use nonoverlapping three-month returns to account for the known staleness in pricing for both credit hedge funds and credit markets generally. The analyses in the prior sections used monthly returns. Exhibit 4.16 summarizes the regression analysis.

The average active (excess of cash) return is 8.66 percent (annualized) across all 51 funds. The average realized tracking error is 10.23 percent (annualized), leading to an average Sharpe ratio (excess of benchmark

EXHIBIT 4.16　Regression analysis for credit long/short hedge funds.

	Active Return	Sharpe Ratio	β_{USTP}	β_{CP}	β_{EP}	α	IR	ρCP
Q1	6.15%	0.64	−0.09	0.43	−0.05	1.40%	0.27	0.62
AVG	8.66%	1.09	0.17	0.69	0.02	3.85%	0.76	0.66
Q2	8.31%	0.84	0.13	0.67	0.03	3.33%	0.73	0.79
Q3	9.67%	1.13	0.36	0.99	0.13	6.20%	1.27	0.91
EW portfolio	10.89%	1.26	0.17	0.61	0.03	8.62%	1.80	0.83

Source: Bloomberg Indices, MSCI indices, and HFR. Q1 (3) is first (third) quartile. AVG is average. Q2 is median. EW portfolio is the equally weighted average across all funds with nonmissing data each month. 1996–2020 period examined.

returns) of 1.09, truly impressive (but keep in mind the survivorship bias with the use of only current live funds). The average Sharpe Ratio is computed across all funds, it is not the ratio of the average active return (8.66 percent) to the average tracking error (10.23 percent), the average of a ratio is not equal to the ratio of the averages. The regression coefficients

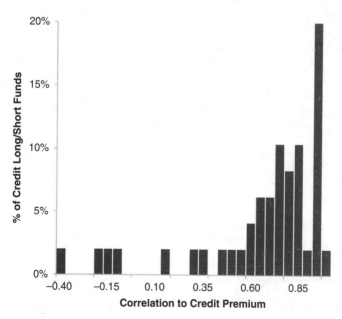

EXHIBIT 4.17　Relative frequency distribution of credit hedge fund correlation of net-of-fee returns and credit premium. Period 1996–2020.
Source: HFRI (HRF database) and Bloomberg Indices.

suggest very positive exposures to the credit premium. The average (median) correlation of active returns to credit premium, ρ_{CP}, is 0.66 (0.79), and Exhibit 4.17 shows how pervasive this passive credit beta capture is across credit hedge funds (this result mirrors the strong evidence of equity beta included in equity long/short funds examined in Asness, Krail, and Liew 2001). Although there are a very small number of credit hedge funds with low or negative correlations to broad credit markets, most have large passive credit betas. And over the last decade, that has been a fabulous return source.

It is important to note that the use of the live set of credit hedge funds as of the end of the sample period means we are examining credit funds over a period in which the credit markets have delivered fantastic risk adjusted returns. Over the 1996–2020 period, the credit premium delivered a 2.6 percent annualized excess return with an annualized volatility of 10.2 percent (0.25 Sharpe ratio); however, over the 2010–2020 period the Sharpe ratio was 0.54 (4.5 percent annualized return). Why is this relevant? The set of 51 credit hedge funds we examine have an average (median) track record of 117 (110) months, which corresponds mostly to the 2010–2020 period. Credit hedge funds do have significant credit beta exposure, and this passive beta has generated a lot of the impressive net-of-fee returns.

Removing the effects of passive exposure to traditional market risk premia reduces the average excess of cash return of 8.66 percent to an "alpha" return of 3.85 percent, a reduction of over 55 percent. Exhibit 4.18 shows the side-by-side relative frequency histograms of annualized excess of cash returns and annualized alpha (both net of fees). The probability mass is very far to the right of zero. Again, formal econometric tests are hardly needed for Exhibit 4.18; every (still live) credit hedge fund has realized a (large) positive annualized return over 1996–2020.

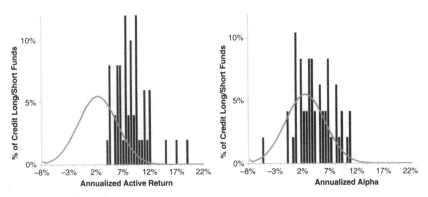

EXHIBIT 4.18 Relative frequency histograms of annualized active returns and annualized alphas for credit long/short hedge funds.
Source: Bloomberg Indices, MSCI indices, and HFR.

Finally, Exhibit 4.19 shows the extent of this passive credit beta capture by credit hedge funds. This scatter plot shows a very strong relation between the average credit hedge fund return and contemporaneous credit excess returns for the US HY market (the full-sample correlation is 0.83). This correlation to the credit premium is pervasive across funds. About half of the credit hedge fund net-of-fee returns is attributable to passive (credit) beta capture. Is that worth a 2/20 fee?

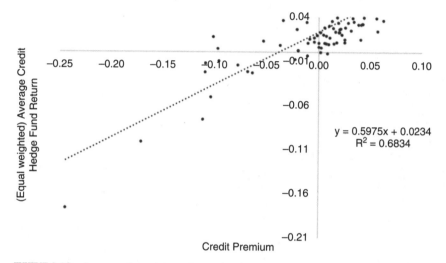

EXHIBIT 4.19 Scatter plot of (equal weighted) net-of-fee credit hedge fund return against US HY index credit excess returns. Period 1996–2020.
Source: HFRI (HRF database) and Bloomberg Indices.

In summary, this chapter has provided an in-depth analysis of the excess of benchmark returns for a broad set of actively managed fixed income funds. There is a very strong general theme that emerges. There is a considerable allocation of active risk taking to passive beta exposures, especially to credit risk. Although estimated alphas are considerably smaller than active returns across all fixed income categories examined, there is still alpha to be found through active fixed income management. The magnitude of that alpha is significantly less than that suggested by a simple analysis of excess of benchmark returns. Asset owners are aware of reaching for yield behavior but may not fully appreciate either the pervasiveness of this behavior or how large an impact it can have on returns.

The challenge for systematic fixed income investing is to harness the investment opportunity set within fixed income, including (i) avoiding bad-selling practices, (ii) asset allocation decisions, (iii) out of benchmark tilts, (iv) liquidity provision, and (v) security selection. We have seen how challenging tactical asset allocation is (Chapter 3) and how pervasive passive credit beta capture is for fixed income managers. For the next three chapters we will focus on the return potential from security selection sources within rate-sensitive bonds (Chapter 5), credit-sensitive bonds (Chapter 6) and emerging-market bonds (Chapter 7). Let's hope we can generate excess of benchmark returns (a necessary condition for successful active fixed income management) and do so with low correlations to traditional market risk premia. If we can manage both, systematic fixed income investing will be highly valuable for asset owners. As we will see in our concluding chapter, I believe this diversification benefit of systematic investing approaches can be realized.

REFERENCES

Asness, C., R. Krail, and J. Liew. (2001). Do hedge funds hedge? *Journal of Portfolio Management*, 28, 6–19.

Baz, J., R. Mattu, J. Moore, and H. Guo. (2017). Bonds are different: Active versus passive management in 12 points. PIMCO Quantitative Research.

Ben Dor, A., A. Desclee, L. Dynkin, J. Hyman, and S. Polbennikov. (2021). *Systematic Investing in Credit*. Wiley.

Brooks, J., T. Gould, and S. Richardson. (2020). Active fixed income illusions. *Journal of Fixed Income*, 29, 5–19.

Brooks, J., S. Richardson, and Z. Xu. (2020). (Systematic) Investing in emerging market debt. *Journal of Fixed Income*, 30, 44–61.

Ilmanen, I. (2011). *Expected Returns*. Wiley.

Palhares, D., and S. Richardson. (2020). Looking under the hood of active credit managers. *Financial Analysts Journal*, 76, 82–102.

CHAPTER 5

Security Selection – Rate-Sensitive Assets

OVERVIEW

This chapter lays out the investment opportunity set for rate-sensitive assets. Our focus is on developed market government bonds, but the insights we cover can also be extended to emerging market government bonds. What seems like a daunting investment challenge spanning over 1,000 bonds can be distilled to a manageable set of well-defined maturity buckets across developed markets. We cover use of principal components to help focus our scarce investment resources. Success in modeling the level, slope, and curvature (which can be achieved with as few as three assets for each country) will capture most of the return opportunities for government bonds. The chapter then discusses the intuition behind representative measures of value, momentum, carry, and defensive investment themes and evaluates the success of these strategies individually and in combination for developed government bond markets.

5.1   WHAT IS THE INVESTMENT OPPORTUNITY SET FOR DEVELOPED MARKET GOVERNMENT BONDS?

We will use a representative broad government bond index to explore our investment opportunity set. The ICE/BAML Global Government Index (W0G1) is our index of choice. W0G1 tracks the performance of publicly issued investment grade sovereign debt denominated in the issuer's own domestic currency. To be included in the index, a country must (i) be a member of the FX-G10 or Western Europe, (ii) have an investment grade foreign currency long term sovereign debt rating (based on an average of Moody's, S&P and Fitch), (iii) have at $50 ($25) billion USD equivalent outstanding face value of Index qualifying debt to enter (remain in) the index, (iv) must be available to foreign investors; and (vi) must have at least one readily available, transparent price source for its underlying securities. The set of countries includes all Euro members, US, Japan, UK, Canada, Australia, New Zealand, Switzerland, Norway, and Sweden. As with most indices, W0G1 is market-capitalization weighted. To be included, each bond must have an issue size more than $1 billion USD or (rough) equivalent, have a fixed coupon schedule, and have at least 18 months to final maturity.

Let's look at the size and composition of the W0G1 index. Exhibit 5.1 shows the market capitalization of the index over the 1996–2020 period and breaks this down across the 10 largest sovereign issuers (United States, Japan, UK, France, Italy, Germany, Spain, Belgium, Canada, and Netherlands) as of the end of the period. The total market capitalization of global government bonds is nearly $35 trillion USD and has grown substantially over the last two decades from around $7 trillion in 2000. The United States and Japan are the largest sovereign issuers accounting for 39 and 25 percent of the current $35 trillion, respectively.

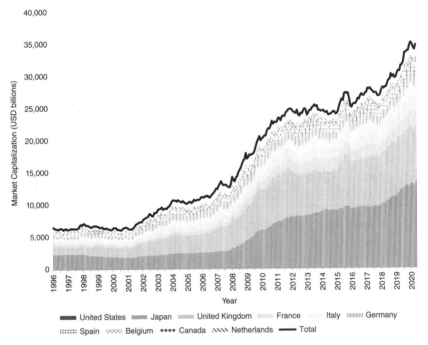

EXHIBIT 5.1   Market capitalization of ICE/BAML Global Government Bond (W0G1) index over 1996–2020 period.
Source: ICE/BAML indices.

The $35 trillion USD index as of December 2020 is made up of 1,087 bonds from 24 sovereign issuers. This looks like a very broad investment opportunity set. Exhibit 5.2 shows the number of unique issuers and number of bonds in the W0G1 index over the 1996–2020 period. Although there has been growth in the number of constituents over time, the number of issuers has remained roughly constant (and notice from Exhibit 5.1 that the largest 10 issuers account for between 90–95 percent of the total market capitalization).

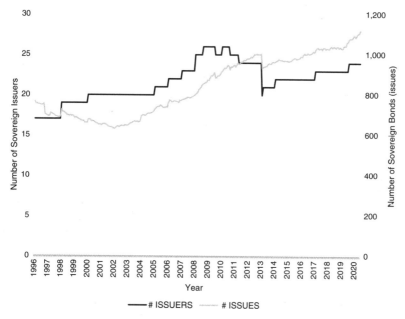

EXHIBIT 5.2 Number of unique issuers and issues in ICE/BAML Global Government Bond (W0G1) index over 1996–2020 period.
Source: ICE/BAML indices.

Another way to look at the relative concentration of rate risk across a small number of issuers is Exhibit 5.3 that shows the distribution of the number of bonds per unique issuer over the 1996–2020 period. The average (median) issuer has about 40 (20) bonds outstanding in any given month. There is considerable skew in this distribution reflecting the fact that the United States and Japan have accounted for 50–65 percent of the total market capitalization of WG01 over the 1996–2020 period, with that fraction increasing toward the end of the period.

EXHIBIT 5.3 Number of unique issues per issuer in ICE/BAML Global Government
Bond (W0G1) index over 1996–2020 period.
Source: ICE/BAML indices.

So how should we be thinking about modeling expected returns and
risks for this set of developed market government bonds? Do we need to
be generating 1,087 individual expected return forecasts? Or is there some
underlying structure in the data that might greatly simplify our forecasting exercise? As we will see, the investment opportunity set can be greatly
reduced by modeling only a small number (e.g., three) of "assets" per issuer.
If there are I issuers in a representative global government bond index, that
means our forecasting challenge is reduced from forecasting 1,087 items to
$3 \times I$ items. Fewer than 13 sovereign issuers account for most of the market
capitalization, so we are really forecasting 39 rate-sensitive assets. How do
we make the determination that three "assets" is sufficient to capture the
available returns opportunity set?

5.2   REDUCING THE DIMENSIONALITY

5.2.1   Zero-Coupon Yields and Principal Component Analysis

There is a large degree of commonality in government bond returns, as evi-
denced by the very high correlation of (i) government bond returns across

countries for a given maturity, (ii) government bond returns across maturities for a given country, and (iii) various fixed income subsectors that share a common rates component (see, e.g., Litterman and Schienkman 1991; Brooks and Moskowitz 2017).

There are a variety of ways to identify that commonality in returns, but first, an apology. We need to introduce some mild technical discussion about principal component analysis (PCA). We will do this by way of example (and this example makes for a fun class case study). Our use of PCA is designed to do one thing: reduce the dimensionality of our return forecasting challenge. If a country (e.g., the United States or Japan) has more than 100 bonds outstanding each month (which they do), do you need to model each bond's return forecast independently? Or do they share sufficient similarity so they can be viewed as close substitutes, and you can get away with forecasting a much smaller set of bonds?

You could measure the pairwise correlation of every possible pair of bonds and then look to group bonds into clusters based on the return co-movement patterns. This approach, although simple (perhaps cumbersome), suffers from a lack of structure. You will find a very high degree of return similarity across bonds of a given sovereign with that return similarity increasing in how close the bonds are in terms of remaining time to maturity (or duration). But this does not provide us any concrete way to reduce dimensionality.

Instead, we can use PCA. What does PCA do? PCA is a technique designed specifically to reduce the number of variables being studied while still retaining as much information as possible. That still doesn't help much. What is the information set we are looking to retain? In Chapter 2 we talked about the importance of yields in determining return potential. For government bonds, we have many bonds for each issuer. It is possible to convert the yields across a set of coupon bonds to a set of "zero-coupon" bonds. Exhibit 5.4 shows the cash flow profile of a zero-coupon 10-year government bond (notice that this looks very similar to Exhibit 1.7 in Chapter 1, just without the small coupon bars). Why are we interested in zero-coupon bonds and their yields? A zero-coupon bond yield is simply a discount rate that can be applied to a specific cash flow (e.g., the two-year zero-coupon yield is the rate that is applied to convert a cash flow two years in the future to today's value). These zero-coupon yields are an efficient way to compare bonds that share different cash flow profiles. A zero-coupon yield is simply the internal rate of return on a cash flow with a fixed maturity; they are a standard way to normalize yield information, allowing for comparisons of fixed income securities with different maturities and from different issuers.

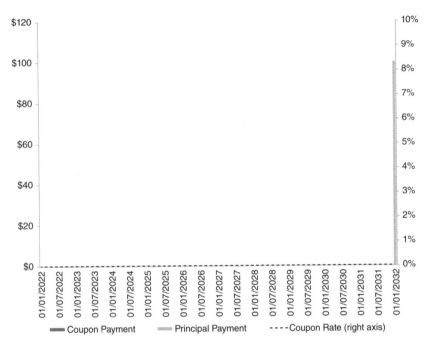

EXHIBIT 5.4 Cash flow profile of a $100 10-year zero-coupon bond issued on January 1, 2022.

How do we compute zero-coupon yields? Assuming all bonds are sufficiently liquid, such that you can trust the quality of prices obtained for each bond, you have an excess of information to create zero-coupon yields. Using simultaneous equations, you can create combinations of regular coupon bonds to create a synthetic zero-coupon bond. How does this work? Let's use a simple example (I have used this example in class for years and it probably comes from Michael Gibbons at University of Pennsylvania Wharton School when I was an assistant professor back in the early 2000s).

Exhibit 5.5 shows the cash flows of three bonds (A, B, and C). The rows correspond to periodic cash flows. The first row is today and contains the prices of the bonds (they have negative values, as that is what you must pay to buy the bond). The next three rows capture the cash flows (coupon and par) from owning each bond. Bond A matures in three years and pays a 5 percent coupon. Bond B also matures in three years but pays a 10 percent coupon (you could think of Bond B as an off-the-run government bond that was issued back in time when prevailing yields were higher, but it now has a similar remaining time to maturity as Bond A). Bond C matures in two years and it has a 15 percent coupon rate. The prices of the bonds should

EXHIBIT 5.5   Cash flows of three risk-free government bonds used to create a synthetic zero-coupon bond.

Year	Price of Zero-Coupon Bond	Bond A	Bond B	Bond C
0		−90.28	−103.00	−111.20
1	?	5	10	15
2	?	5	10	115
3	?	105	110	0

all make sense, given they are issued by the same (risk-free) government; the bonds with higher coupons should command a higher price.

We are interested in creating a synthetic zero-coupon one-year bond. We would like a bond that has the following cash flows: (i) 100 in year 1, (ii) 0 in year 2, and (iii) 0 in year 3. What would be the price of such a bond? We can find a combination of the three other coupon-bearing bonds that match these desired cash flows (i.e., we would buy N_A units of bond A, buy N_B units of bond B, and buy N_C units of bond C). This system of equations would be:

$$5N_A + 10N_B + 15N_C = 100 \tag{5.1}$$

$$5N_A + 10N_B + 115N_C = 0 \tag{5.2}$$

$$105N_A + 110N_B + 0N_C = 0 \tag{5.3}$$

Although we could estimate this longhand, matrix algebra helps a lot. These equations can be written in matrix form as:

$$\begin{bmatrix} 5 & 10 & 15 \\ 5 & 10 & 115 \\ 105 & 110 & 0 \end{bmatrix} \begin{bmatrix} N_A \\ N_B \\ N_C \end{bmatrix} = \begin{bmatrix} 100 \\ 0 \\ 0 \end{bmatrix} \tag{5.4}$$

A solution to this system of equations is found by solving Equation (5.5) and Exhibit 5.6 shows the resulting positions across the three bonds that create our synthetic zero-coupon bond. This creation of synthetic zero-coupon bonds can continue for two-year and three-year zero-coupon bonds in our example (e.g., for a two-year zero-coupon bond, Equation (5.4) would be modified to have $\begin{bmatrix} 0 \\ 100 \\ 0 \end{bmatrix}$ as the desired cash flows on the right-hand side, and for a three-year zero-coupon bond, Equation (5.4) would be modified

to have $\begin{bmatrix} 0 \\ 0 \\ 100 \end{bmatrix}$ as the desired cash flows on the right-hand side). Exhibit 5.6

shows the prices of all three synthetic zero-coupon bonds, and using a

simple yield formula, $P = \frac{100}{(1+y)^T} \rightarrow y = \left[\frac{1}{P}\right]^{\frac{1}{T}} - 1$, also the corresponding

zero-coupon yields.

$$\begin{bmatrix} N_A \\ N_B \\ N_C \end{bmatrix} = \begin{bmatrix} 5 & 10 & 15 \\ 5 & 10 & 115 \\ 105 & 110 & 0 \end{bmatrix}^{-1} \begin{bmatrix} 100 \\ 0 \\ 0 \end{bmatrix} \tag{5.5}$$

EXHIBIT 5.6   Synthetic zero-coupon bond prices and yields for our case study of three risk-free government bonds.

Bond	Unit	One-Year Zero	Two-Year Zero	Three-Year Zero		Price	Yield
A	N_A	−25.3	3.3	2	One-year zero	−92.16	8.50%
B	N_B	24.15	−3.15	−1	Two-year zero	−84.67	8.68%
C	N_C	−1	1	0	Three-year zero	−77.56	8.84%

This example is a useful in-class exercise for students to appreciate how zero-coupon yields are computed. All calculations can easily be performed in Excel. Now that we know where zero-coupon yields come from, let's look at a large dataset of zero-coupon yields. For this we will use the dataset from Wright (2011; https://econ.jhu.edu/directory/jonathan-wright). To save space, we will only explore US yields and focus on the period 1971–2009 using 1–10 year zero-coupon yields. We are focused on yields as the current shape of the yield curve and future movements in the shape of the yield curve generate returns (see Chapter 1).

Our aim is to assess whether, and how, we can reduce the investment opportunity set from 10 zero-coupon bonds to a smaller number. We will use the PCA approach described in Campbell, Lo, and MacKinlay (1996). The zero-coupon yield dataset consists of one row for each month starting in November 1971 and ending in May 2009 (451 months) and each row contains 10 columns (one column for each year, 1 through 10). This is our [451×10] data matrix, X. We will work with the natural logarithm of zero-coupon yields (Cochrane and Piazzesi 2005) and will standardize each data series (i.e., for each zero-coupon bond series we subtract the full-sample mean and divide by the full sample standard deviation). The objective of PCA is to reduce the dimension from 10 to K factors ($K < 10$) while retaining as much of the variation in yields as possible. Principal components can be thought of as factors (linear combinations) of the 10 zero-coupon yields. The first principal component is the linear combination of yields with the maximum variance. The second principal component is the linear combination of yields with the maximum variance that is uncorrelated to the first principal component. The third principal component is the linear combination of yields with the maximum variance that is also uncorrelated to the first and second principal components.

Mathematically, the solution for the first principal component can be written as:

$$\max_{w_1} w_1 \sum w_1^T, \text{subject to } w_1 w_1^T = 1 \tag{5.6}$$

where w is the linear combination of zero-coupon yields to be solved for (a [1×10] array of weights), and Σ is the sample covariance matrix (a [10×10] matrix computed as $X^T X$ (the square of our standardized dataset, capturing how zero-coupon yields at each point evolve over time individually and with each other). Subsequent principal components then have additional constraints of the type $w_2 w_1^T = 0$ (for the second component), ensuring that the factors (principal components) are orthogonal (uncorrelated) to each other.

Exhibit 5.7 shows the first three principal components of US zero-coupon bond yields over the 1971–2009 period. These three principal

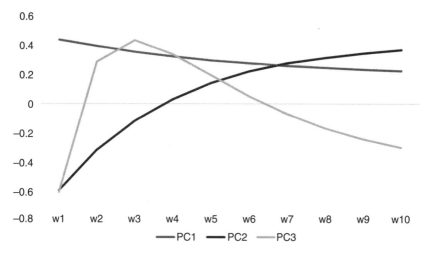

EXHIBIT 5.7 First three principal components (PC1, PC2, PC3) for US zero-coupon yields.
Source: Wright (2011).

components capture 99 percent of the total variation in zero-coupon yields. The first (second) principal components account for 96.7 (2.9) percent of the total variation, respectively. This is the basis for reducing our investment opportunity set. Bonds share a common component that is reflected in the level of yields and common movements in the level of the yield curve account for most of the variation in yields.

5.2.2 Forming Maturity Bucket Assets

The first three principal components have natural interpretations (see e.g., Litterman and Scheinkman 1991). The first component is a "level" factor, the second component is a "slope" factor, and the third component is a "curvature" factor. If we link these principal components with our investment opportunity set, it will look something like this: (i) select a representative bond for each country or an average across bonds for a given country to capture the "level" factor, (ii) select a pair of bonds (buying the longer-dated bond and shorting the short-dated bond) to capture the "slope" factor, and (iii) selecting a triplet of bonds (buying a moderate-duration bond and shorting both a short- and longer-duration bond) to capture the "curvature" factor. Thus, with three representative bonds for a given sovereign issuer, we will be able to capture most of the variation in the yield curve and hence expected returns.

Choices need to be made for constructing the level, slope, and curvature "assets." First, we need to select representative points across curves. A feasible approach might be to group all bonds into three buckets according to their remaining time to maturity. Brooks, Palhares, and Richardson (2018) partition bonds in each country into (i) 1–5 year (short), (ii) 5–10 year (medium), and (iii) 10–30 year (long). This will exclude bonds with a maturity greater than 30 years, but it captures most bonds in the index. Within each maturity bucket we can aggregate across all bonds by market capitalization weighting. This will generate three representative assets: short, medium, and long. Second, we need to combine these representative assets to create the assets we wish to trade (level, slope, and curvature). The level asset can be computed as the average across the short, medium, and long assets. The slope asset can be computed by buying the long asset and then shorting the short asset. The curvature asset can be computed by buying the medium asset and then shorting a combination of the short and long asset.

Our systematic investment approach is designed to capture idiosyncratic returns from security selection and *not* from capture of traditional market risk premia. In government bond markets, the primary risk premia is term risk, and that is linked to duration. To ensure we do not inadvertently capture term premia via our level, slope, and curvature assets, we want to "neutralize" them with respect to duration. As discussed in Chapter 1, duration is a first-order approximation of how yield curve changes affect bonds prices, and it will leave our level, slope, and curvature assets relatively immune from general shifts in the yield curve. The level asset is already duration balanced as it (duration-weighted) averages bonds across three maturity buckets, so selection across countries will not generate directional views on global yields.

The slope and curvature assets need to be constructed in a duration-neutral, not dollar-neutral, manner. This can be achieved in a variety of ways, but perhaps the simplest way to think of this is that each maturity bucket has a given duration and all returns and signals used to forecast returns can be normalized by duration (e.g., if the duration of the long maturity bucket is D_L years and the duration of the short maturity bucket is D_L years, then the returns for a duration neutral slope asset could be defined as $+D_L$ times the return of the long maturity bucket plus $-\frac{D_L}{D_S}$ times the return of the short maturity bucket). Your dataset is then ready to compare cross-sectionally without any directional duration tilts.

In what follows, we will focus on how a systematic approach can generate outperformance via country-level selection (we will only briefly touch on the slope and curvature assets). We will use two datasets. First, we will examine nearly a century of data on style-based measures in fixed income (see e.g., Ilmanen, Israel, Lee, Moskowitz, and Thapar 2021). Second, we will examine a more recent dataset based on the constituents of the JPMorgan Government Bond Index (see e.g., Brooks, Palhares, and Richardson 2018). The more recent dataset has the advantage of a broader set of bonds allowing consideration of level, slope, and curvature investment possibilities. The longer dataset only allows for analysis of country-level views but has the benefit of a much longer time series.

5.3 A FRAMEWORK FOR SECURITY SELECTION OF GOVERNMENT BONDS (INVESTMENT THEMES)

In this section we will revisit some of the well-known investment themes discussed in Chapter 3 when we covered tactical timing decisions around the term premium. In that earlier chapter we were interested in active risk-taking decisions in the temporal dimension (i.e., do you want to be long- or short-rate sensitive assets at a given point in time). Now we are looking at active risk-taking decisions in the cross-sectional dimension (i.e., do you want to be long or short, or over- or underweight, a specific country or country-tenor at a given point in time). These decisions (temporal vs. cross-sectional) are directly related to each other. We are treating them as separate investment decisions, to cleanly separate market-timing decisions (temporal) from security-selection decisions (cross-sectional). In Chapter 4 we saw how much of the cross-sectional investment skill of active fixed income managers could be explained by passive exposure to traditional market risk premia. We will ex ante try to mitigate this by focusing our security selection on dimensions of attractiveness across countries that do not inherit direct exposure to duration risk. Our framework will look very similar to that discussed in Chapter 3.

5.3.1 Value

Equation (3.4) in Chapter 3 discussed how expected returns can be broken down into an initial yield ("carry") and an expected change in yields component. Value is a type of investment idea designed to identify yields that are out of synch with underlying fundamentals that should determine the level and shape of the yield curve. Those fundamentals might include information about expected central bank monetary policy decisions, inflation expectations, economic growth, business cycle forecasts, and risk aversion. A variety of models can be used to extrapolate from current short-term interest rates to build an expected path of future interest rates. In Exhibit 5.8, that would be the dashed black line (this is where you believe interest rates are likely to move to). The solid black line is the current zero-coupon yield

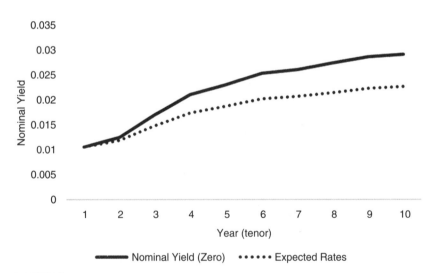

EXHIBIT 5.8 Visualizing value opportunities along the yield curve.
Source: Author.

curve, the rates implied from the market pricing of government bonds. The gap between the solid and the dashed lines we can think of as our value opportunity. What does the gap represent? Ideally, it reflects that component of yield not attributable to what you have modeled (i.e., a premium component). Of course, there is always the risk of a "value trap" where market prices (yields) are aware of something that your model is missing. Therein, lies the source of risk with this type of investment signal. But that is also your opportunity as an investor: continue to refine and develop your understanding of fundamental (and nonfundamental) drivers of yields.

For our purposes, we will use a simple measure of value for global government bonds. In the longer dataset the measure of value is taken directly from Ilmanen, Israel, Lee, Moskowitz, and Thapar (2021) as the 10-year real bond yield. This is calculated as the difference between nominal yields and expected inflation. The measure of expected inflation here is the trailing three-year change in the country-specific Consumer Price Index (this ensures a consistent measure over the entire period). In the more recent dataset, we will use a measure of real bond yield that is specific to each country-maturity bucket. This is computed as the market capitalization average yield of all bonds in the respective country-maturity bucket less a maturity-matched inflation-expectation forecast from Consensus Economics. Again, note that the real bond yield is one simple way to operationalize value for rate-sensitive assets, but there are many other possible measures.

As an aside, how do you know if your valuation measure is any good? The most obvious empirical test is to see whether your value measure (distance between where yields are compared to where you think they should be) correlates with future excess returns. Although this approach is useful, it is arguably incomplete. Future excess returns will include a component of the current yield level ("carry"). A better empirical test would be to assess whether, and how quickly, your value measure correlates with future changes in yields (see e.g., Correia, Richardson and Tuna 2012, for a similar exercise in the case of value signals for credit-sensitive assets). Standard statistical tests (e.g., Dickey and Fuller 1979) can be used to assess the speed and magnitude of mean reversion in yields implied by your valuation signals. Further empirical analysis of non-price-based tests (see discussion in Chapter 1) can add comfort that your value signal is capturing the expected yield change as hypothesized. One such test might be to assess whether, and how quickly, your forecast of yield changes is reflected in the forecasts of capital market participants such as the Survey of Professional Forecasters or Consensus Economics. An ability to forecast the forecaster is valuable, because their forecasts are associated with contemporaneous changes in prices (see e.g., Bradshaw, Richardson, and Sloan 2001, who introduced this type of analysis in equity markets).

5.3.2 Momentum

Again, linking back to Equation (3.4) from Chapter 3, we can think broadly of momentum as an investment insight designed to forecast changes in yields. The general idea is that recent performance is expected to continue (return continuation is linked to behavioral biases from investors such as the disposition effect, e.g., Frazzini 2006; fundamental momentum is generally pervasive and that is not fully appreciated by capital market participants, e.g., Brooks 2017). Measures of momentum can be price-based for the specific asset (i.e., own momentum) or based on returns of related asset classes. Despite the vast choices available to us for measuring momentum, we are going to use the simplest measure: own price momentum. Specifically, we will use the 12-month arithmetic average of government bond excess returns. In our longer dataset, consistent with Ilmanen, Israel, Lee, Moskowitz, and Thapar (2021), the momentum measure skips the recent month's return to avoid any market microstructure effects, such as bid–ask bounce, which may induce negative short-term autocorrelation. Given this measure is applied across countries at the 10-year point, there is no need for further adjustments. In the more recent sample, we will use duration adjusted returns to ensure comparability in returns across maturity buckets (see e.g., Brooks, Palhares, and Richardson 2018).

It is important to remember that own price momentum is but one measure of momentum. Asset owners and investors should pay attention to the breadth of investment insights under the "momentum" label. Recent price changes of other related assets might also be useful for government bond returns. The key economic risks driving government bond yields (e.g., inflation expectations, economic growth expectations, risk aversion/sentiment) are also relevant in other assets (e.g., currencies and equities). Recent price changes from these markets may also be informative for government-bond price changes. Similarly, the breadth of business cycle indicators that a typical fundamental analysis would look at (e.g., industrial production forecasts, inflation surveys, central bank forecast) are all relevant for the systematic investor as well. Arguably, a systematic investor is better suited to make full use of the information content across a broad set of general economic indicators. As an example of the breadth of data inputs and modeling techniques available to aggregate across a wide set of predictor variables, the interested reader can explore the popular "Nowcasting" (e.g., https://www.newyorkfed.org/research/policy/nowcast) approach, which claims to have the ability to extract information from a large quantity of data series, at different frequencies, and with different publication lags, and create a sensible view on underlying economic conditions (e.g., growth). If measured well, this can be a useful addition to a systematic investor under both the momentum and value investment themes.

5.3.3 Carry

Exhibit 3.1 provides a simple representation of what "carry" is. If nothing happens but the passage of time, carry is the return you will receive. As with our tactical timing model, we will use the term spread, $y_t^{LT \ Bond} - y_t^{ST \ Bond}$, the difference in the nominal long-term government bond yield and the nominal short-term government yield as our measure of carry. This is an approximation for the full "carry" because it ignores curvature in the yield curve and the associated "roll-down" component. But it has the benefit of simplicity and ease of measurement over a long period. You only need two yields (for a short-term and long-term bonds) to measure the term spread, whereas a comprehensive measure of carry requires multiple bonds allowing construction of the zero-coupon yield curve we discussed earlier in this chapter.

A general question that students often ask around security selection for government bonds is the effect of foreign currency movements. The bonds that we are selecting from are issued in the native (local) currency of the respective sovereign (i.e., US government bonds are issued in USD, UK government bonds are issued in GBP, German sovereign bonds are issued in EUR, at least for now, and so on). We abstract away from currency effects on returns by looking at our ability to forecast excess government bond returns. The excess simply means the return of a government bond in excess of the local short-rate (cash) instrument. The signals that we look at also abstract away from currency effects given how we measure them (e.g., momentum is based on excess returns, and our measure of carry, the term spread, is in excess of the local cash rate).

A final consideration for carry, in fact this is important for all investment signals as we will see in Chapter 8, is whether you want to volatility scale the measure or not. In the analysis that follows, we do not volatility scale any of our investment signals, but there is merit to exploring whether you want exposure to carry irrespective of the volatility of returns or whether you want your exposure to carry to be conditional on recent (or expected) volatility. There is a literature linking carry returns to episodic crashes and volatility conditioning may be a way to mitigate the episodic crashes (see e.g., Koijen, Moskowitz, Pedersen, and Vrugt 2018).

5.4 A FRAMEWORK FOR SECURITY SELECTION OF GOVERNMENT BONDS (LEVEL, SLOPE, AND CURVATURE)

5.4.1 Long Sample Evidence

Our long dataset covers the 1926–2020 period. Ilmanen, Israel, Lee, Moskowitz, and Thapar (2021) describe the full details of the dataset. The source data is the same Global Financial Data used in earlier chapters and focuses on the 10-year bond or whatever is closest to a 10-year bond. The cross-section of government bonds varies through time (starting with 10 countries back in the 1920s and expanding to 28 countries by the end of the period). This analysis only considers the level asset (i.e., the security selection is simply across developed government bonds at the 10-year point). For each investment signal (value, momentum, and carry) portfolio weights are constructed based on the strength of the signal (in Chapter 8 we will call this "signal strength weighting"). Thus, all government bonds will receive weight in the thematic portfolio, with the weight increasing in the strength of the signal. Each signal is converted to standardized ranks and these standardized ranks are the basis of portfolio weights (i.e., you will have the largest positive weight for countries with the highest rank and have the largest negative weight for countries with the lowest rank). For example, if there are three assets to choose from, you rank them 1, 2, and 3 (where 3 is the country with the strongest signal) and the average rank is 2. The weights for each asset are $(1 - 2)/6$, $(2 - 2)/6$, and $(3 - 2)/6$, respectively (i.e., -1, 0, $+1$). These weights are then rescaled to ensure a consistent notional position on the long and short side through time (i.e., avoid temporal variation in gross notional positions based on the number of assets at any one point in time). This ensures that the weights are balanced across the negative (short) and positive (long) views. This is what is commonly referred to as dollar-neutral portfolios. It is important to note that there is no volatility scaling in these portfolios, so at each point in time the amount of risk taking in active security selection across government bonds will vary. We will come back to risk targeting in Chapter 8.

Exhibit 5.9 summarizes the performance of our three investment signals – value, momentum, and carry – both individually and as an equally weighted average combination. The bottom section of the exhibit reports information about the return series (averages, volatilities, Sharpe ratios, and correlations). The value and carry investment themes have the most attractive return profile and the equally weighted combination is superior to any one individual theme due to the low pairwise correlations you see at the bottom of Exhibit 5.9, especially the reduced volatility of the combination, which generates a much higher Sharpe ratio. The (relatively) weaker performance of momentum is consistent with the weak evidence of price momentum to help with tactical investment decisions in global government bonds (see Chapter 3).

To assess whether security selection based on value, momentum, and carry themes are diversifying with respect to traditional market risk premia

EXHIBIT 5.9 Properties of systematic investment themes (V for value, M for momentum, C for carry and COMBO for an equally weighted average) for global government bonds over 1926–2020 period.

	α	β_{CP}	β_{TP}	β_{EP}	β_{SMB}	β_{HML}	β_{MOM}	R^2	IR
V	0.01	−0.01	0.04	0.01	0.00	−0.00	−0.02	0.96%	0.30
	2.80	*−0.23*	*1.41*	*1.54*	*0.27*	*−0.50*	*−1.80*		
M	0.00	0.00	0.03	−0.00	−0.00	−0.00	0.03	1.14%	0.04
	0.41	*0.03*	*1.06*	*−0.44*	*−0.06*	*−0.40*	*2.59*		
C	0.03	−0.02	0.03	−0.01	−0.00	0.00	0.01	0.88%	0.64
	5.91	*−0.70*	*1.20*	*−0.70*	*−1.71*	*1.19*	*1.07*		
COMBO	0.01	−0.01	0.03	0.00	−0.00	0.00	0.01	0.66%	0.54
	4.98	*−0.49*	*2.05*	*0.23*	*−0.80*	*0.14*	*1.06*		

	V	M	C	COMBO		AVG	STDEV	SR
V	1	−0.23	0.28	0.58		1.35%	4.57%	0.30
M		1	0.07	0.48		0.50%	4.70%	0.11
C			1	0.74		2.83%	4.35%	0.65
COMBO				1		1.56%	2.71%	0.58

Source: Ilmanen, Israel, Lee, Moskowitz, and Thapar (2021); data found at: https://www.aqr.com/Insights/Datasets/Century-of-Factor-Premia-Monthly. Additional factor mimicking portfolio returns found at https://mba.tuck.dartmouth.edu/pages/faculty/ken.french/data_library.html. T-statistics reported in italics beneath regression coefficients, intercept (alpha) is annualized.

(and some well-known factor risk premia from equity markets), we run the following regression:

$$THEME = \alpha + \beta_{CP}CP + \beta_{TP}TP + \beta_{EP}EP + \beta_{SMB}SMB + \beta_{HML}HML + \beta_{MOM}MOM + \varepsilon \tag{5.7}$$

THEME is the return on the respective investment theme. *CP*, *TP*, and *EP* are the credit premium, term premium and equity premium as defined in Chapter 4. *SMB*, *HML*, and *MOM* are the factor-mimicking portfolio returns based on size, value, and momentum, respectively, in the US equity market. Exhibit 5.9 reports estimated regression coefficients and, in italics below, the corresponding test-statistics. The value and carry investment themes are not significantly associated with either traditional market risk premia (*CP*, *TP*, and *EP*), or equity style returns. The intercepts (annualized) are 1.38 percent and 2.8 percent for value and carry, respectively.

Their information ratios, IR, are 0.30 and 0.64. An information ratio is computed as the regression intercept divided by the standard deviation of regression residuals (it is a common measure to assess the attractiveness of risk-adjusted returns after controlling for other return sources). Momentum has an even lower IR than its standalone Sharpe ratio due to the positive exposure to the equity momentum style (there is commonality in momentum across markets as shown in Asness, Moskowitz, and Pedersen 2013). The combination portfolio exhibits some exposure to term premium (while each theme individually was only moderately exposed to term premium, the combination shares that exposure). Importantly, the regression intercept is strongly significant (1.46 percent return with a 4.98 test statistic) and the combined portfolio has a respectable IR of 0.54. For those interested in even longer time-series evidence of the efficacy of systematic investing for government bonds, please read Baltussen, Martens, and Penninga (2021), which contains data back to 1800!

5.4.2   Recent Evidence – Level Asset

The more recent dataset uses information from the JP Morgan Government Bond Index (GBI). The analysis here was originally reported in Brooks, Palhares, and Richardson (2018), and we are now extending that data analysis up to the most recent period. The GBI is a market-cap-weighted index of all liquid government bonds across 13 markets (Australia, Belgium, Canada, Denmark, France, Germany, Italy, Japan, Netherlands, Spain, Sweden, the UK, and the United States). As discussed earlier, bonds are partitioned into maturity buckets: 1–5 year (short), 5–10 year (medium), and 10–30 year (long). For our country "level" asset, we form views across the 13 countries by taking an equal duration-weighted average across the three maturity buckets within each country. Each country asset is scaled to have the same duration to remove any directional duration tilt when we rank across countries.

The country "level" views are formed by ranking across the 13 countries by each investment theme individually or in combination. Specifically, each month we form tercile portfolios of the country assets based on rankings of each theme. We form long-short style portfolios by going long the third tercile portfolio (most attractive) and short the first tercile portfolio (least attractive) each month. Countries are equally weighted within each tercile, and all returns are in excess of the local cash rate. These portfolios are neutral to an equal parallel shift across global yield curves as they are formed in a duration-neutral manner.

Exhibit 5.10 summarizes the performance of our three investment signals – value, momentum, and carry – both individually and as an equally weighted average combination. The bottom section of the exhibit reports information about the return series (averages, volatilities, Sharpe ratios, and correlations). All three investment themes have attractive risk-adjusted returns with Sharpe ratios ranging from 0.31 for momentum to 0.67 for value. Again, the equally weighted combination is superior to any one individual theme due to the low pairwise correlations you see at the bottom of Exhibit 5.10, especially the negative correlation between momentum and both carry and value. Although momentum is less attractive unconditionally, it is a powerful diversifier when added to value and carry signals (value and carry are more positively correlated in the recent sample than they were over the longer time series examined earlier).

EXHIBIT 5.10 Properties of country "level" systematic investment themes (V for value, M for momentum, C for carry, and VMC for an equally weighted average) for global government bonds over 1995–2020 period.

	α	β_{CP}	β_{TP}	β_{EP}	β_{SMB}	β_{HML}	β_{MOM}	β_{QMJ}	β_{BAB}	R^2
V	0.02	−0.01	0.07	0.03	−0.00	−0.00	−0.00	−0.01	0.01	3.01%
	2.45	*−0.22*	*1.22*	*1.71*	*−0.36*	*−1.06*	*−0.20*	*−0.35*	*0.78*	
M	0.01	−0.05	0.06	0.03	0.00	−0.00	0.03	0.02	0.00	3.30%
	0.83	*−0.78*	*0.94*	*1.26*	*0.50*	*−0.06*	*2.07*	*0.55*	*0.10*	
C	0.02	0.24	0.08	−0.01	0.00	0.00	−0.01	−0.02	−0.01	10.04%
	2.33	*4.06*	*1.40*	*−0.70*	*−1.58*	*1.56*	*−0.41*	*−0.66*	*−0.38*	
VMC	0.02	0.06	0.07	0.02	−0.00	0.00	0.01	−0.00	0.00	4.78%
	3.40	*1.77*	*2.18*	*1.44*	*−0.83*	*0.25*	*0.99*	*−0.24*	*0.31*	

	V	M	C	VMC		AVG	STD	SR	IR
V	1	−0.29	0.49	0.71		2.48%	3.72%	0.67	0.55
M		1	−0.36	0.26		1.25%	4.04%	0.31	0.19
C			1	0.67		1.91%	3.80%	0.50	0.52
VMC				1		1.88%	2.08%	0.90	0.76

Sources: Brooks, Palhares, and Richardson (2018), JP Morgan Index data, Bloomberg Indices. Additional factor mimicking portfolio returns found at https://mba.tuck.dartmouth.edu/pages/faculty/ken.french/data_library.html, and https://www.aqr.com/Insights/Datasets. T-statistics reported in italics beneath regression coefficients, intercept (alpha) is annualized

We run a modified version of Equation (5.7) adding in two additional equity-market factor-mimicking portfolio returns (*BAB*, the betting against beta factor from Frazzini and Pedersen 2014; and *QMJ*, the quality minus junk factor from Asness, Frazzini, and Pedersen 2019). We estimate it for the individual theme returns and the equally weighted combination, and Exhibit 5.10 reports the results. Exhibit 5.10 reports estimated regression coefficients and, in italics below, the corresponding test statistics. Consistent with the longer sample evidence, we see attractive risk-adjusted returns for the value and carry investment themes, but we now also see attractive returns for momentum. Part of this difference is the sample period (the Sharpe ratio of momentum from the longer sample is 0.23 limiting that period to 1995–2020 vs. 0.31 shown in Exhibit 5.10) and part of it is the different cross-section of countries examined and the weighting of all bonds across each country with positions carefully duration neutralized each month.

The combination portfolio exhibits some exposure to traditional market risk premia (*CP*, *TP*, and *EP*) but those exposures are modest leaving a very significant intercept of 1.55 percent and test statistic of 3.4, yielding an *IR* of 0.76. These exposures to traditional beta are important to keep in mind. A criticism of incumbent active fixed income managers is that a lot of their active returns are little more than passive exposure to traditional market risk premia. We want to ensure our systematic investment approach does not also suffer from that same criticism. The results in Exhibits 5.9 and 5.10 suggest that this is not a large concern, but there is still some residual exposure. However, these portfolios are more academic in nature and do not make comprehensive use of risk modeling and exposure control tools that should be an integral part of a systematic investment process. We will return to these portfolio considerations in Chapter 8.

5.4.3 Recent Evidence – Slope and Curvature Asset

Using the same (recent) dataset, Brooks and Moskowitz (2017) extended the analysis in Brooks, Palhares, and Richardson (2018) to explore the return performance of value, momentum, and carry signals for the country "slope" and "curvature" assets. Given the formation of country-maturity buckets, it is relatively easy to then form duration-balanced combinations. The "slope" asset is long the 10–30 year maturity bucket and short the 1–5 year maturity bucket. Although the bonds within each bucket are weighted on a market capitalization basis, we use a different weighting scheme when combining the maturity buckets. The slope asset is dollar imbalanced to ensure an equivalent duration exposure on the long and short side. Similarly, for the curvature asset we compute that as long the 5–10 year maturity bucket and short a combination of the 1–5 year and 10–30 year maturity buckets (the curvature asset is a net zero duration position, with the 1–5 year maturity bucket having the same duration contribution as the 10–30 year maturity bucket). Again, complete details of the construction of the slope and curvature assets can be found in Brooks and Moskowitz (2017).

Exhibits 5.11 and 5.12 report the return properties of the value, momentum and carry investment themes individually and in combination for the slope and curvature asset, respectively. For both the slope and curvature assets, value and carry have attractive risk-adjusted returns with Sharpe ratios ranging from 0.30 to 1.08. Momentum has weaker returns, actually negative for the curvature asset. The equally weighted combination for the slope and curvature assets has a Sharpe ratio of 0.84 and 0.87, respectively. Controlling for traditional market risk premia and the broad set of equity-style factor returns also does not reduce the attractiveness of risk-adjusted returns, because the *IRs* are quite similar to the reported *SRs*. The only notable exposure to traditional market risk premia is the positive loading that carry has to the credit premium. This is not surprising given the known episodic crash risk from carry that coincides with negative shocks to credit risk.

EXHIBIT 5.11 Properties of country "slope" systematic investment themes (V for value, M for momentum, C for carry, and VMC for an equally weighted average) for global government bonds over 1995–2020 period.

	α	β_{CP}	β_{TP}	β_{EP}	β_{SMB}	β_{HML}	β_{MOM}	β_{QMJ}	β_{BAB}	R^2
V	0.01	−0.04	−0.02	0.02	0.00	0.00	−0.01	0.02	0.02	3.59%
	1.33	*−0.97*	*−0.67*	*1.90*	*−0.80*	*−0.86*	*−0.60*	*0.86*	*1.91*	
M	0.01	0.02	0.04	−0.00	−0.00	0.00	0.00	−0.02	0.00	1.02%
	1.47	*0.43*	*0.98*	*−0.22*	*−0.99*	*−0.55*	*0.07*	*−0.93*	*0.17*	
C	0.02	0.13	0.07	−0.00	−0.00	−0.00	−0.01	0.02	0.00	4.65%
	2.54	*2.86*	*1.68*	*−0.22*	*−1.41*	*−1.61*	*−0.55*	*0.96*	*0.07*	
VMC	0.01	0.04	0.03	0.01	−0.00	−0.00	−0.00	0.01	0.01	5.15%
	3.32	*1.54*	*1.32*	*0.81*	*−1.99*	*−1.87*	*−0.65*	*0.51*	*1.25*	

	V	M	C	VMC	AVG	STD	*SR*	*IR*
V	1	−0.42	0.04	0.33	0.96%	2.46%	0.39	0.30
M		1	0.18	0.51	0.82%	2.71%	0.30	0.33
C			1	0.77	1.81%	2.73%	0.66	0.57
VMC				1	1.20%	1.43%	0.84	0.74

Sources: Brooks and Moskowitz (2017), JP Morgan Index data, Bloomberg Indices. Additional factor mimicking portfolio returns found at https://mba.tuck.dartmouth .edu/pages/faculty/ken.french/data_library.html, and https://www.aqr.com/Insights/ Datasets. T-statistics reported in italics beneath regression coefficients, intercept (alpha) is annualized.

EXHIBIT 5.12   Properties of country "curvature" systematic investment themes (V for value, M for momentum, C for carry and VMC for an equally weighted average) for global government bonds over 1995–2020 period.

	α	β_{CP}	β_{TP}	β_{EP}	β_{SMB}	β_{HML}	β_{MOM}	β_{QMJ}	β_{BAB}	R^2
V	0.01	0.01	0.02	−0.00	−0.00	0.00	0.00	−0.01	0.00	3.42%
	3.31	1.21	1.78	−0.63	−1.58	0.00	0.57	−1.88	0.76	
M	0.00	−0.02	0.01	0.00	0.00	0.00	0.00	0.00	0.00	1.23%
	−1.56	−1.47	0.50	0.84	0.58	0.48	−0.38	−0.36	−0.64	
C	0.01	0.03	0.01	0.00	0.00	0.00	0.00	0.00	0.00	2.11%
	4.89	2.15	1.96	−0.39	0.03	−0.75	−0.45	0.27	−0.04	
VMC	0.004	0.01	0.01	−0.00	0.00	0.00	−0.00	−0.00	0.00	2.63%
	3.92	1.07	1.94	−0.04	−0.47	−0.16	−0.22	−1.11	−0.02	

	V	M	C	VMC	AVG	STD.	SR	IR
V	1	−0.58	−0.06	0.14	0.53%	0.75%	0.71	0.74
M		1	0.36	0.57	−0.29%	0.88%	−0.33	−0.35
C			1	0.85	0.92%	0.85%	1.08	1.10
VMC				1	0.39%	0.44%	0.87	0.88

Sources: Brooks and Moskowitz (2017), JP Morgan Index data, Bloomberg Indices. Additional factor mimicking portfolio returns found at https://mba.tuck.dartmouth .edu/pages/faculty/ken.french/data_library.html, and https://www.aqr.com/Insights/ Datasets. T-statistics reported in italics beneath regression coefficients, intercept (alpha) is annualized.

In summary, for both the longer time series and the more recent sample of bond index data, there is robust evidence of the efficacy of a systematic investment approach for security selection among developed-market government bonds. Most important, not only may a systematic investment approach generate attractive risk-adjusted returns, those returns are diversifying with respect to traditional market risk premia and alternative risk premia in the equity asset class. Brooks and Moskowitz (2017) and Ilmanen, Israel, Lee, Moskowitz, and Thapar (2021) examine the diversifying potential of systematic investing approaches across multiple asset classes. The empirical analysis contained in Exhibits 5.9–5.12 make for excellent in-class exercises for readers to appreciate the choices in signal measurement, portfolio weighting, and the potential diversification benefits of a systematic approach.

5.5 EXTENSIONS

5.5.1 Selecting Which Bond to Trade

The astute reader will notice that trading the country "level," "slope," and "curvature" assets discussed in the previous sections may be unnecessarily complicated, as each maturity bucket consisted of *all* bonds within. Do you want to trade up and down an entire basket of bonds in each country-maturity bucket when the attractiveness of that bucket changes? A simpler approach is to model country-maturity buckets as quasi-assets whose portfolio weights will change over time in response to your investment views. When trading toward your desired position for a given country-maturity bucket, you need to select an actual bond to buy when that bucket is more attractive and select an actual bond to sell when that bucket is less attractive. Let's consider the buy decision. At a time to buy into a country-maturity bucket, there will be multiple bonds available to purchase. It is wise to focus your attention on the more liquid bonds in that bucket (cheaper to trade in and out) and those bonds with a more attractive carry profile (expected return) at time of purchase. So over time, you may hold multiple bonds in each country-maturity bucket as liquidity and expected returns evolve across bonds within that bucket. For the sell decision, this is more limited in a benchmark aware, long-only portfolio, because you can only sell what you hold. However, a similar set of logic may apply; look to sell the bond in the relevant bucket with the least attractive carry profile and/or the oldest bond with a deteriorating liquidity profile.

5.5.2 Europe (Countries with a Shared Monetary Policy Framework)

The security selection across developed-market government bonds treated all sovereigns within an index equally. For example, Germany, France, Italy, and Spain are all treated as independent assets to select from and the investment signals for these sovereigns share the same expected path of interest rates (European Union members, at least at time of writing). An investor may be able to improve their security-selection efforts by decoupling the core from the periphery for European countries. This could be achieved by trading, say, Germany as a representative EU asset or trading a basket of EU countries together when comparing EU to other developed countries. If the basket option is selected, attention needs to be given to the weighting choice across EU members. Using market capitalization weights will give over 40 percent allocation to Italy and Spain. The volatility of excess returns for the peripheral European countries has been considerably higher than core EU countries over the last decade, as concerns about an EU breakup and fiscal weakness of peripheral countries intensified. An investor may think of modifying measures of value, momentum, and carry (and other signals) to explicitly model the "spread risk" giving rise to the additional yield on peripheral EU countries, rather than have simple value and carry signals push you into these peripheral countries.

5.5.3 Emerging Market (Local Currency) Sovereign Bonds

The empirical analysis in this chapter focused on developed-market government bonds. The framework we developed is applicable to all rate-sensitive assets, whether they be issued by developed or emerging sovereigns. Some care needs to be taken when extending the investment universe to include emerging markets. There are several topics worth highlighting.

First, simply extending the universe to include both developed and emerging markets may not be feasible. Asset owners typically have matrix approaches to asset classes and subgroups within asset classes. Emerging markets in fixed income are typically a separate allocation from core fixed income. But even for an unconstrained asset owner, care needs to be taken if combining developed and emerging markets together. Signal ideas do not always carry over cleanly (e.g., sensitivity to growth, which we will discuss shortly). But risk can be quite different across developed and emerging markets, in terms of both the magnitude of risk and the drivers of that risk. Careful attention is needed for risk modeling when there is considerable heterogeneity in the cross-section, which would be the case if blending developed and emerging markets. We will discuss some aspects of how heterogeneity affects risk modeling in Chapter 8.

Second, the sensitivity of rates to growth is typically negative for rate-sensitive assets. This is true for developed markets but is less true for emerging markets. Yields on emerging government bonds do share the central bank channel via which positive shocks to growth ultimately lead to interest rate hikes, but there is a more direct channel where the spread of the emerging government bond relative to a developed government bond is negatively related to the health of the country. Therefore, improvements in economic conditions for emerging countries can have an off-setting negative affect on yields. Simply cutting and pasting a model from developed to emerging markets is not encouraged.

Third, there is no defensive or quality theme discussed in this chapter. A pure defensive theme could be expressed in developed and emerging markets via the betting against beta insight in Frazzini and Pedersen (2014). This would entail a long position in the bonds with the lowest beta and a short position in the bonds with the highest beta. This collapses to a passive steepener position (long the front end of the curve and short the long end of the curve) because duration is the primary source of risk in rate-sensitive markets. Such a position entails the use of leverage (indeed leverage aversion is the basis for the betting against beta effect), making it less attractive in benchmark-aware portfolios. But there is the possibility of "quality" measures to be used for country selection. Candidate measures could be reduced-form indicators of the quality of government management such as (i) the level of inflation (lower is better), (ii) the level of government debt relative to GDP (lower is better), (iii) return-based measures potentially reflecting the health of the underlying economy (e.g., stock returns or credit spreads on companies domiciled in that country or the local banking system), and (iv) measures of the robustness of the local economy (e.g., looking at measures of sectoral concentration in the local equity index). These quality measures do not have as much natural variation across developed markets, but they do for emerging markets, so they are worth including as part of a broad systematic model.

5.5.4 Market-Capitalization Weighting

Over the years there has been criticism of market-capitalization-weighted indices, especially in fixed income. Market-capitalization-weighted indices have the natural benefit of (i) requiring minimal active trading decisions to replicate an index (as prices change the weights of bonds change automatically), and (ii) harnessing the (relative) efficiency of capital markets. Although markets are never perfectly efficient and active trading decisions are needed to replicate a benchmark (e.g., index inclusions/exclusions and a variety of actions by issuers that change the nature and size of outstanding bonds), market-capitalization-weighted indices still make a lot of sense.

The criticism for fixed income indices typically amounts to a criticism of index inclusion rules. Indices will include all bonds from an issuer that meet certain criteria. As we saw earlier in Section 5.1, for the W0G1 global government bond index from ICE/BAML, the United States and Japan account for nearly 65 percent of the total government debt outstanding in that index. This concentration of weights in the index is not limited to government indices; you also see this for corporate bond indices and equity indices, but not to the same extent where two issuers account for 65 percent of the total. Is this index concentration an issue? Some argue that it places too much weight on the issuers who have issued the most. While I would agree with the investment thesis to avoid issuers that have taken on too much debt, simply asserting that market capitalization indices fail because they don't account for debt issuance is wrong. The weights in the index are based on market prices. Given markets are reasonably efficient, concerns about excessive indebtedness or poor fiscal and monetary policy decision-making by indebted sovereigns will be reflected in prices and hence index weights.

What could you do if you felt market capitalization weights are too concentrated? There are not many liquid alternatively weighted indices, but some approaches might include equal weighting across sovereigns or weighting based on the strength/size of the underlying economy (e.g., GDP weighting). Some investors take combinations of these approaches by blending different weighting schemes together. A benefit of these alternative weighting schemes can be the improved risk profile of the reweighted (and less concentrated) basket of government bonds. This can make for an excellent class exercise:

Step 1: Start with the constituent information from a global government bond index; then roll up all bonds to the country level.

Step 2: Compute weights for each country using market capitalization weights, equal weights, GDP weights, and possibly a measure inversely related to recent volatility.

Step 3: Compute index level returns using these alternative weighting schemes.

Step 4: Evaluate the return profile of these alternative index level returns (i.e., average returns, volatility of returns, and Sharpe ratios).

Question: Do the alternative weighting schema deliver on their promise of a "better" return profile? In what way are the return series better? Distinguish between numerator and denominator effects.

One closing thought on index weighting choices. If your investment hypothesis is to avoid issuers that are overly indebted, then bet on that directly (I agree with this investment hypothesis). Switching to an equally weighted index is *not* the best way to pursue that investment hypothesis. If you dislike issuers with too much outstanding debt, then measure the leverage of the issuer directly and use that as a "signal" to take active positions relative to the benchmark (or active risk generally in a hedge fund). Simply using an equally weighted benchmark in lieu of a market capitalization weighted benchmark is deficient in two key respects: (i) the magnitude of active risk (tracking error) relative to benchmark is unmodeled and may be outsized relative to your conviction, and (ii) the difference between equal and market capitalization weights reflects the size of the issuer, not leverage, so the resulting portfolio is a noisy reflection of your investment hypothesis.

REFERENCES

Asness, C., A. Frazzini, and L. Pedersen. (2019). Quality minus junk. *Review of Accounting Studies*, 24, 34–112.

Asness, C., T. Moskowitz, and L. Pedersen. (2013). Value and momentum everywhere. *Journal of Finance*, 68, 929–985.

Baltussen, G., M. Martens, and O. Penninga. (2021). Factor investing in sovereign bond markets: Deep sample evidence. *Journal of Portfolio Management*, 48, 209–225.

Bradshaw, M, R. Richardson, and R. Sloan. (2001). Do analysts and auditors use information in accruals? *Journal of Accounting Research*, 39, 45–74.

Brooks, J. (2017). A half century of macro momentum. AQR working paper.

Brooks, J., and T. Moskowitz. (2017). Yield curve premia. Working paper, AQR.

Brooks, J., D. Palhares, and S. Richardson. (2018). Style investing in fixed income. *Journal of Portfolio Management*, 44, 127–139.

Campbell, J., A. Lo, and C. MacKinlay. (1996). The Econometrics of Financial Markets. Princeton University Press.

Cochrane, J., and M. Piazzesi. (2005). Bond risk premia. *American Economic Review*, 95, 138–160.

Correia, M., S. Richardson, and I. Tuna. (2012). Value investing in credit markets. *Review of Accounting Studies*, 17, 572–609.

Dickey, D., and W. Fuller. (1979). Distribution of the estimators for autoregressive time series with a unit root. *Journal of the American Statistical Association*, 74, 427–431.

Frazzini, A. (2006). The disposition effect and underreaction to news. *Journal of Finance*, 61, 2017–2046.

Frazzini, A., and L. Pedersen. (2014). Betting against beta. *Journal of Financial Economics*, 111, 1–25.

Ilmanen, I., R. Israel, R. Lee, T. Moskowitz, and A. Thapar. (2021). *Journal of Investment Management*, 19, 15–57.

Koijen, R., T. Moskowitz, L. Pedersen, and E. Vrugt. (2018). Carry. *Journal of Financial Economics*, 127, 197–225.

Litterman, R., and J. Scheinkman. (1991). Common factors affecting bond returns. *Journal of Fixed Income*, 1, 54–61.

Wright, Jonathan H. (2011). Term premia and inflation uncertainty: Empirical evidence from an international panel dataset." *American Economic Review*, 101(4): 1514–1534.

CHAPTER 6

Security Selection – Credit-Sensitive Assets

OVERVIEW

This chapter lays out the investment opportunity set for credit-sensitive assets. Our focus is on developed market corporate bonds, but the insights we cover can be extended to emerging market government bonds. We look at the vast number of investment grade (IG) and high yield (HY) corporate bonds in developed market indices and note the first order importance of across issuer security selection. While security selection among corporate bonds shares some similarities with security selection among stocks, we note important differences between credit and equity investing. The chapter discusses the intuition behind representative measures of value, momentum, carry, and defensive investment themes and evaluates the success of these strategies individually and in combination for developed corporate bond markets.

6.1 WHAT IS THE INVESTMENT OPPORTUNITY SET FOR DEVELOPED MARKET CORPORATE BONDS?

We will use a representative broad corporate bond index to explore the potential investment opportunity set. We will use indices from ICE/BAML for this purpose. To get a sense of the current size of the corporate bond markets, how those markets have grown over the past 20 years, and what the typical corporate issuer looks like, we examine four distinct categories of corporate bonds: (i) US IG includes all CAD- and USD-denominated bonds issued by corporate issuers domiciled in developed markets within the ICE/BAML G0BC index, (ii) US HY bonds (ICE/BAML H0A0 index), (iii) European (EU) IG includes all GBP- and EUR-denominated bonds issued by corporate issuers domiciled in developed markets within the ICE/BAML G0BC index, and (iv) EU HY bonds (ICE/BAML HP00 index).

All bonds are issued by corporations domiciled in developed markets. There is nothing limiting the efficacy of systematic investing approaches for emerging market corporate bonds, but the challenges of data access and liquidity in emerging markets can make that effort more challenging. We will not be looking at emerging corporate bonds in this chapter.

What types of bonds are included in these indices? The G0BC index, from which we construct our two IG universes, contained nearly 17,000 bonds as of December 31, 2020. And our US (EU) IG subuniverses contained 8,802 (3,443) corporate bonds, respectively. The G0BC index is designed to track the performance of investment grade corporate debt publicly issued in the major domestic and Eurobond markets. All securities are IG rated based on an average rating across the main rating agencies, have a minimum of 12 months remaining to final maturity, a fixed coupon schedule, and meet minimum issue size requirements (e.g., $250 million USD for a USD denominated bond). The H0A0 (HP00) index used for our US (EU) HY universes contained 2,030 (808) bonds, respectively, as of December 31, 2020. The H0A0 index is designed to track the performance of USD denominated subinvestment grade corporate debt publicly issued in the US domestic market. The HP00 index is designed to track the performance of EUR and GBP denominated sub investment grade corporate debt publicly issued in the eurobond, sterling domestic, or euro-domestic markets. Both H0A0 and HP00 follow similar index inclusion rules to G0BC (i.e., all securities are HY rated based on an average rating across the main rating agencies, have a minimum of 12 months remaining to final maturity, a fixed coupon schedule, and meet minimum issue size requirements). H0A0 has the additional requirement that eligible securities must have risk exposure to FX-G10 countries (Euro members, US, Japan, UK, Canada, Australia, New Zealand, Switzerland, Norway, and Sweden), so emerging corporate issuers are explicitly excluded. All four corporate bond universes are market capitalization weighted (see the discussion at the end of Chapter 5 for arguments for and against this weighting choice).

Exhibit 6.1 shows the market capitalization in USD trillions for the four corporate bond universes. There has been a huge growth in these markets. As of December 2020, the total market capitalization of corporate bonds across our four universes is $14.05 trillion dollars, led by US IG ($8.12T) and European IG ($3.84T). The HY markets are smaller with $1.55T ($0.54T) outstanding for US (European) markets, respectively.

What is the composition of corporate issuers across our corporate bond universes? As with government bonds, there are multiple corporate bonds outstanding for a given corporate issuer. The concentration of issues per issuer is not as great as was seen in the government bond market.

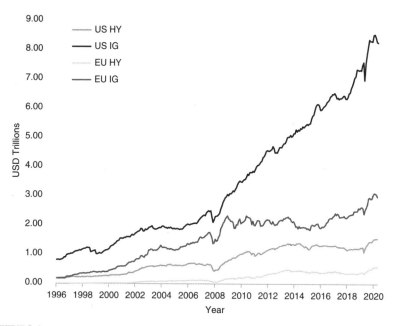

EXHIBIT 6.1 Market capitalization (USD) of developed-market corporate bond indices. US IG includes all CAD and USD denominated bonds issued by corporate issuers domiciled in developed markets within the ICE/BAML G0BC index. US HY is the US High Yield Index from ICE/BAML (ticker H0A0). EU IG includes all EUR and GBP denominated bonds issued by corporate issuers domiciled in developed markets within the ICE/BAML G0BC index. EU HY is the European Currency High Yield Index from ICE/BAML (ticker HP00).
Source: ICE/BAML indices.

Exhibit 6.2 plots the number of unique issuers across the four indices. There has been substantial growth in the number of corporate issuers over the 1996–2020 period. So part of the growth in the overall corporate bond market is attributable to a growing number of companies seeking to raise debt financing in public bond markets. As of December 31, 2020, there were 1,206 (602) issuers in the US (EU) IG markets, and 860 (384) issuers in the US (EU) HY markets.

Exhibit 6.3 plots the number of issues across the four indices. There is a clear increase in the number of issues (bonds) over time reflecting the general increase in the size of corporate bond markets. The occasional "'drops'" in number of issues are attributable to changes in index inclusion rules (e.g., changes in the minimum allowable size of the bond). As of

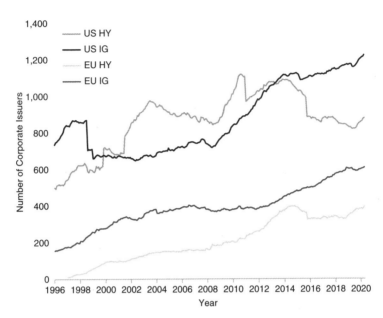

EXHIBIT 6.2   Number of corporate issuers across developed market corporate bond indices. US IG includes all CAD and USD denominated bonds issued by corporate issuers domiciled in developed markets within the ICE/BAML G0BC index. US HY is the US High Yield Index from ICE/BAML (ticker H0A0). EU IG includes all EUR and GBP denominated bonds issued by corporate issuers domiciled in developed markets within the ICE/BAML G0BC index. EU HY is the European Currency High Yield Index from ICE/BAML (ticker HP00).
Source: ICE/BAML indices.

December 31, 2020, there were 8,802 (3,443) issues in the US (EU) IG markets, and 2,030 (808) issues in the US (EU) HY markets. Exhibits 6.2 and 6.3 imply that the average issuer in the US (EU) IG market currently has about seven (six) bonds outstanding, and the average issuer in the US (EU) HY market currently has about two (two) bonds outstanding. This creates potential for both across and within issuer security selection, but note that the breadth of within issuer investment choices is much smaller relative to government bonds, especially for HY corporate bonds.

What does the duration of corporate bonds look like? The duration profile of corporate bonds is considerably shorter than government bonds. Exhibit 1.12 in Chapter 1 showed that the duration of the global treasury component of the Global Aggregate Index was about nine years as of December 31, 2020. Exhibit 6.4 shows the duration profile of our four corporate bond universes.

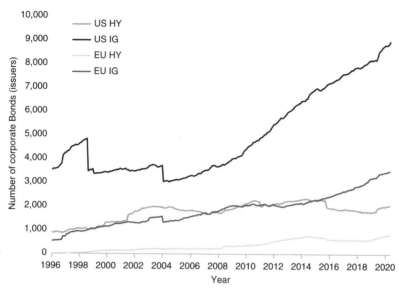

EXHIBIT 6.3   Number of corporate bonds (issues) across developed-market corporate bond indices. US IG includes all CAD and USD denominated bonds issued by corporate issuers domiciled in developed markets within the ICE/BAML G0BC index. US HY is the US High Yield Index from ICE/BAML (ticker H0A0). EU IG includes all EUR and GBP denominated bonds issued by corporate issuers domiciled in developed markets within the ICE/BAML G0BC index. EU HY is the European Currency High Yield Index from ICE/BAML (ticker HP00).
Source: ICE/BAML indices.

The average duration for the US (EU) IG universe is 8.21 (5.82) years as of December 31, 2020, and for the US (EU) HY universe it is 3.55 (3.32) years, respectively. Corporate bonds tend to have a lower duration than government bonds, and there is a striking difference between IG and HY bonds. This difference is a direct consequence of the heightened credit risk of HY rated corporate issuers. Lenders rationally lend to riskier issuers for shorter periods of time. There is also a much greater skew to the duration distribution for US IG corporate bonds. This is a direct consequence of the long-duration corporate bond market in the United States. Many corporate and public pension plans demand longer dated "'safe'" fixed income assets to help with asset-liability matching needs, and US-based corporates can tap into that demand by issuing longer dated bonds. We will discuss systematic approaches to long duration corporate bond indices in Chapter 11.

What do credit spreads look like across our corporate bond universes? Exhibit 6.5 shows the cross-sectional distribution of option adjusted

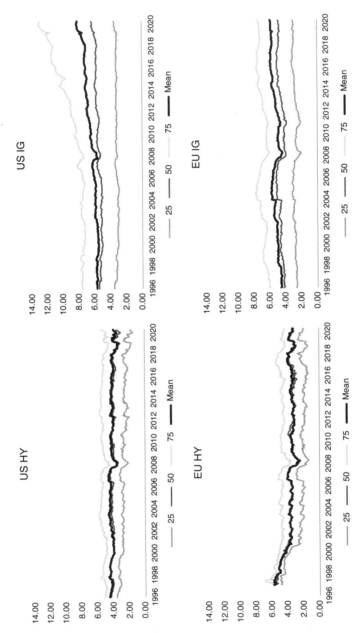

EXHIBIT 6.4 Duration of corporate bonds (issues) across developed-market corporate bond indices. The bold black line is the average duration, the other three lines labeled 25, 50, and 75 represent percentiles. The vertical axis is effective duration measured in years.
Source: ICE/BAML indices.

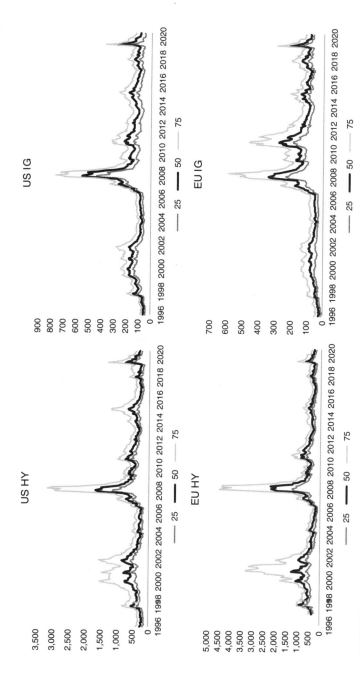

EXHIBIT 6.5 Option adjusted spreads (OAS) of corporate bonds (issues) across developed- market corporate bond indices. The bold black line is the median OAS (labeled as 50). The other two lines labeled 25 and 75 represent percentiles (25 for lower qua-tile, and 75 for upper quartile). The vertical axis is credit spread measured in basis points (i.e., 300 means 3 percent)
Source: ICE/BAML indices.

spreads. An option-adjusted spread is the credit spread adjusted for embedded optionality (e.g., calls) that reduces the duration profile of the corporate bond, which in turn affects the computed spread (i.e., you are matching the option-adjusted cash flows to riskless government bond securities, not the full set of cash flows). It is clear across all corporate bond universes that there is a strong countercyclical pattern with credit spreads and the business cycle. Credit spreads widen considerably, and quickly, during periods of economic stress (e.g., the end of the dot.com boom in 2000–2001, the great financial crisis of 2008, and the COVID crisis in early 2020). The scales of the IG and HY charts are very different: high–yield-rated corporate issuers are riskier and that is reflected in the considerably high credit spreads on average across the IG and HY markets.

There are interesting dynamics in credit spreads across IG and HY corporate bond markets. For most corporate issuers the credit spread term structure is upward sloping, especially for IG-rated corporate issuers. The slope of the credit curve (i.e., the pattern in credit spreads as a function of maturity or duration) is typically flatter the riskier the corporate issuer (see, e.g., Arora, Richardson, and Tuna 2014). One well-known feature of fixed income markets is that the return per unit of risk tends to be higher toward the front of the curve (see, e.g., Ilmanen 2011). We will capture that as part of our investment framework within the defensive theme. Leveraging the front end of credit (or yield) curves, via a passive steepener, has historically generated attractive risk-adjusted returns. It is a return opportunity that is not without risk, as there can be large drawdowns from curves flattening, especially in times of crisis. For corporate bond investors this was a very sore point in March 2020 (during the start of the COVID crisis).

There is at least one other aspect of the corporate bond market that is important to highlight up front. Newcomers to the corporate bond markets need to appreciate that many corporate issuers do not have publicly listed equity. This can pose challenges sourcing relevant data for your investment process. It does not mean you cannot, or should not, invest into these "private" issuers, but it does mean you need to be careful in sourcing your data. Exhibit 6.6 shows the fraction of corporate issuers across our four corporate bond universes that do not have publicly listed equity. A sizable portion of corporate issuers are private, particularly in Europe. This will reduce the investment opportunity set for security selection when equity market data or data that comes with equity listings (e.g., quarterly financial statements and analyst coverage) is unavailable.

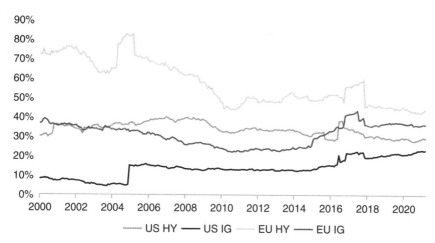

EXHIBIT 6.6 Fraction of private issuers across developed market corporate bond indices.
Source: ICE/BAML indices.

6.2 DIMENSIONS OF ACTIVE RISK TAKING WITHIN CORPORATE BONDS

6.2.1 Importance of Across Issuer Relative to Within Issuer

The cross-section of corporate bonds is much larger than government bonds. US (EU) IG indices contain over 1,200 (600) issuers compared to the 13 sovereign entities in the JP Morgan Government Bond Index (GBI). Security selection for corporate bonds will, therefore, naturally focus on the across-issuer dimension. The principal component analysis undertaken in Chapter 5 we will not repeat here for corporate bonds. But, to emphasize the importance of "level" effects and justify our focus on across issuer security selection, we will decompose credit-spread changes at the issuer level into a common-issuer component and a maturity-specific component.

We can start with an approximation for credit excess returns (R_{XS}):

$$R_{XS} \approx S - D * \Delta S \qquad (6.1)$$

where S is credit spread and D is spread duration. For each issuer that has multiple bonds outstanding, we can measure (i) the average spread change across all outstanding bonds, ΔS_{LEVEL}, akin to the "level" approach taken for government bonds, and (ii) the relation between spread change and bond spread duration, ΔS_{SLOPE}, akin to the "slope" approach taken for government bonds. This allows for an additive decomposition of spread change: $\Delta S = \Delta S_{LEVEL} + \Delta S_{SLOPE} + \varepsilon$ (the residual here is necessary as we will estimate this decomposition empirically). ΔS_{LEVEL} reflects the average widening or tightening of credit spreads across all bonds and represents a parallel shift in the credit curve. ΔS_{SLOPE} captures how longer-term bonds widened (or tightened) relative to shorter-term bonds and represents a widening or flattening of the credit curve. The portion of credit-excess returns attributable to spread changes can be written as $R_{XS} = [-D_i \Delta S_{LEVEL}] + [-D_i[\Delta S_{SLOPE}](D_i - \overline{D})] + \varepsilon$, where D_i is the spread duration for a specific bond for an issuer and $\overline{D}$ is the average spread duration across bonds of the issuer. This may be easier to grasp visually (see Exhibit 6.7).

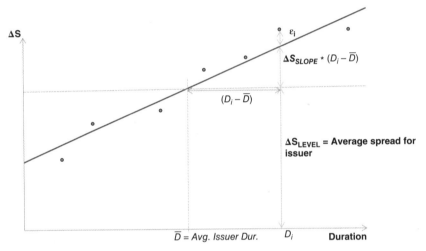

EXHIBIT 6.7   Breakdown of credit spread changes into level and slope components.

The dots in Exhibit 6.7 correspond to specific bonds for a corporate issuer. The vertical axis measures the change in spreads over a month, and the horizontal axis is the spread duration of each bond. The slope of the estimated regression line is ΔS_{SLOPE}, and ΔS_{LEVEL} is the average across all bonds (indicated by the dashed horizontal line in Exhibit 6.7). The portion of R_{XS} attributable to the level and slope components need to be multiplied by spread duration. In the case of the slope component, the contribution to credit excess returns utilizes simple geometry: the "rise" is equal to the product of the "slope" (ΔS_{SLOPE}, estimated via regression) and the "run" $(D_i - \overline{D})$.

We can estimate this regression for all IG and HY issuers that have multiple bonds outstanding. This allows us to quantify the fraction of variation in R_{XS} that we can explain with either ΔS_{LEVEL} or ΔS_{LEVEL} and ΔS_{SLOPE}

in combination. Estimating this using the full-time series of returns for each corporate issuer, the level-only specification can explain on average 60 (77) percent of variation in credit-excess returns for IG (HY) corporates. Using both level and slope increases the return variation explained to an average 75 (90) percent for IG (HY), respectively. If you had a crystal ball, you would want to know the average credit spread change for the corporate issuer because this explains most of the credit-excess returns. Thus, the level of credit spread changes, across issuer, will be the primary focus in the rest of the chapter.

6.2.2 Investing in Credit Markets Is Not the Same as Investing in Equity Markets

A gentle reminder of the interdependence, but not equivalence, of claims across the capital structure is warranted. Even academics sometimes fail to remember this (I have seen multiple papers get submitted to academic journals where the analysis is simply a cut/paste from equity markets to credit markets). Expecting the same result in credit markets as you would expect for equity markets may be appropriate in some settings, but not always.

An equity investor participates in the free cash flow after all other claims have been paid; equity is the residual claim. There is no limit to the upside participation. An investor in a senior claim, such as a corporate bond or loan, participates in the free cash flow before the equity holder but only up to the point specified by the contractual terms of the fixed income security; the upside is strictly limited. Equity investing is very much about expectations of earnings and earnings growth (see, e.g., Penman 2001, and Penman, Reggiani, Richardson, and Tuna 2018). Equation (6.2) is a useful tautology based on a combination of the dividend discount model and clean surplus accounting:

$$E[R_{EQUITY,t}] = \frac{E[EARNINGS_{t+1}]}{P_t} + \frac{E[(P_{t+1} - B_{t+1}) - (P_t - B_t)]}{P_t} \quad (6.2)$$

$E[R_{EQUITY,t}]$ is the expected return for the equity claim, $E[EARNINGS_{t+1}]$ is the expected (comprehensive) income for the next period, and $E[(P_{t+1} - B_{t+1}) - (P_t - B_t)]$ is the expected change in the premium of price over book value of equity. This latter term is what makes Equation (6.2) true (tautological), but it also captures the spirit of what equity investing is about: the long-run future. You can think of the premium of price over book value as capturing expected earnings growth. Equity price integrates across all future periods for free cash flow (residual income) participation. So expected equity returns have an initial expected return component, $\frac{E[EARNINGS_{t+1}]}{P_t}$, and additional expected returns that come from (risky) future earnings growth.

In contrast, the expected returns for the corporate credit claim as shown in Equation (3.8) was linked to credit spreads and how they are expected to change. What determines credit spreads? The primary determinant of credit spreads is the expected loss given default (LGD) (see, e.g., Kealhofer 2003, and Correia, Richardson, and Tuna 2012). Technically, this is all in what is called "risk-neutral" terms. That's just a fancy of way saying that there is a risk premium embedded in risky corporate bonds and the spreads that we infer from prices include that risk premium. Equation (6.3) captures this intuition:

$$Spread \approx E[LGD] = E[PD] * E[1 - R] \qquad (6.3)$$

$E[PD]$ is the expected (risk neutral) default probability and $E[1 - R]$ is expected loss in the event of default (i.e., R is the recovery rate). Combining Equations (3.8) and (6.3) it should be clear that expected credit excess returns are driven by changing expectations of default and/or recovery rates. This is the downside focus of the credit investor who does not get to participate fully in future earnings growth. Credit investing is *different* from equity investing. In this chapter we will discuss how $E[PD]$ is a relevant fundamental input across our investment themes (e.g., value, momentum, and quality). We will not spend much time on recovery-rate modeling because our focus is on security selection primarily across corporate issuers on a within sector basis. The key determinants of recovery rates are: (i) when you default (i.e., recovery rates are cyclical; lower in economic downturns), (ii) seniority (i.e., recovery rates are higher for loans than for secured bonds than for unsecured bonds), and (iii) sector/industry (i.e., recovery rates are linked to the nature of the assets that can be sold in the event of default to satisfy contractual commitments). As our security selection is in the cross-section, within sector groups, and among corporate bonds that are similar in seniority (e.g., senior unsecured), recovery rates are of second-order importance for us.

Although credit and equity claims originate from the same corporate issuer, they are less than perfectly correlated. Exhibit 3.17 introduced the concept of differential deltas for credit and equity claims (the safer the corporate issuer the less sensitive is the value of the credit claim to changing enterprise value and the greater the sensitivity of the equity claim to changing enterprise value). Lok and Richardson (2011) show empirically that the return correlation between corporate bond excess returns and stock excess returns is higher for riskier corporates (see their Figure 2). This is important; as a credit investor, the riskier (safer) the company you are examining, the greater (less) the relevance of equity market and enterprise-level information.

Another important aspect linking equity and credit markets relates to agency considerations. Corporations are run by management teams on behalf of the equity investors. There is a myriad of agency conflicts inherent in the modern, equity centric, corporation. Credit investors need to pay attention to operating, investing, and financial decisions that may be made in the interests of equity holders at the expense of other stakeholders. The most common examples relate to changes in the capital structure through financing events that alter either the amount or mix of financial obligations of the firm. This could include (i) leveraged corporate actions such as buyouts or acquisitions, and (ii) stock buybacks. These financing activities may be great for equity holders but can have the opposite effect for creditors (i.e., buybacks are typically good news for equity holders due to signaling and reduction in agency costs, but bad for creditors because they reduce the distance to default).

So, what are main lessons for credit investors? First, the relevance of an equity-investor perspective increases for riskier corporates (both the types of information and the relative weight assigned to each piece of information). Second, beware the pitfalls of wealth transfer events. What may be good for the equity investor need not be good for the credit investor. As Israel, Palhares, and Richardson (2018) noted: "simply documenting that: (i) X is correlated with equity excess returns, (ii) equity excess returns and credit excess returns are correlated, and hence (iii) X is therefore correlated with credit excess returns is not that exciting." I would add to that comment: it is also not intelligent as it misses important differences across credit and equity claims.

6.3 A FRAMEWORK FOR SECURITY SELECTION OF CORPORATE BONDS (INVESTMENT THEMES)

In this section we will revisit some of the well-known investment themes discussed in Chapter 3 when we covered tactical timing decisions for the credit premium. As with our framework on security selection for government bonds, we are now exploring cross-sectional investment opportunities (i.e., do I prefer issuer A or issuer B, or do I prefer the 2030 or 2025 maturing bond for issuer A?). Our focus here is to isolate attractive idiosyncratic sources of returns that are minimally correlated with traditional market risk premia. As we saw in Chapter 4, credit dedicated funds tend to have a very large passive exposure to the credit premium (credit beta). This is something we want to avoid, and we will handle via careful portfolio construction choices to beta-neutralize our investment themes. More on portfolio construction in Chapter 8.

Before we discuss our investment themes, it is useful to remember why we invest in corporate bonds. In Chapter 3 we decomposed the total returns of corporate bonds into a component attributable to risk-free discount rates and a component attributable to risky discount rates. This latter component is what we are looking for: credit-excess returns. Therefore, our investment signals need to be anchored to credit spreads (carry) and forecasted changes in credit spreads (signals other than carry).

6.3.1 Value

Equation (6.3) provides all the intuition we need for the value investment theme. Credit spreads are proportional to $E[PD]$, and given a default forecast, the "gap" between spreads and default risk is your measure of value. Alternatively, you can think of the quoted credit spread as containing an implied default probability forecast and the active investor is challenging the quality of that implied default forecast.

What is this "default" that we are trying to forecast? Technical default occurs when an entity is unable to meet its contractual commitments (i.e., nonpayment or late payment of coupons or principal, or perhaps breaching some other contract feature of the obligation). The precise rules governing default vary based on the jurisdiction of where the debt was issued. Our purpose is not to understand the precise details of the default process (that is important for the distressed market where a deep understanding of the legal jurisdiction and precise details of the lending agreement can be first order determinants of investment success). We are typically looking at going-concern corporations where the key risk is changes in its underlying credit risk. So, when we talk about "default" forecasts, we really mean we care about changing expectations of the underlying credit risk of the corporation.

How could you forecast this default event? First, we need some data that reflects the default events. Correia, Richardson, and Tuna (2012) identify a variety of sources that are typically used for formal default forecasting. These data sources identify "default" as a nonpayment type event. Such datasets identify defaults across many thousands of corporate entities over the past 40-plus years. This is a very rich dataset to train forecasting models on. A challenge for the systematic investor is building this default dataset to ensure as comprehensive coverage as possible. But we also do not need to limit ourselves only to forecasting the actual default event. We care about firms migrating to a different credit quality. Our modeling could be expanded to look at ratings changes and at the limit forecasting large spread changes directly. Second, we need a method to generate our default forecast. Correia, Richardson, and Tuna (2012) and Correia, Kang, and Richardson (2018) examine a variety of methodologies to forecast defaults. These methods include (i) basic probability models (e.g., Beaver 1966, Altman 1968, and Ohlson 1980), (ii) structural models (e.g., Merton 1974), (iii) combinations of both approaches (e.g., Beaver, Correia, and McNichols 2012), and (iv) more general machine learning models such as random forests and ensemble forecasting (see e.g., Correia, Kang, and Richardson 2018).

Default and credit migration forecasting should be done on an out-of-sample basis. That means if you are interested in forecasting defaults for the 860 issuers in the US HY index as of December 31, 2020, you should only be using information that is available to you as of that date. That covers the data attributes used in the forecast as well as parameters of the forecast itself (e.g., regression coefficients in the case of basic probability models or tree structure in the case of machine learning approaches). This out-of-sample condition is easy to satisfy for the current active investor (you don't get to see the future without a crystal ball), but for the systematic researcher who is building a model, this is a serious challenge. The data you use for forecasting needs to be point-in-time (as discussed in Chapter 3), but most importantly your model parameters also need to be point-in-time. You cannot calibrate a model on the full time series of data and then go back to assess its investment efficacy. This is in-sample fitting. Many academic papers that have been written about default forecasts do not satisfy this out-of-sample condition, so those analyses are, at best, useful for descriptive purposes only. The standard way to assess out-of-sample classification accuracy is the use of ROC (receiver operating characteristic) curves, which formally assess the diagnostic ability of a given binary classification scheme (our default models are binary classifiers: a firm either defaults or it does not over your forecasting horizon). Exhibit 6.8 shows the relative performance of four default forecasting models using these ROC curves (the full details of each model can be found in Correia, Richardson, and Tuna (2012).

The horizontal axis plots the false positive rate (FPR) and the vertical axis plots the true positive rate (TPR). FPR and TPR are computed for various thresholds (e.g., pick X percent from your default model as the threshold and see what fraction of defaults are captured for firms you say have a default probability greater than X percent, that's your TPR, and your FPR is the fraction of firms with a default forecast above X percent that did not default). So, if you have a sample of 1,000 corporate issuers, you can rank them from highest to lowest probability of default and then wait, say, 12 months and see where the defaults happen. If there are 30 defaults in the next 12 months (a 3 percent default rate is about average for a broad cross-section of corporate issuers), then a "perfect" model will identify the 30 defaulting firms as those with the highest probability of default. In Exhibit 6.8 this would be a straight line starting at the origin going to 1 along the vertical axis (i.e., FPR = 0 for all threshold values up to the in-sample default rate and TPR increases to 1 once the threshold value equals the in-sample default

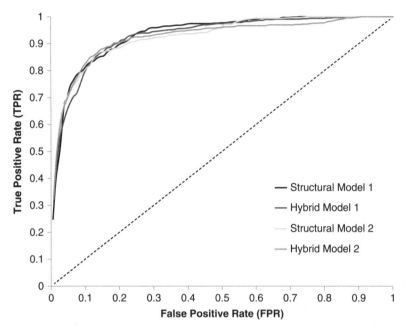

EXHIBIT 6.8   Receiver operating characteristic (ROC) curve for evaluation of four default forecasting models.
Source: Correia, Richardson, and Tuna (2012).

rate) and then another straight line extending from the vertical axis at 1 (i.e., TPR = 1 for all threshold values, but FPR increases as you increase the threshold). A model that has no ability to discriminate would be the dashed 45-degree line. The farther the ROC curve is from that line, the higher the model's predictive power. It is possible to measure the area under a respective model's ROC ("Area Under the Curve" or "AUC"), and the best model has the highest AUC.

An added benefit of the formal analysis of default forecasts is the ancillary (see Chapter 1) nature of the test. If we can demonstrate (out-of-sample) skill in forecasting defaults and credit migrations, then when we see such measures are correlated with future credit excess returns, we have greater comfort about our investment process. We can forecast returns via the channel of forecasting the relevant fundamentals.

How do we use our default forecasts to generate a value measure? The simplest value measure would be the ratio of credit spreads to your default forecast (e.g., $\frac{Spread}{E[PD]}$), and then we can compare this ratio in the cross-section (one company relative to another) or in the time series (same company relative to its own history). While this approach captures the intuition of value (a cheap corporate bond is one in which the credit spread is wide relative to your fundamental view on default risk), the ratio is limited in that it doesn't allow for controlling for other aspects of credit spreads. Generally, a type of regression (linear or otherwise) is used to link credit spreads to default forecasts and other relevant variables (e.g., recovery rates if your cross-section has heterogeneity on the seniority dimension, or duration to capture credit curve if the cross-section has heterogeneity on the maturity dimension). The regression residual is then the measure of "value." Equation (6.4) is a generalization of value signals for credit sensitive assets:

$$Spread = \alpha + \beta_{PD}E[PD] + \beta_{OTHER}OTHER + \varepsilon_{VALUE} \qquad (6.4)$$

Other than looking at future credit-excess returns, what else might we do to convince ourselves our value measure, ε_{VALUE}, is a good one? Implicit in Equation (6.4) is the notion that we have identified the component of credit spreads that is "unexplained." If the model is well specified, this unexplained portion should be strongly mean reverting. This can be tested directly via the same statistical tests discussed in Chapter 5 (e.g., Dickey and Fuller 1979). Specifically, the following regressions can be run for each corporate issuer:

$$\Delta\varepsilon_{VALUE,k+\tau} = \alpha + \beta_1\varepsilon_{VALUE,t} + \vartheta \qquad (6.5)$$

$$\Delta Spread_{k+\tau} = \alpha + \beta_2\varepsilon_{VALUE,t} + \vartheta \qquad (6.6)$$

Equation (6.5) captures mean reversion in the value signal directly. This can be estimated over the next few (k) months. For a good value measure, you will see $\beta_1 < 0$, and as you cumulate across the next k months, $\sum_{k=1}^{K}\beta_{1,k} \to -1$, indicative of a full closure of the valuation opportunity (there is one coefficient for each of the k months ahead). Of course, you also need to check which "leg" of the value signal (credit spreads or your model of implied credit spreads) is converging, so you also need to see $\beta_2 < 0$, and $\sum_{k=1}^{K}\beta_{2,k} \to -1$ when estimating Equation (6.6). This is the exact approach taken in Correia, Richardson, and Tuna (2012).

For our purposes here, we will use an equal-weighted combination of two value measures (see e.g., Israel, Palhares, and Richardson 2018). First, we use the structural model approach from Correia, Richardson, and Tuna (2012) and regress credit spreads onto "distance of default" (*D2D*) estimated as in Bharath and Shumway (2008). This can only be estimated for corporate issuers that have public equity and, as was noted at the start of the chapter, this means it cannot be estimated for a sizable minority of corporate issuers. Second, to expand coverage, we will examine a linear model based on regression residuals from a cross-sectional regression of credit spreads onto credit ratings, spread duration, and 12-month credit-excess-return volatility (this model is very similar to that used for timing credit premium in Chapter 3).

Hang on, we have another term: distance to default (*D2D*). What is this? Distance to default is central to structural models of credit, so it is important the intuition of this measure is well understood. Merton (1974) introduced the idea of distance to default to link prices of debt and equity to underlying enterprise value. Kealhofer (2003) and Correia, Richardson, and Tuna (2012) describe approaches to measure *D2D*, and that is our focus here. Equation (6.7) links *D2D* to measurable characteristics of a firm:

$$D2D = \frac{log\left(\frac{V_A}{X}\right) + \left(\mu - \frac{\sigma_A^2}{2}\right)t}{\sigma_A \sqrt{t}} \qquad (6.7)$$

The relevant characteristics are: (i) V_A, the market value of the enterprise (asset value as academics call it), which is simply the sum of the market value of all outstanding claims against the firm, (ii) X, the book value of the total outstanding contractual commitments the firm currently has (default barrier or threshold as academics call it), (iii) σ_A, the standard deviation of the return on assets of the enterprise (asset volatility), (iv) μ, the expected return on enterprise value due to systematic risk, and (iv) t, the remaining maturity of the contractual commitments. Let's use the visualization in Exhibit 6.9 to make the intuition clear. We are interested in quantifying the credit risk of a company that has debt and equity outstanding. On the vertical axis we measure the market value of the enterprise (asset value). This is a number. Bloomberg or Reuters or any other data vendor can provide you the data to measure this (sum up outstanding claims). Let's call this V_A. We then read the financial statements for the company and identify all outstanding contractual commitments. This is the default barrier. Let's call it X (shown by the horizontal line labeled "Default Threshold" in Exhibit 6.9). It is clear that $V_A > X$, today and the firm is not in "default" (i.e., the market value of the enterprise exceeds the total amount owed to creditors). But what we really care about is whether V_A will fall below X at some future point. I don't know that with certainty, nor do you. But we can estimate that probability, and that is what *D2D* is all about. The normal distribution that is turned 90 degrees in Exhibit 6.9 reflects the uncertainty with respect to what V_A will be in the future. The shape of that distribution is determined by two things: (i) the average value, which is the starting value, V_A, plus the expected return for that risky enterprise, μ (drift), and (ii) the standard deviation, which is σ_A (the greater the uncertainty the flatter the 90 degree rotated normal distribution). Now we have a way to think about the likelihood that V_A will fall below X. In Exhibit 6.9 the shaded area labeled "Default Probability" is the *PD* implied by Equation (6.7). This is very intuitive. The distance between the current market value of the enterprise, V_A,

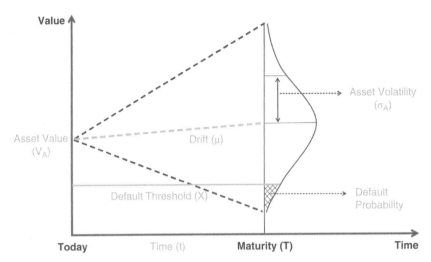

EXHIBIT 6.9   Graphical representation of *D2D* (distance to default).
Source: Correia, Richardson, and Tuna (2012).

and current contractual commitments, X, is scaled by a measure of volatility, σ_A, that reflects the uncertainty of the business model (the drift adjustment in the numerator and the $\sqrt{t}$ adjustment in the denominator allow comparisons across issuers with differing systematic risk levels and debt maturity profiles). *D2D* closely resembles a t-statistic, and in our case the null hypothesis is that $V_A = X$ (how big a shock in asset value, measured in standard deviation units, is needed to move the firm into default?) The inputs are also very intuitive (just remember that *D2D* is inversely related to *PD*). All else equal, if a firm (i) increases its contractual commitments, *D2D* will fall, or (ii) experiences an increase in underlying volatility, *D2D* will fall. These are the essential ingredients of structural models of credit risk (i.e., leverage, $\frac{V_A}{X}$, and volatility).

There is a lot of choice in measuring the components of *D2D* and combining them together (see e.g., Kealhofer 2003, Correia, Richardson, and Tuna 2012, and Correia, Kang, and Richardson 2018). The final step is mapping of *D2D* to default probability (*PD*). While it is possible to assume the world is normally distributed and use normal distributions to map *D2D* to *PD*, this fails to recognize that the default generating process is far from normal and firms with a low normal distribution implied *PD* may still have an economically meaningful *PD*. For example, if *D2D* = 5 this would imply a 5 standard deviation shock in asset value is needed to move a firm into default. In the world of normal random variables, this implies a *PD* of 0.00015 percent (hardly worth worrying about), but empirically the default rate of firms with $D2D = 5$ is considerably greater. Therefore, most active credit investors working with default model will calibrate their forecasts to actual default data. This stresses the importance of quality data access.

6.3.2 Momentum

Although both valuation and momentum investment themes for credit-sensitive assets are about forecasting changes in credit spreads, valuation rests on credit spreads mean reverting to an expected level and momentum rests on continuation in movement of credit spreads (and other market and fundamental performance measures linked to the corporate issuer). The success of momentum depends on a combination of persistence in performance measures and the markets lagged response to these measures.

We will use the same two measures of momentum examined in Israel, Palhares, and Richardson (2018). First, we use "own" momentum defined as the trailing six-month bond credit excess return. Issuers with higher recent credit excess returns are expected to outperform issuers with lower recent credit excess returns. Second, we use "related" momentum measured as the trailing six-month momentum of the bond issuer's equity returns. This use of equity momentum for corporate bond investing was first written about by Kwan (1996). Issuers with higher recent stock returns are expected to outperform issuers with lower recent stock returns. Of course, equity momentum can only be computed for public corporate issuers so this measure will be missing for the private issuers that we discussed in Section 6.1. The equity momentum measure for credit markets does not skip the most recent month as is typically done for equity-momentum investing. Why? The potential for bid-ask bounce effects to contaminate prices across markets is less of an issue, and empirically there is no evidence of any short-term across-markets reversal. If anything, the more recent equity returns are more predictive in credit markets.

Although our measures of momentum are both simple and transparent, the systematic investor in credit markets can look further for relevant momentum measures. There are multiple measures of fundamental health linked directly to the company, and recent changes in expectations of these variables are all candidate measures of momentum. This could include the various forecasts of default discussed earlier in the chapter. Likewise, under the heading of "related" momentum, there are many ways to identify economically linked firms (e.g., supply-chain linkages as done in Cohen and Frazzini 2008). Measures of momentum can be projected from economically linked firms to the corporate issuer you are evaluating. Momentum can become a very broad investment theme for systematic credit investors.

6.3.3 Carry

The investment thesis for carry in corporate bonds is identical to that for carry in government bonds. We are looking to identify the expected return from holding the asset assuming nothing happens to the credit-risk profile of the issuer as time passes. A comprehensive measure of carry requires estimation of the credit term structure. Similar to the discussion in Chapter 5 about curve fitting through zero-coupon bond yields, identification of an issuer-specific credit curve requires specifying the maturity structure of credit spreads that can then be used to discount corporate bond cash flows (coupon and principal). This involves obtaining pricing data for all relevant corporate bonds and the associated terms and conditions for each bond. For the purposes of this chapter we will work with a simple measure of carry, namely, the corporate bond option adjusted spread (see, e.g., Israel, Palhares, and Richardson 2018).

6.3.4 Defensive

There are two broad, but related, themes within defensive. First, we have measures related to low-risk where the investment thesis is to capture the higher risk-adjusted returns from lower-risk securities, in part due to leverage aversion within fixed income markets (see e.g., Frazzini and Pedersen 2014). We will use spread duration of the corporate bond as a measure of low risk. In credit markets, beta can be approximated by the product of spread duration and spread, or DTS (e.g., Ben Dor et al. 2007). One could use DTS as a measure of risk, and under the defensive theme seek exposure to credit-sensitive assets with lower values of DTS. This would, however, mix two ideas as discussed in Israel, Palhares, and Richardson (2018). The first component, spread duration, our focus here, has been shown to be negatively associated with risk-adjusted returns in multiple asset classes (see e.g., van Binsbergen and Koijen 2017). The second component, credit spread, is our measure of carry for corporate bonds. Measures of beta and/or measures of volatility based on credit excess returns therefore combine two conflicting measures that have opposite effects on expected returns. We decompose beta (DTS) into its components and seek lower spread duration here as part of the defensive theme (low risk).

The second set of measures within defensive relates to "quality." A wide set of potential measures could be included here: (i) measures of default probability (these were used conditionally with spread in our valuation signal, but could be used unconditionally here as a part of quality), and (ii) measures of profitability and components of profitability (a vast literature has explored the efficacy of financial statement analysis to better understand the persistence of corporate profitability and that literature is directly relevant here). In this chapter we will examine only the two measures from Israel, Palhares, and Richardson (2018): (i) market leverage (preference for corporate issuers with lower levels of leverage), and (ii) gross profitability (preference for corporate issuers with higher levels of profitability).

6.4 A FRAMEWORK FOR SECURITY SELECTION OF CORPORATE BONDS (PERFORMANCE)

Let's assess how well investing based on the systematic themes could have worked. We will start with a combined universe of IG and HY bonds as described in Israel, Palhares, and Richardson (2018). In each month, one representative bond is kept for each issuer from the US IG and US HY indices described at the start of the chapter. The two universes are combined, and each issuer is ranked based on the four investment themes, both individually and in combination (equal weighted). Simple academic portfolios are constructed that are long the most attractive 20 percent of issuers each month (market capitalization weighted) and short the least attractive 20 percent of issuers each month (market capitalization weighted). It is important to stress the academic nature of these portfolios. They make *no* attempt to address the various implementation challenges an investor faces with credit sensitive assets (e.g., sourcing liquidity, trade size limits, position limits, risk constraints, expected transaction costs, etc.). Our purpose here is to assess whether the systematic return profile is worthy of further exploration. The implementation challenges we will discuss in Chapters 8 and 9.

Exhibit 6.10 summarizes the performance of our four investment signals (value, momentum, carry, and defensive), both individually and as an equally weighted average combination. The bottom section of the exhibit reports information about the return series (Sharpe ratios, information ratios, and correlations). Except for carry, all investment themes have attractive risk-adjusted returns with Sharpe ratios ranging from 0.98 for momentum to 1.71 for value. The Sharpe ratios and information ratios are much higher than we saw for the analysis of government bonds (these are *not* implementable portfolios). The equally weighted combination is superior to any one individual theme due to the low pairwise correlations you see at the bottom of Exhibit 6.10.

EXHIBIT 6.10 Properties of corporate bond security selection investment themes (V for value, M for momentum, C for carry, D for defensive, and VMCD for an equally weighted average) for the 1997–2020 period using a combined IG and HY universe.

	α	β_{CP}	β_{TP}	β_{EP}	β_{SMB}	β_{HML}	β_{MOM}	β_{QMJ}	β_{BAB}	R^2
V	0.13	0.16	0.04	−0.06	−0.03	−0.00	−0.01	−0.10	−0.07	5.32%
	8.56	*1.55*	*0.38*	*−1.70*	*−0.66*	*−0.01*	*−0.39*	*−1.62*	*−2.77*	
M	0.07	−0.71	−0.11	0.07	−0.01	−0.01	0.05	0.07	−0.03	27.32%
	4.81	*−7.02*	*−1.15*	*2.02*	*−0.16*	*−0.39*	*2.20*	*1.18*	*−1.28*	
C	0.01	0.51	−0.33	0.07	0.04	0.01	−0.01	−0.10	0.00	63.52%
	1.55	*8.19*	*−5.77*	*3.63*	*1.54*	*0.65*	*−0.40*	*−2.74*	*−0.25*	
D	0.10	−0.94	−0.11	−0.01	0.00	−0.05	−0.03	0.04	−0.08	46.85%
	8.60	*−10.74*	*−1.37*	*−0.50*	*0.03*	*−1.72*	*−1.42*	*0.84*	*−3.43*	
VMCD	0.17	−0.58	−0.26	0.05	0.02	−0.01	0.01	−0.05	−0.08	17.62%
	12.70	*−6.05*	*−2.85*	*1.51*	*0.62*	*−0.34*	*0.28*	*−1.01*	*−3.34*	

	V	M	C	D	VMCD		SR	IR
V	1	−0.32	0.19	0.05	0.43		1.71	1.99
M		1	−0.50	0.56	0.38		0.98	1.12
C			1	−0.51	0.03		0.09	0.36
D				1	0.64		1.26	2.00
VMCD					1		2.42	2.95

Sources: Israel, Palhares, and Richardson (2018), ICE/BAML indices, https://mba .tuck.dartmouth.edu/pages/faculty/ken.french/data_library.html, and https://www .aqr.com/Insights/Datasets.

To assess whether security selection based on value, momentum, carry, and defensive themes are diversifying with respect to traditional market risk premia (and some well-known factor risk premia from equity markets) we run the following regression (with all explanatory variables as defined in Chapter 5):

$$THEME = \alpha + \beta_{CP}CP + \beta_{TP}TP + \beta_{EP}EP + \beta_{SMB}SMB + \beta_{HML}HML$$
$$+ \beta_{MOM}MOM + \beta_{QMJ}QMJ + \beta_{BAB}BAB + \varepsilon \tag{6.8}$$

The top half of Exhibit 6.10 reports estimated regression coefficients and, in italics below, the corresponding t-statistics. The value investment theme is not significantly associated with either traditional market risk premia (CP, TP, and EP), or equity style returns, with an information ratio of 1.99. Of note is the insignificant β_{HML} regression coefficient. This means that systematic value investing in credit markets is uncorrelated with systematic investing in equity markets. At first glance, this may be puzzling to you. Aren't we talking about identifying cheap assets (bonds or stocks) linked to companies? Surely those types of investment approaches must be similar. Not necessarily. There are multiple reasons for this. First, the credit market and the equity market, while positively correlated, are diversifying with respect to each other (we covered that in Chapter 3). Second, the set of companies where we are taking active risk in equity and credit markets are different (some companies have public equity but not debt, and some companies have public debt but no equity). Third, and perhaps most important, the measures of value are very different. As discussed earlier in the chapter, equity investing is about the long term and the equity value measures ($\frac{X}{P}$, where X is a fundamental measure extracted from the primary financial statements) are deliberately constructed to be very different from the credit value measures ($\frac{Spread}{PD}$). For those who have been locked in the world of fixed income markets and have not looked at the equity markets recently (read last decade) this is a very useful result. Value-based investing in equity markets (systematic and traditional discretionary) has been very tough over the past decade (see e.g., Israel, Laursen, and Richardson 2021).

Momentum has an attractive Sharpe and information ratio, even though it has the expected positive association with the equity momentum factor (in this case it is a common measure across equity and credit markets, but it is still diversifying). The simple academic long-short momentum portfolio has a strong negative correlation with the credit premium. While this creates a headwind over the sample period (the credit premium was strongly positive over this period and a signal that is short that exposure inherits a negative return as a consequence), it is the consequence of poor portfolio construction choices. A simple sort on momentum will identify better recent performers as more attractive and, all else equal, such issuers will have tighter spreads, creating the negative correlation. Better portfolio construction choices can be made to neutralize signals to traditional market risk premia (more on this in Chapter 8). Defensive also shares this strong negative correlation to credit markets (issuers with lower leverage and higher profitability tend to have lower credit spreads too). Carry has the expected positive directionality with risky markets (credit and equity) and the resulting negative loading on the term premium is a direct consequence of the strong negative stock-bond correlation over this period (see discussion in Chapter 2).

The combination portfolio exhibits some exposure to traditional market risk premia (negative to credit premium and term premium) but they are generally muted relative to individual investment themes. The adjusted R^2

of the combined signal is 17.62 percent and the regression intercept has a test statistic of 12.7! Yes, too good to be true, but it suggests if you could implement these investment themes, they would be a powerful diversifier to an asset owner portfolio.

As an appetizer for what is to come in later chapters, Exhibits 6.11 and 6.12 repeat the same exercise but separate the corporate bond markets into the IG and HY universes separately and also examine a wider set of measures within each of the respective investment themes implemented in a manner consistent with some of the principles to be discussed in Chapter 8 (e.g., sector demeaning signals, beta-neutralizing signals). Separating the IG and HY universes has at least two benefits. First, it reduces heterogeneity in risk in the cross-section making for better (more balanced) security selection. Second, it allows for differential weighting choices to be made across

EXHIBIT 6.11   Properties of corporate bond security selection investment themes (V for value, M for momentum, C for carry, D for defensive, and VMCD for an equally weighted average) for the 1997–2020 period using the US HY universe.

	α	β_{CP}	β_{TP}	β_{EP}	β_{SMB}	β_{HML}	β_{MOM}	β_{QMJ}	β_{BAB}	R^2
V	1.04	−0.39	0.51	−0.21	−0.00	−0.01	−0.02	0.27	0.09	16.16%
	26.21	*−1.26*	*1.92*	*−2.19*	*−0.02*	*−0.14*	*−0.26*	*1.66*	*1.31*	
M	0.69	−0.53	−0.38	−0.04	0.09	0.01	0.12	0.81	0.23	26.39%
	16.45	*−1.64*	*−1.36*	*−0.43*	*0.78*	*0.11*	*1.63*	*4.76*	*2.99*	
C	0.62	0.66	2.19	−0.39	−0.28	0.23	0.08	−1.04	−0.15	15.50%
	9.85	*1.35*	*5.22*	*−2.55*	*−1.59*	*1.41*	*0.78*	*−4.06*	*−1.28*	
D	0.03	−0.14	−0.21	-0.12	0.06	0.07	0.04	0.18	−0.04	12.24%
	1.33	*−0.77*	*−1.31*	*−2.05*	*0.88*	*1.17*	*1.00*	*1.88*	*−0.90*	
VMCD	1.25	−0.25	1.10	−0.31	−0.10	0.10	0.08	0.07	0.09	21.01%
	28.47	*−0.73*	*3.76*	*−2.92*	*−0.80*	*0.86*	*1.05*	*0.37*	*1.17*	

	V	M	C	D	VMCD			SR	IR
V	1	0.47	−0.09	0.18	0.83			5.75	6.24
M		1	−0.45	0.15	0.44			3.59	3.92
C			1	0.02	0.38			2.03	2.35
D				1	0.22			0.26	0.32
VMCD					1			6.07	6.78

Sources: Author calculations, ICE/BAML indices, https://mba.tuck.dartmouth .edu/pages/faculty/ken.french/data_library.html, and https://www.aqr.com/Insights/ Datasets.

EXHIBIT 6.12 Properties of corporate bond security selection investment themes (V for value, M for momentum, C for carry, D for defensive, and VMCD for an equally weighted average) for the 1997–2020 period using the US IG universe.

	α	β_{CP}	β_{TP}	β_{EP}	β_{SMB}	β_{HML}	β_{MOM}	β_{QMJ}	β_{BAB}	R^2
V	1.45	−1.20	1.18	−0.36	0.10	−0.27	−0.11	−0.13	−0.14	18.53%
	25.90	−2.75	3.16	−2.69	0.62	−1.90	−1.17	−0.58	−1.35	
M	0.43	−0.71	0.59	−0.02	0.00	−0.05	−0.02	0.39	0.03	19.47%
	12.26	−2.62	2.52	−0.18	0.02	−0.51	−0.37	2.74	0.50	
C	1.16	0.72	1.48	−0.28	0.01	−0.38	−0.05	−0.48	−0.20	8.64%
	16.45	1.32	3.15	−1.66	0.05	−2.10	−0.38	−1.67	−1.52	
D	0.03	−0.01	0.08	−0.05	−0.02	0.02	0.03	0.08	0.09	8.55%
	1.37	−0.08	0.66	−1.18	−0.47	0.47	1.05	1.05	2.58	
VMCD	1.61	−0.78	1.53	−0.37	0.07	−0.35	−0.09	−0.16	−0.15	16.05%
	25.85	−1.60	3.70	−2.50	0.39	−2.16	−0.83	−0.64	−1.36	

	V	M	C	D	VMCD		SR	IR
V	1	0.21	0.77	0.14	0.96		5.40	6.17
M		1	−0.12	0.35	0.31		2.78	2.92
C			1	−0.01	0.85		3.63	3.92
D				1	0.17		0.45	0.33
VMCD					1		5.51	6.16

Sources: Author calculations, ICE/BAML indices, https://mba.tuck.dartmouth .edu/pages/faculty/ken.french/data_library.html, and https://www.aqr.com/Insights/ Datasets.

investment themes where you have *priors* for differential performance. As we have seen earlier in this book the efficacy of momentum is stronger for riskier credit sensitive assets and the efficacy of carry is stronger for safer credit-sensitive assets. For both the HY and IG universes, the systematic investment themes are diversifying with respect to traditional market risk premia and well-known equity factors. The adjusted R^2 for Equation (6.8) ranges from 12 to 26 percent for HY and from 8 to 19 percent for IG. These are much lower than the R^2 reported in Exhibit 6.10 for the combined universe and simpler portfolio construction. The correlation structure across investment themes is also different, partly attributable to improved portfolio construction choices (e.g., beta-neutralizing and sector demeaning), but also due to a wider set of measures. In both markets the combination of systematic investment signals has the promise of something very attractive.

6.5 EXTENSIONS

6.5.1 Why Not Size or Liquidity?

Over the years working in systematic fixed income, I have been asked why we never tried to harvest a size effect in credit markets. My answer has always been this: What does size capture? It is not obvious what size means in the credit market. Are you taking a view on the size of the enterprise (sum of all debt and equity outstanding)? Are you taking a view on the equity capitalization? Are you taking a view on the amount of debt outstanding? Is that view based on the sum of all debt outstanding or is it specific to each bond? I don't know, and given I am not the one advocating this investment theme all I can do is discuss what folks might be trying to get at when they talk about "size" as an investment factor in credit markets.

I think it could be one of two things: liquidity or leverage. If the investment view is leverage, then measure that directly. Looking at the amount of debt outstanding by an issuer in an index (preference for issuers with less debt) is an imperfect way to do this. A similar discussion occurred in Chapter 5 when we discussed the potential limitations of market capitalization weighted indices. If leverage is part of your investment view, I agree with that completely, but let's agree to call it what it is; it is part of the defensive/quality theme!

If the investment view behind a preference for smaller-sized bonds or issuers with less debt outstanding is related to liquidity (i.e., a belief in a premium to be harvested from holding less liquid assets), then it is better to measure liquidity directly. Indeed, that is exactly what Palhares and Richardson (2019) do. Theoretically, I agree with the idea of a liquidity premium. If an investor is forced to bear the risk of uncertainty with respect to selling an asset at low cost in the future, they will rationally demand a premium from holding such an asset. A liquid asset is one that can be bought/sold at a reasonable price, in a relatively short period of time, at a reasonable cost with minimal impact on its value. Not asking for too much, are we?

Palhares and Richardson (2019), using a broad sample of US IG and US HY corporate bonds, measure liquidity in six different ways: (i) issue size (smaller bonds are perceived to be less liquid), (ii) bid-ask spreads, BAS (bonds with wider bid-ask spreads are less liquid), (iii) market impact, MI (bonds with a larger price impact from trading, defined as the change in price for a given trading volume, are less liquid), (iv) daily trading volume, DTV (bonds that trade in smaller dollar amounts are less liquid), (v) percentage of no-trading days, PNT (bonds that trade on fewer days are less liquid), and (vi) time since issuance, age (older bonds may be perceived to be less liquid). Palhares and Richardson (2019) examine whether these six measures of liquidity can explain cross-sectional variation in future credit excess returns and whether long/short portfolios designed to target the less liquid bonds generate attractive risk-adjusted returns. What was the result? Not much.

Perhaps the easiest, and cleanest, way to assess the impact of liquidity on credit markets is to look across bonds issued by the same corporate issuer that are maximally different on each respective liquidity measure. In this way, you control for any credit risk affects of the corporate issuer, and any remaining difference in credit spreads or credit excess returns is then likely attributable to liquidity. Exhibit 6.13 summarizes the analysis on credit spreads for this within issuer design from Palhares and Richardson (2019). The first two taller bars serve as a benchmark of comparison for the average level of credit spreads (AVG) and the interquartile range (IQR). The remaining smaller bars measure the average difference in credit spreads within issuer pairs of assets (i.e., what is the difference in credit spreads between the least and most liquid bond for that issuer). If there is a liquidity premium, you would expect a positive spread difference. Exhibit 6.13 shows a generally positive result, albeit small relative to the average spread level.

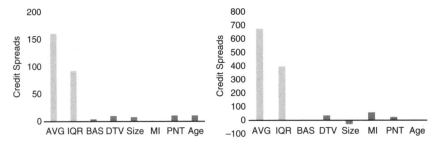

EXHIBIT 6.13   Effect of liquidity on corporate bond spreads for US IG (left) and US HY (right).
Sources: Data from Palhares and Richardson (2019), TRACE, ICE/BAML indices.

However, when looking at the difference in future credit excess returns across bonds issued by the same corporate there is no statistical evidence of a positive risk-adjusted returns from seeking exposure to the less liquid corporate bonds. Exhibit 6.14 shows this lack of a result (all test-statistics are below conventional levels of significance). This lack of a result, while puzzling from an academic perspective, is very important from an asset-owner perspective. If you cannot find reliable evidence of positive risk-adjusted returns from holding less liquid corporate bonds in an academic setting, which assumes frictionless trading, the result after incurring transaction costs and the challenge of sourcing these less liquid bonds is likely to be a negative return investment proposition. Furthermore, holding less liquid corporate bonds in an investment vehicle with frequent dealing introduces a redemption risk that seems to be uncompensated.

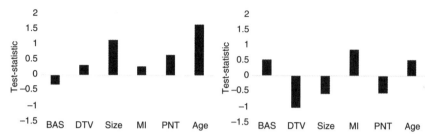

EXHIBIT 6.14 Effect of liquidity on corporate bond credit-excess returns for US IG (left) and US HY (right).
Sources: Data from Palhares and Richardson (2019), TRACE, ICE/BAML indices.

6.5.2 Within Issuer (Maturity Dimension)

All the empirical analysis discussed in this chapter emphasized the across-issuer dimension of security selection. Although this is the most important source of return potential, it is still possible to engage in within issuer security selection, especially for IG issuers that tend to have multiple issues outstanding. Such models will typically include measures specific to the bond rather than using corporate-issuer-level information (e.g., carry measures can be localized to specific points, value measures are localized to specific bonds, and other measures may naturally be unique to a bond). An added benefit of modeling multiple bonds for a given issuer is additional flexibility in portfolio construction. For example, having views on an issuer propagated across multiple bonds allows for better liquidity provision in corporate bond secondary markets. We will revisit this in more detail in Chapter 9.

6.5.3 Data Issues

A general caveat for all analysis in systematic fixed income investing is the integrity of your data. But this is especially true for credit sensitive assets. We have discussed some of these issues throughout the book, but it is worth collecting our thoughts on this topic. First, the returns data are not maintained by a central exchange and will need to be sourced directly.

The most common source is from an index provider who can provide monthly (even daily) constituent-level information on total and excess returns. Index-provider returns are generally of high quality, but for the less liquid bonds, choices will be made to interpolate prices, or spreads, and hence returns. To help mitigate issues from poor pricing, a good systematic investment approach should source returns data from multiple sources and assess robustness across those sources. An alternative source, and one increasingly used by academics, is returns data from TRACE (trade reporting and compliance engine). Returns estimated from TRACE reported trades are problematic in several ways: (i) price-based measures of returns are total returns, not credit-excess returns, so they capture both rate and credit effects on corporate bonds (and we have seen earlier that these two components are negatively correlated); (ii) returns estimated from TRACE cover only a small portion of corporate bonds (especially if you require a trade at the start and end of a month); (iii) returns estimated from TRACE data are negatively serially correlated and can be predicted by index provider returns (suggesting the TRACE returns suffer from staleness issues). Andreani, Palhares, and Richardson (2022) discuss the limitations of TRACE estimated corporate bond returns.

Other important data integrity issues are related to mapping. Think of the vast array of fundamental data that needs to be mapped from a parent entity down to the entity that has issued the bond who you are thinking about buying. For some companies, the organizational structure is simple. There is one operating company with one class of stock and one type of senior unsecured debt. Alas, this is the exception. In practice, organizational forms are complicated and sometimes drastically so. Choices need to be made to link information from parent entity to issuing entity in a thoughtful manner. Not everyone agrees on how this should be done in some of the more complicated cases. As with returns, try to source multiple-reference entity-mapping tables to assess the robustness of your investment performance to different choices.

6.5.4   IG versus HY

As a rule, I dislike market segmentation, because it unnecessarily reduces your investment opportunity set. In corporate bond markets the extent of market segmentation is extreme. IG and HY markets are treated as separate asset classes by asset owners. This segmentation needs to be respected, which is unfortunate from an investment breadth perspective, but on the other hand it can allow tailoring of your investment themes across IG and HY markets. As we saw earlier in this chapter, momentum measures work better (worse) in HY (IG) markets and carry measures work worse (better) in HY (IG) markets. Safer corporate bonds tend to trade close to par with considerably lower spread volatility. This translates to greater spread mean reversion in IG markets, consistent with the differences in performance for momentum and carry. Take advantage of these insights in your investing. For less constrained investors, do what you can to be downgrade tolerant and expand your investment set across IG and HY markets. Even if a complete combination of IG and HY markets is a step too far, at least entertain a spillover into the neighboring rating buckets. This will allow you to avoid bad-selling practices and improve on your security selection opportunities.

6.5.5 Sustainability/ESG

The push into sustainable investing, which started in equity markets, is gathering momentum in fixed income, especially for corporate bonds. This is an area where systematic investing approaches are uniquely positioned to be able to accommodate the joint investing challenge of delivering attractive risk-adjusted returns but also simultaneously delivering on sustainability objectives. This topic is so vast and important that we have a later chapter dedicated to it (Chapter 10).

6.5.6 Machine Learning

I hesitate to add a subtitle with such a loaded topic. I am no expert in machine learning techniques, but I have used them successfully in the investment process. I remain skeptical of the general applicability of many of the techniques that fall under the machine learning category. There is considerable variability in the quality of investment analysis that falls under this category. One thing that seems to be generally accepted is the need for a lot of data for machine learning techniques to add value. Investing in corporate bonds does not bring with it ample trading data, so machine learning is unlikely to be helpful from a trading perspective (unlike with high frequency trading where these techniques could credibly add value, because there is very rich data at a very fine frequency). But where investing in corporate bonds may lend itself to machine learning techniques is with ancillary testing, particularly with the default forecasting models discussed earlier in the chapter as part of the valuation theme.

How might machine learning techniques be used here? There are large datasets that cover the default experience of thousands of corporates over the last 50 years. A dataset of that size lends itself to machine learning techniques. A benefit of these techniques is that they allow for consideration of a larger set of correlated forecasting variables, and the techniques also allow for potential nonlinearities and interactions among a large set of predictors.

Do these techniques help investors? Luckily, I can refer to some recent research from Correia, Kang, and Richardson (2018) that used a type of machine learning technique, random forests, to assess whether, and how, a variety of fundamental and market data could help improve out-of-sample forecasts of bankruptcy. Exhibit 6.15 is an example of a pruned tree that demonstrates how these techniques can improve classification of an investor-relevant outcome (bankruptcy) using many variables in some nonobvious ways. This technique starts with all data points (68,040 firm-year observations with a probability of bankruptcy of 0.6 percent for the entire sample) in the top box. The full sample is then partitioned using a variety of predictor variables, and the technique keeps the predictor variable that generates the maximal difference in bankruptcy probability above and below a given threshold. This generates two boxes at the first branch, which differ in bankruptcy probability by 4.8 to 0.2 percent using $\frac{V_A}{X}$ (a measure of leverage we discussed earlier in this chapter). The relation is intuitive: firms with more leverage (lower $\frac{V_A}{X}$) have higher probabilities of bankruptcy. This process is repeated to generate further branches in the tree. In the second branch a measure of volatility is important (the higher the volatility the higher the risk of bankruptcy). In so doing, this tree uncovers the important interaction between leverage and volatility that is at the heart of structural models, but it does so in a data-driven way that can identify further interactions. There is, of course, a large risk of data mining (in-sample fitting for the politically correct reader), but that can be mitigated by cross-validation techniques (i.e., build the tree on one set of data and assess its classification accuracy on another dataset) and randomizing across the construction of many trees (hence the name random forest). This is a promising area of future work for systematic fixed income investing.

6.5.7 Importance of Attribution

A general challenge for systematic investors is communicating the investment narrative and explaining performance. Over the years, I have seen this done very well but also very poorly. Asset owners vary immensely in their ability and willingness to fully understand any investment process, not just systematic investment approaches. Good portfolio managers, whether they be systematic or traditional discretionary, must be able to communicate succinctly what the investment narrative is ex ante (to get the asset owner to invest), and they must be able to explain performance ex post (to retain that investment). Of course, poor performance is a reason for asset owners to redeem their investments. But failure to communicate clearly what they are doing (both ex ante and ex post) can create sufficient confusion and distrust that it may expedite that redemption risk.

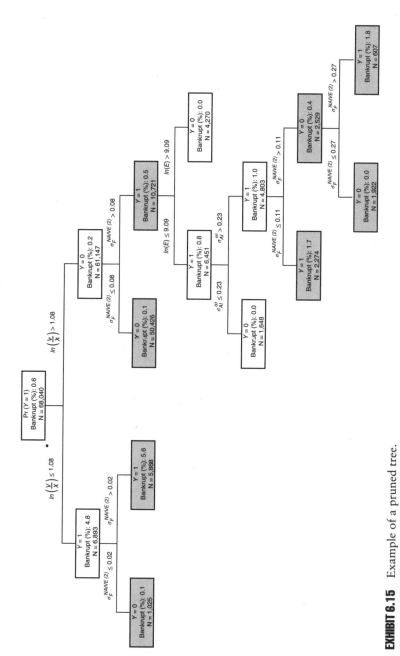

EXHIBIT 6.15 Example of a pruned tree.

Source: Based on data analysis contained within Correia, M., J. Kang, and S. Richardson. (2018). Asset volatility. Review of Accounting Studies, 23, 37–94.

So, what can/should an investor do? I am not going to provide the recipe for communication, but I cannot overemphasize how important this is and how poorly many seem to execute this dimension. Part of the asset management service is building trust and confidence with the asset owner, and this is greatly helped by a clear understanding of your investment thesis/narrative. Although a systematic manager does not, and will likely never, have a story for each bond in their portfolio, it is possible to build visual tools that allow an asset owner to look through the portfolio to the active-risk positions and understand what the drivers are of various positions (e.g., how did your valuation measures lead to your current portfolio positioning, and how did the performance of valuation themes explain your excess of benchmark performance?) All of this, and more, is feasible with a systematic investment process. There is no right or single way to do this. It is a journey that you and your investors will need to take together.

REFERENCES

Altman, E. (1968). Financial ratios, discriminant analysis and the prediction of corporate bankruptcy. *Journal of Finance*, 23, 589–609.

Andreani, M., D. Palhares, and S. Richardson. (2022). *Computing corporate bond returns form TRACE: A word (or two) of caution*. Working paper.

Arora, N., S. Richardson, and I. Tuna. (2014). Asset reliability and security prices: Evidence from credit markets. *Review of Accounting Studies*, 19, 363–295.

Beaver, W. H. (1966). Financial ratios as predictors of bankruptcy. *Journal of Accounting Research*, 4, 71–111.

Beaver, W. H., M. Correia, and M. McNichols. (2012). Do differences in financial reporting attributes impair the predictive ability of financial ratios for bankruptcy? *Review of Accounting Studies*, 17, 969–1010.

Ben Dor, A., L. Dynkin, J. Hyman, P. Houweling, E. Van Leeuwen, and O. Penniga. (2007). DTS (Duration Times Spread). *Journal of Portfolio Management*, 33, 77–100.

Bharath, S., and T. Shumway. (2008). Forecasting default with the Merton Distance-to-Default Model. *Review of Financial Studies*, 21, 1339–1369.

Binsbergen, J., and R. Koijen. (2017). The term structure of returns: Facts and theory. *Journal of Financial Economics*, 124, 1–21.

Cohen, L., and A. Frazzini. (2008). Economic links and predictable returns. *Journal of Finance*, 63, 1977–2011.

Correia, M., J. Kang, and S. Richardson. (2018). Asset volatility. *Review of Accounting Studies*, 23, 37–94.

Correia, M., S. Richardson, and I. Tuna. (2012). Value investing in credit markets. *Review of Accounting Studies*, 17, 572–609.

Dickey, D., and W. Fuller. (1979). Distribution of the estimators for autoregressive time series with a unit root. *Journal of the American Statistical Association*, 74, 427–431.

Frazzini, A., and L. Pedersen. (2014). Betting against beta. *Journal of Financial Economics*, 111, 1–25.

Ilmanen, I. (2011). *Expected Returns*. Wiley.

Israel, R., K. Laursen, and S. Richardson. (2021). Is (systematic) value investing dead? *Journal of Portfolio Management*, 47, 38–62.

Israel, R., D. Palhares, and S. Richardson. (2018). Common factors in corporate bond returns. *Journal of Investment Management*, 16, 17–46.

Kealhofer, S. (2003). Quantifying credit risk II: Debt valuation. *Financial Analysts Journal*, 59, 78–92.

Kwan, S. H. (1996). Firm-specific information and the correlation between individual stocks and bonds. *Journal of Financial Economics*, 40, 63–80.

Lok, S., and S. Richardson. (2011). Credit markets and financial information. *Review of Accounting Studies*, 16, 487–500.

Merton, R. (1974). On the pricing of corporate debt: The risk structure of interest rates. *Journal of Finance*, 29, 449–470.

Ohlson, J. (1980). Financial ratios and the probabilistic prediction of bankruptcy. *Journal of Accounting Research*, 18, 109–131.

Palhares, D., and S. Richardson. (2019). (Il)liquidity premium in credit markets: A myth? *Journal of Fixed Income*, 28, 5–23.

Penman, S. (2001). *Financial Statement Analysis and Security Valuation*. McGraw-Hill Irwin.

Penman, S., F. Reggiani, S. Richardson, and I. Tuna. (2018). A framework for identifying accounting characteristics for asset pricing models, with an evaluation of book-to-price. *European Financial Management*, 24, 488–520.

CHAPTER 7

Security Selection – Emerging Markets (Hard Currency)

OVERVIEW

This chapter lays out the investment opportunity for emerging market fixed income. Although estimates on the size of emerging market fixed income vary considerably, this is a large and growing area. We will focus on hard currency bonds issued by sovereign and quasi-sovereign entities. A hard currency bond typically refers to a USD denominated bond issued by an emerging market country. These bonds contain a risk-free and a risky component, with the risky component being our area of focus. Security selection for credit excess returns in emerging market hard currency shares some similarities with security selection for credit-sensitive assets generally, but data challenges mean our measures need to be modified. This chapter introduces a set of systematic investment themes and assesses their efficacy individually and in combination for emerging market hard currency bonds.

7.1   WHAT IS THE INVESTMENT OPPORTUNITY FOR EMERGING MARKET FIXED INCOME?

Obtaining clear estimates on the size of emerging market fixed income is difficult. Indices that are used as typical policy benchmarks for asset owners only include bonds that meet stringent index inclusion criteria. Countries are typically included only if the Gross National Income (GNI) is below a certain threshold (distinguishes emerging countries from developed countries). Bonds are typically included only if they are investible. A key use of benchmarks is for relative performance evaluation and/or tracking. If a bond does not trade or capital market participation is limited to foreign investors, then that renders the bond less suitable for benchmarking purposes. Index provider liquidity and investability filters can greatly reduce the size of the emerging market investment opportunity set.

I often use a short annual report from Ashmore Group PLC to introduce emerging market fixed income to students. Using a variety of sources including data from the Bank for International Settlements, Ashmore provides high-level information on the size of the emerging market (EM) fixed income asset class. Their most recent piece was published in August 2020 (Dehn 2020) and noted that the EM fixed income asset class was $29.6 trillion USD. Local-currency-denominated bonds accounts for 82 percent, and the remaining 18 percent consists of what they call "external debt" but we are calling "hard currency." Government-issued debt accounts for 44 percent of the total, and the remaining 56 percent are issued by corporates (36 percent by financial corporates and 20 percent by nonfinancial corporates). Governments and corporates account for roughly 50 percent each of the local currency debt, but corporates account for more of the external debt (especially financial corporates). Exhibit 7.1 shows a breakdown of issuance across the largest 15 emerging countries. China is by far the largest issuer of emerging market bonds (52 percent) and that concentration is true for local currency and external debt and for government and corporate issuance.

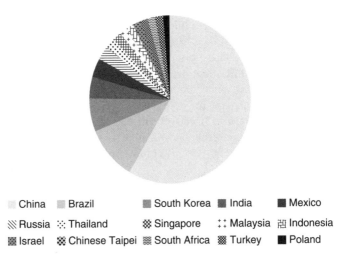

China	Brazil	South Korea	India	Mexico
Russia	Thailand	Singapore	Malaysia	Indonesia
Israel	Chinese Taipei	South Africa	Turkey	Poland

EXHIBIT 7.1 Country representation in emerging markets fixed income.
Sources: Ashmore (2020) and Bank of International Settlements.

We will focus our analysis on the efficacy of systematic investment approaches in emerging markets fixed income on the JP Morgan Emerging Market Bond Index Global Diversified (EMBIGD). This is a weighted USD-denominated emerging markets sovereign index. The weighting schema enforces additional diversification than what would be evident if simply using market capitalization weights (a 10 percent cap is applied for each country). Countries are included if they have a rating of BBB or below. Individual bonds need to have a face value of at least $500 million USD, pass certain liquidity filters (bid-ask spreads and interdealer quote requirements), and have at least 2.5 years remaining to maturity to be added to the index. In addition to sovereign bonds, the index includes bonds issued by quasi-sovereign entities, which refers to entities that are either fully guaranteed or fully owned by the national government.

Exhibit 7.2 shows a breakdown of the number of sovereign and quasi-sovereign issuers in EMBIGD over the 2002–2019 period. The cross-section has grown considerably over the past two decades in line with the overall growth in emerging markets. The EMBIGD had a market capitalization of $203 billion USD in 2002, which has grown to over $1 trillion USD in 2020.

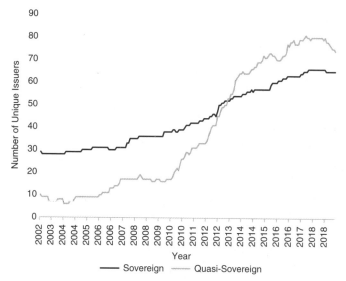

EXHIBIT 7.2 Number of sovereign and quasi-sovereign issuers of emerging market hard currency bonds.
Source: JP Morgan Emerging Market Bond Index Global Diversified (EMBIGD).

Exhibit 7.3 shows a breakdown of the credit ratings for EMBIGD over the 2002–2019 period. Most bonds are rated BBB and below with a sizable portion not rated (NR). There is a noticeable shift in the ratings distribution in September 2012 when ratings became more widely available for included bonds. Exhibit 7.3 also provides a cumulative count of the number of bonds in EMBIGD. The index has grown from 140 bonds in 2002 to over 750 bonds toward the end of the period.

Exhibits 7.4 and 7.5 show how the distribution of credit spreads and spread duration, respectively, have changed over the 2002–2019 period for EMBIGD bonds. Similar to corporate bonds (Chapter 6), we see counter-cyclical movements in credit spreads of hard currency emerging market bonds as the credit risk gets larger during challenged economic

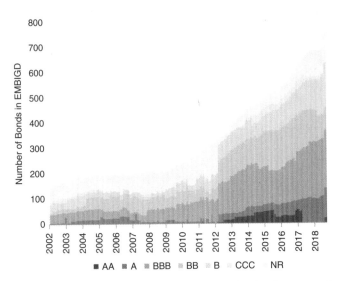

EXHIBIT 7.3   Credit rating breakdown of emerging market hard currency bonds.
Source: JP Morgan Emerging Market Bond Index Global Diversified (EMBIGD).

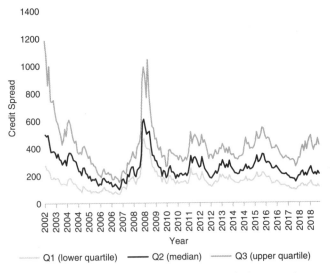

EXHIBIT 7.4   Cross-sectional distribution of credit spreads for emerging market hard currency bonds.
Source: JP Morgan Emerging Market Bond Index Global Diversified (EMBIGD).

environments. Spread duration has remained relatively constant over the sample period; the drop in spread duration around the great financial crisis (2008/2009) is attributable to the sudden large increases in spreads (a risky annuity shortens in duration when spreads widen).

EXHIBIT 7.5 Cross-sectional distribution of spread duration for emerging market hard currency bonds.
Source: JP Morgan Emerging Market Bond Index Global Diversified (EMBIGD).

As of December 31, 2020, the JP Morgan EMBI Global Diversified Index contained 861 individual bonds. Of these bonds, 546 were issued by sovereign entities and 315 were issued by quasi-sovereign entities. Two hundred distinct entities issued these 861 bonds (87 unique sovereign entities and 113 unique quasi-sovereign entities). There is considerable breadth in the emerging market hard currency universe. The investment opportunity set shares more similarity with corporate bonds than government bonds, with the across-issuer dimension having the greater breadth (i.e., the median sovereign issuer has four bonds outstanding, and the median quasi-sovereign issuer has two bonds outstanding).

It is useful to compare the composition of EMBIGD to the broad emerging market fixed income universe identified in Dehn (2020). EMBIGD includes bonds from 73 countries compared to 185 countries covered in the Bank for International Settlements data. The EMBIGD has a market valuation of about $1.15 trillion USD in 2020 compared to the nearly $30 trillion USD for the entire emerging market fixed income universe. It is important to keep this in mind as we continue this chapter. We have very good coverage of hard currency emerging sovereign debt (the $1.15 trillion USD is the bulk of external sovereign debt), but we are not looking at emerging market local currency government debt (we discussed security selection for rate-sensitive assets in Chapter 5) nor are we examining local or hard currency emerging market corporate debt (we discussed security selection for credit sensitive assets in Chapter 6).

Hard currency bonds contain two primary sources of risk (and hence return potential). First, there is a risk-free component. Because these bonds are all issued in USD, the risk-free component is the US government bond yield curve. Second, there is a risky component. The risk for an investor in a hard currency bond is that the issuing entity (sovereign or quasi-sovereign) will be unable to satisfy the USD contractual commitments in the future. This is a type of credit risk, unlike the rate risk that dominates regular local currency government bonds. The mismatch in foreign currency obligations to local currency cash flow sources for repayment is the source of risk. An emerging sovereign cannot issue more local currency to satisfy foreign currency obligations (they need to repay in *foreign* currency). To quantify the relative importance of the risk-free and risky components of hard currency emerging debt, we can undertake a return-variance decomposition similar to what was done in Chapter 2 (see Equations 2.2–2.13). Over the 2002–2020 period the return variation attributable to the risky (risk-free) portion is 82 (18) percent. Most of the return potential in hard currency emerging market bonds is due to spread risk, and that is the focus of our security selection for the remainder of the chapter.

7.2   A FRAMEWORK FOR SECURITY SELECTION OF HARD CURRENCY EMERGING MARKET BONDS (INVESTMENT THEMES)

There is not a section on the dimensions of active risk taking for emerging market hard currency bonds (e.g., the importance of level, slope, curvature). The breadth available to investors is in between what we have seen for developed market corporate bonds (Chapter 6) and developed market government bonds (Chapter 5). Corporate bond markets had over 1,000 issuers and each issuer had a small number of bonds outstanding (about two for each HY corporate issuer and about seven for each IG corporate issuer). Government bond markets had less than 20 sizable issuers, but each issuer had many bonds outstanding. Exhibit 7.2 (number of issuers) and Exhibit 7.3 (number of issues) imply about three to four bonds outstanding for each emerging sovereign issuer. So, there is the opportunity to engage in security selection both across issuers (country selection) and within issuer (maturity selection). We will focus on country selection in what follows.

The framework described in the following subsections was originally developed in Brooks, Richardson, and Zu (2020). They examine the efficacy of systematic investment themes across long/short and long only emerging market hard currency portfolios. We will examine only the long/short portfolios in this chapter. Our framework will cover a broad set of investment themes (carry, defensive, momentum, and valuation), but we will only discuss simple measures within each theme. The basis for each investment theme builds on Chapter 6 where we covered credit sensitive assets more generally. Kang, So, and Tziortziotis (2019) also find evidence that simple measures of value and momentum can explain cross-sectional variation in emerging market bond (excess of cash, not credit excess) return variation, and that these simple measures can be incorporated into an optimized long-only portfolio.

7.2.1 Value

A belief in the efficacy of value themes is supported by extensive evidence across many asset classes, many geographies, and many time periods (see e.g., Asness, Moskowitz, and Pedersen 2013). Value is the tendency for relatively cheap assets to outperform relatively expensive assets on a risk-adjusted basis. Emerging market hard currency bonds entail credit risk, and that is the return source we are looking for through our security selection. So, our value measures will condition credit spreads on relevant fundamental information. But what should/could that set of fundamental information be? Chapter 6 illustrated a structural model approach (distance to default, or *D2D*), where the expected probability of default implied by *D2D* is the theoretical anchor for credit spreads. A cheap emerging market hard currency bond would then be the bond (or credit default swap [CDS] contract linked to that bond) where the credit spread is wide relative to that expected default probability. This looks the same as the analysis in Chapter 6 for corporate bonds.

So what is different here for emerging market bonds? Data. Prior research examining the efficacy of value measures for corporates has generated relatively sophisticated distance to default and expected default probability measures using a rich set of market and fundamental data sources (e.g., Correia, Richardson, and Tuna 2012; Correia, Kang, and Richardson 2018). For emerging sovereign entities, it is difficult to compute a clean measure of distance to default. How do you get a clean measure of the indebtedness of the sovereign entity? How do you get a precise measure of the volatility of the sovereign entity? Is it possible to link the constructs of leverage and volatility in a parsimonious way? Rather than trying to force proxies for leverage and volatility into a structural model, we will use a reduced form approach and measure these aspects directly and use them as explanatory variables in a regression-based value signal.

We estimate the regression in Equation (7.1) on an expanding window basis:

$$Spread = \alpha + \beta_{RATING} RATING + \beta_{VOLATILITY} VOLATILITY + \varepsilon \quad (7.1)$$

RATING is the average credit rating across the primary rating agencies that are used in EMBIGD. *VOLATILITY* is the trailing standard deviation of the monthly country equity returns over the most recent 12 months. Equation (7.1) is estimated using a panel regression because each cross-section is small (typically less than 25 sovereign entities have liquid CDS contracts each month). Time fixed effects are included to account for temporal variation in credit spreads driven by common macroeconomic factors. This regression framework captures the two essential ingredients of default forecasts (leverage and volatility), and it does so in a flexible way that allows for estimation across our universe. The residual from Equation (7.1) is our value measure.

Extensions to value measures could (i) expand the set of information used to identify the indebtedness and credit quality of the emerging sovereign, and (ii) expand the set of market assets used to measure volatility (this could include historical measures of volatility from the debt market itself or currency markets). Our aim here is not to exhaust all possible measures of value but to present a framework for thinking about operationalizing value for emerging market hard currency bonds.

7.2.2 Momentum

As with value, our belief in momentum is supported by extensive evidence across many asset classes, many geographies, and many time periods (see e.g., Asness, Moskowitz, and Pedersen 2013). Momentum is the tendency for an asset's recent performance to continue, leading to outperformance of recent winners relative to recent losers. The challenge is how to best measure momentum for emerging market hard currency bonds. Recent performance can be measured using return data from the asset itself, as well as return data from other related assets. We will measure momentum as an equal-weighted combination of three monthly return-based metrics: (i) six-month trailing emerging market CDS returns, (ii) six-month trailing foreign exchange (FX) returns, and (iii) six-month trailing country equity returns. We prefer to sell protection on CDS contracts (equivalent to a long position in emerging market bonds) with positive CDS returns, positive local currency returns relative to USD, and positive country equity returns.

Extensions to momentum could include a variety of nonprice, or fundamental, measures. As was discussed in Chapter 5 in the context of security selection for rate-sensitive assets, improvements in expectations of the health of the emerging sovereign should be a positive signal for the embedded credit risk in hard currency bonds. Such fundamental measures of momentum could include (i) changing expectations of economic growth, and components thereof, sourced from a variety of forecasting agencies (positive), and (ii) changes in leverage or indebtedness of the sovereign entity (negative).

An investor should put their fundamental hat on to identify relevant country level statistics.

As with all momentum signals that are designed to forecast changes in credit spreads (for all credit sensitive assets) it may be necessary to convert that spread change forecast to an expected return forecast by making an adjustment for any cross-sectional difference in spread duration. For our examination of long/short strategies within a set of liquid five-year CDS contracts, there is minimal cross-sectional variation in spread duration, so these adjustments do not matter much, but for security selection within the full EMBIGD, consideration should be given to duration adjustments.

7.2.3 Carry

By now this should start to feel somewhat repetitive. That is part of the systematic investor experience. You are looking for economically sound investment insights that travel well across your asset classes. So it should be no surprise to hear, again, that carry is the tendency for higher-yielding assets to outperform lower-yielding assets (it is the return you *will* get if nothing changes with the passage of time). But, of course, as time passes there will be changes in expectations of credit risk, and hence returns. Carry is a source of risk, but one that has generated a positive risk-adjusted return across many asset classes and time periods (e.g., Koijen, Moskowitz, Pedersen, and Vrugt 2018). We will use a very simple measure of carry, based only on the five-year CDS contract at the start of each month. We seek exposure to emerging sovereigns where the CDS contract has a higher spread level. We ignore roll-down and higher-order measures of curve shape, which can be a useful extension of the carry investment theme (as was the case for government and corporate bond security selection as well).

7.2.4 Defensive

Defensive is the tendency of safer, lower-risk assets to deliver higher risk-adjusted returns relative to their low-quality, higher-risk counterparts. This is a multifaceted construct requiring multiple measures. As with value measures, access to reliable and relevant data for emerging sovereigns makes measurement of this theme more challenging. Ideally, we would like access to a clean set of financial statements that give an (audited) assessment of the sovereign entities financial health, cash flow (tax) generating capabilities, and a transparent assessment of its capital structure. Alas, this does not exist. Not even close. Countries do not practice accrual-based accounting, and tracking what sovereigns ultimately owe is hard even in developed markets. We will do what we can in reduced form. First, we will use a measure based on the level of inflation (based on forecasted levels of inflation).

A "better" sovereign entity is one that can target and achieve low levels of inflation. A lower quality sovereign is one that has higher levels of inflation. We use a constant 12-month ahead forecast of inflation from Consensus Economics. We prefer to sell protection on CDS contracts (long risk) where there is a lower level of expected inflation. Second, we use a measure of indebtedness (i.e., asset/debt ratio). The "asset" value for the sovereign combines foreign reserves (obtained from Thomson Reuters International Comparable Economics, TRICE) and the level of GDP grossed up by expectations of GDP growth for the next 12 months (GDP growth expectations are obtained from Consensus Economics). Estimating "debt" precisely for sovereign entities is a challenging task, because there are often many implicit government guarantees linked to government sponsored entities. We take a simple approach and compute "debt" as the sum of government external debt and 50 percent of nongovernment external debt (reflecting the contingent nature of external private sector debt, which the sovereign may assume in the event of default). External debt data is obtained from TRICE. The log of asset/debt is our measure of sovereign indebtedness. We prefer to sell protection on CDS contracts (long risk) for countries with higher Asset/Debt ratios (i.e., lower leverage). Our defensive theme is an equal-weighted combination of the two measures (inflation and indebtedness).

7.3   A FRAMEWORK FOR SECURITY SELECTION OF EMERGING MARKET HARD CURRENCY BONDS (PERFORMANCE)

To assess whether systematic exposures to carry, defensive, value, and momentum are potentially useful in an emerging market bond context, we construct long/short portfolios using five-year CDSs. Over the 2004–2018 period, we can measure the four systematic investment themes over 25 emerging sovereign reference entities. We are discussing the return performance using CDS instruments, rather than EMBs, as CDSs are standardized, liquid contracts that allow for relatively easier cross-country comparisons and long/short implementation.

This is the first time we have examined CDS contracts in detail, so a short discussion is useful. CDS contracts provide insurance against the likelihood of nonpayment of USD hard currency reference bond obligations by emerging sovereign reference entities. We use five-year "on the run" CDS contracts linked to (i) reference entities that are "emerging sovereign," (ii) have reference obligations denominated in USD, and (iii) are sufficiently liquid as captured by membership in the EMBIGD+ index (the + is not a typographical error, it refers to a modified EMBIGD index that ensures each sovereign is sufficiently liquid).

At the start of each month we rank the universe of liquid CDS contracts on our four investment themes, either individually or in combination (equal weighted across the four investment themes). Our investment view is continuous in each measure, and we ensure that it is beta-neutral (ensuring that the notional exposures on the long and short side of the portfolio are equal in beta amounts). Our long/short CDS portfolio is a little more advanced than the simpler long/short top/bottom tercile/quantile approach discussed in earlier chapters for government and corporate bonds. We are now moving to a stage in the book where portfolio construction/design choices are coming into focus. To estimate beta, we use an asset-by-asset variance-covariance matrix, modeling correlation and volatility separately (this matrix is based on historical credit excess returns). Portfolios are scaled to 10 percent volatility (using the return covariance matrix), are rebalanced monthly, but do not account for transaction costs. Again, our purpose is to assess the potential efficacy of a systematic approach for security selection in emerging market hard currency bonds. View this as a necessary but not sufficient condition for success. If we find evidence of return predictability at this stage, we cannot yet claim success. Are we able to implement these exposures in a cost-effective way?

Exhibit 7.6 summarizes the performance of our four investment signals (value, momentum, carry, and defensive), both individually and as an equally weighted average combination. The bottom section of the exhibit reports information about the return series (Sharpe ratios, information ratios, and correlations). All investment themes have attractive risk-adjusted returns with Sharpe ratios ranging from 0.34 for defensive to 0.68 for momentum. The equally weighted combination, Sharpe ratio of 1.11, is superior to any one individual theme due to the low pairwise correlations evident at the bottom of Exhibit 7.6.

To assess whether security selection based on value, momentum, carry, and defensive themes are diversifying with respect to traditional market risk premia (and some well-known factor risk premia from equity markets), we run the following regression (with all explanatory variables as defined in Chapter 5):

$$THEME = \alpha + \beta_{CP}CP + \beta_{TP}TP + \beta_{EP}EP + \beta_{SMB}SMB + \beta_{HML}HML$$
$$+ \beta_{MOM}MOM + \beta_{QMJ}QMJ + \beta_{BAB}BAB + \varepsilon \tag{7.2}$$

The top half of Exhibit 7.6 reports estimated regression coefficients and, in italics below, the corresponding test statistics. Across all four investment themes, individually and in combination, there is minimal exposure to either traditional market risk premia or equity style returns. The adjusted R^2 for Equation (7.2) ranges from 2.83 percent for value to 13.61 percent for momentum. Momentum has the expected positive correlation with equity momentum (there is a commonality to momentum returns across

EXHIBIT 7.6 Properties of emerging market hard currency bond security selection investment themes (V for value, M for momentum, C for carry, D for defensive, and VMCD for an equally weighted average) for the 2004–2019 period.

	α	β_{CP}	β_{TP}	β_{EP}	β_{SMB}	β_{HML}	β_{MOM}	β_{QMJ}	β_{BAB}	R^2
V	0.04	0.24	−0.10	−0.02	−0.12	0.09	−0.01	−0.02	−0.03	2.83%
	1.49	*1.04*	*−0.45*	*−0.30*	*−1.10*	*0.84*	*−0.15*	*−0.17*	*−0.33*	
M	0.07	−0.38	0.09	−0.02	0.19	−0.01	0.11	−0.14	−0.13	13.61%
	3.01	*−2.15*	*0.54*	*−0.26*	*2.28*	*−0.13*	*2.23*	*−1.22*	*−1.81*	
C	0.05	0.57	0.21	−0.08	0.10	0.15	−0.03	0.03	−0.20	8.89%
	1.56	*2.35*	*0.91*	*−0.95*	*0.88*	*1.31*	*−0.54*	*0.21*	*−2.12*	
D	0.03	−0.37	−0.09	0.15	−0.09	−0.21	0.03	0.06	−0.01	6.50%
	0.88	*−1.63*	*−0.42*	*1.82*	*−0.81*	*−1.94*	*0.44*	*0.44*	*−0.14*	
VMCD	0.13	−0.16	0.01	0.02	0.09	0.06	0.07	−0.03	−0.24	6.85%
	4.39	*−0.72*	*0.04*	*0.31*	*0.85*	*0.58*	*1.25*	*−0.23*	*−2.80*	

	V	M	C	D	VMCD				SR	IR
V	1	−0.29	0.07	0.04	0.45				0.37	0.44
M		1	−0.13	0.24	0.58				0.68	0.89
C			1	−0.75	0.12				0.36	0.46
D				1	0.32				0.34	0.26
VMCD					1				1.11	1.30

Sources: Brooks, Richardson, and Xu (2020), JP Morgan indices, https://mba
.tuck.dartmouth.edu/pages/faculty/ken.french/data_library.html, and https://www
.aqr.com/Insights/Datasets.

asset classes) but that correlation is muted and does not detract from the very strong intercept (test statistic of 3.01). Carry has the expected positive association with the credit premium, and that reduces the orthogonal return contribution from the carry investment theme. Importantly, the information ratios (and associated test statistics for the regression intercepts) are all positive, and statistically so for momentum and the combination portfolio.

7.4 EXTENSIONS

7.4.1 Maturity Dimension

The analysis in Section 7.3 covered long/short portfolios based on five-year CDS contracts for emerging market sovereigns. The systematic investment model can equally be applied in a benchmark-aware long-only context where active risk is taken relative to the EMBIGD benchmark. Brooks, Richardson, and Xu (2020) and Kang, So, and Tziortziotis (2019) both assess the efficacy of long-only implementations of systematic emerging market bond portfolios. They both find attractive risk-adjusted returns from long-only implementations suggesting the potential of diversified return sources for asset owners.

A benefit of examining long-only benchmark-aware portfolios is the additional investment breadth. For sovereign issuers with more than one liquid bond, you are able to enhance investment capacity by (i) taking positions in multiple bonds for that sovereign issuer (e.g., you can define a country "level" asset similar to what we did in Chapter 5 for government bonds), (ii) taking positions in different bonds for a sovereign issuer (e.g., you can define a country slope asset, again similar to the analysis in Chapter 5 for government bonds). For country-level views, we can aggregate across multiple issues proportional to the inverse of spread duration. For example, if an issuer has three bonds with spread durations of 2, 5, and 7, the weights for the country asset would be 59, 24 and 17 percent, respectively. For country slope views, we can define a country specific "steepener" that is spread-duration-neutral for that country.

There are choices on whether to include sovereign and quasi-sovereign issuers together when defining the country-level and country-slope asset. Likewise, there are choices on tailoring the investment for country-level and country-slope views. For example, the front end of the credit curve may be more sensitive to underlying fundamentals (e.g., economic growth, indebtedness, etc.) and this differential sensitivity can be captured when modeling the country slope asset (i.e., you may prefer a country steepener for higher quality and improving emerging sovereigns, because the front end of the credit curve is more responsive to those insights).

7.4.2 Emerging Market Corporate Bonds

As noted at the start of this chapter, there is a very large set of emerging market corporate bonds. A representative index is the J.P. Morgan Corporate Emerging Markets Index (CEMBI), which tracks the returns of USD denominated bonds issued by emerging market corporate entities, which had a market capitalization of nearly $500 billion USD as at December 31, 2020.

Dekker, Houweling, and Muskens (2021) examine the effectiveness of systematic investing signals using factor definitions of Houweling and Van Zundert (2017), including size (preference for emerging corporate issuers with lower market value of debt outstanding), low-risk (preference for emerging corporates with better credit ratings and emerging corporate bonds with lower remaining time to maturity), value (preference for emerging corporate bonds with spreads that are wide relative to rating category, maturity, and historical change in spreads), and momentum (preference for emerging corporate bonds with higher recent bond excess returns). Although I don't agree with the size signal (see discussion in Chapter 6), the set of investment signals here is representative. Dekker, Houweling, and Muskens (2021) find across long/short and long-only portfolios evidence of attractive risk-adjusted returns from investing based on systematic investment themes either individually or in combination.

Operationally, sourcing/providing liquidity is more challenged in emerging markets. Relationships may need to be cultivated with a broader set of trading counterparties to ensure depth of market liquidity access. While there is nothing in principle limiting the success of active investing (systematic or otherwise) in emerging markets, it is more challenging to implement portfolios in emerging markets.

REFERENCES

Asness, C., T. Moskowitz, and L. Pedersen. (2013). Value and momentum everywhere. *Journal of Finance*, 68, 929–985.

Brooks, J., S. Richardson, and Z. Xu. (2020). (Systematic) investing in emerging market debt. *Journal of Fixed Income*, 30, 44–61.

Correia, M., S. Richardson, and I. Tuna. (2012). Value investing in credit markets. *Review of Accounting Studies*, 17, 572–609.

Correia, M., J. Kang, and S. Richardson. (2018). Asset volatility. *Review of Accounting Studies*, 23, 37–94.

Dehn, J. (2020). The EM fixed income universe version 9.0. Ashmore, *The Emerging View* (August).

Dekker, L., P. Houweling, and F. Muskens. (2021). Factor investing in emerging market credits. *Journal of Index Investing*, 12, 28–46.

Houweling, P., and J. Van Zundert. (2017). Factor investing in the corporate bond market. *Financial Analysts Journal*, 73, 100–115.

Kang, J., K. So, and T. Tziortziotis. (2019). Embedded bets and better bets: Factor investing in emerging market bonds. *Journal of Investment Management*, 17, 27–46.

Koijen, R., T. Moskowitz, L. Pedersen, and E. Vrugt. (2018). Carry. *Journal of Financial Economics*, 127, 197–225.

CHAPTER 8

Portfolio Construction Considerations

OVERVIEW

This chapter describes the portfolio construction process. There are many decisions that need to be made to convert your "signals" into portfolio positions. A successful systematic investment process needs to be excellent across many dimensions. These dimensions include: (i) breadth of investment themes covered, (ii) depth of measures across investment themes, (iii) choices in combining multiple investment themes and converting them to an expected return forecast, (iv) identifying a suitable set of fixed income securities that are appropriate for a systematic investment process (liquidity screening), (v) tracking error and risk modeling generally, and (vi) selecting sensible constraints to maximize risk-adjusted returns while avoiding poorly compensated exposures. At the end of the chapter the reader should have a full appreciation of the challenges of portfolio construction, and hence understand the opportunity for skillful portfolio craftsmanship to improve the investor experience.

8.1 CHOICES IN THE INVESTMENT PROCESS (DESIGN AND INVESTMENT UNIVERSE)

Exhibit 8.1 is a simple visualization of the necessary ingredients for a successful investment process. There is nothing here that is specific to a systematic investment process since all aspects need to be implemented well for investment success for any investor. The previous three chapters have focused on Step 2 in the investment process: How do we rank the relative attractiveness of our assets? We now need to think more holistically about portfolio construction. Let's walk through each step and highlight the many choices that need to be made by the systematic investor along the way.

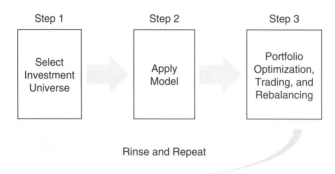

EXHIBIT 8.1   Visualization of the systematic investment process.

The first step in any investment process is defining the sandbox of eligible securities. In the case of comingled investment vehicles (e.g., US mutual funds formed under the Investment Company Act of 1940, or European-domiciled UCITS funds [UCITS is short for Undertakings for the Collective Investment in Transferable Securities]), the prospectus that underlies the investment vehicle will contain the specific details of what is an eligible security. In the case of separately managed accounts there will be a formal document containing the investment guidelines that specify what the asset manager can and cannot do. The investment guidelines will typically specify a benchmark. For long-only portfolios this is your starting point for eligible securities. The guidelines may then allow for out of benchmark securities that meet certain criteria (e.g., an IG corporate bond mandate may allow for a certain percentage of fund assets to be invested in non-IG rated corporate bonds). For long–short unconstrained portfolios the benchmark is typically a cash rate (e.g., LIBOR or the new bank reference rates such as SONIA), and the investment guidelines will then specify the type of securities allowed in the investment vehicle.

Let's try to make this more concrete as we walk through the portfolio construction choices in this chapter. We will use credit-sensitive assets as our working example for this chapter, but note that these choices need to be made for all fixed income securities (e.g., a Global Aggregate Index benchmarked portfolios will need to make choices on government bonds, corporate bonds and securitized assets). Our asset owner has decided to make an allocation to the US HY corporate bond market. They have selected the ICE/BAML H0A0 index as their policy benchmark for this asset allocation. As of December 31, 2020, the H0A0 index had 2,003 corporate bonds. Not all these bonds are suitable for the systematic investment process. Let's walk through some important dimensions that the investor needs to consider.

- Liquidity

    A necessary condition for a successful systematic investment process is your ability to buy and sell assets in a cost-effective way. It is no use modeling the attractiveness of an asset if it has not been traded for the past six months. I wish you all the best for discussions with your trading execution team if you keep modeling illiquid securities: they will never be able to buy the assets that you think are attractive, and you will keep telling them to look – not a recipe for success. Instead, a reasonable alternative is to prescreen your eligible universe based on "liquidity." Yes, you will exclude the less liquid assets, but this does not come with a loss in expected return, as was discussed in Chapter 6 there is no evidence of a liquidity premium for public corporate bond markets.

    How might you identify those bonds with less liquidity? Corporate bonds (government bonds, too, for that matter) do not trade on a centralized exchange. Consequently, it can be challenging to get reliable, comprehensive data on trading activity of individual bonds. Absent data it is not possible to identify whether a bond is liquid or not. So where might we source data on liquidity? In the United States, the TRACE engine provides sufficient data to be able to compute a variety of measures related to liquidity (e.g., fraction of no trading days, dollar volume traded, turnover, bid-ask spreads, and market impact as measured in Palhares and Richardson 2019). Relationships with broker-dealers can allow for aggregation of indicative quotes to get a sense for potential live bid-ask spreads, depth, and frequency of market making opportunities. Aggregating across these data sources will allow you to remove from your investment universe bonds that are insufficiently liquid (exclusion). Some of this data will also be important later in the chapter when we discuss optimization and objective functions. Modeling expected transaction costs, inclusive of market impact, can be part of the systematic process. Likewise, trade size and position size constraints should also be liquidity aware (i.e., you should be able to trade large sizes and build larger positions for more liquid bonds).

- Seniority

    Corporate bond indices will contain significant variability in seniority ranging from senior secured to unsecured to junior bonds. I have seen some investment approaches remove bonds that are too senior (e.g., secured) or too junior in the capital structure to help improve cross-sectional comparability of eligible bonds. If the investor retains bonds that span the entire capital structure, careful attention should be given to forecasts of expected returns, especially for measures that are based on credit spreads (carry and value investment signals especially). All else being equal, seniority affects spreads directly through expected recovery rates. At a minimum, adjustments need to be made for expected recovery rates to ensure cross-sectional comparability for value and carry signals.

- Remaining Time to Maturity

  As we will see in Chapter 9, trading is operationally challenging and very costly relative to the return potential for credit-sensitive assets. This has a direct impact on the optimal amount of turnover for a portfolio. A good investor will look to ration their turnover budget very carefully. You want to be buying bonds that you think have the highest expected return potential from your set of eligible securities and then selling bonds from your portfolio that have the least attractive expected return potential. As we discussed in Chapter 1, fixed income assets have a natural life; they die when they mature. It may therefore be rational to limit your enthusiasm for buying bonds that have the shortest duration or, at a minimum, do not force trading out of a bond as it exits an index or gets close to exit based on declining maturity. This would be a suboptimal use of your scarce turnover budget.

- Private Issuers

  As discussed in Chapter 6, there are many private issuers in the corporate bond markets. As of December 31, 2020, 29 percent of the US HY index is comprised of private issuers. These are corporate entities for which it is more difficult to source relevant information to generate expected return forecasts. Does the systematic investor want to keep private issuers? If yes, should you entertain a minimum information threshold for retention in the investment universe? If you are not able to source sufficient information you will not be able to create an expected return forecast, so how can you include such assets in your portfolio? Excluding all private issuers is too extreme, but requiring a minimal information threshold is not.

- Domicile of Issuer

  Attention needs to be paid to the domicile of the corporate issuer. In some cases, you will have corporate issuers who have issued in USD, but they are domiciled in emerging markets. Do you want to keep these issuers in the investment universe? Ideally, you want to increase the homogeneity of corporate issuers to increase your ability to identify relative value opportunities in the cross-section.

Once you have made decisions on these dimensions, it is important to then understand how different your eligible universe is relative to the starting benchmark of securities. While you may have a sound basis for excluding securities, this set of excluded securities introduces what is called "tracking error" to your portfolio process. Formally, tracking error is a statistical measure of distance. How different is the performance of one portfolio from another? We had discussed tracking error earlier (Chapter 4) as an ex post return attribute (i.e., what was the volatility of the excess of benchmark returns). Here we are talking about tracking error from an ex ante perspective. Given a set of exclusions how different is your eligible security universe from the starting benchmark? The measure of difference is weighted by the riskiness of each security. For credit sensitive assets, as was discussed in Chapter 6, DTS (the product of spread duration and credit spread) is a useful proxy for risk. Let's assume you either exclude (i) a corporate bond (A) that has 1 percent weight in the benchmark and a DTS of 2,240 (a credit spread of 560 and spread duration of four years), or (ii) a corporate bond (B) that has 1 percent weight in the benchmark and a DTS of 5,550 (a credit spread of 1,850 and spread duration of three years). Both bonds have the same weight in the benchmark (i.e., you would exclude 1 percent of the benchmark in both cases), but they have a very different risk profile – B is riskier than A. Tracking error captures the difference in risk across the portfolios, which is a function of the weight of an asset and its contribution to risk (return volatility and correlation structure). This discussion is related to the topic of active share that we briefly discussed in Chapter 1. Simple differences in portfolio weights are a poor measure of distance between two portfolios. This limitation becomes more problematic as the degree of heterogeneity in risk in the cross-section increases. And in the corporate bond universe, both IG and HY have very significant differences in risk contributions across index constituents.

The tracking error implications of investment universe exclusions need to be measured and monitored. We will come back to this later in the chapter when we discussion optimization and objective functions. Constraints are typically added to the objective function to limit the amount of active risk that is allowed on certain dimensions that you think are not well compensated (i.e., dimensions that are not part of your investment view). Examples might include maturity categories, rating categories, or industry groups that your exclusions affect, but for which you do not have an explicit view on expected return potential. So, it may then be prudent to limit the amount of active risk you take across those dimensions.

8.2 CHOICES IN THE INVESTMENT MODEL (EXPECTED RETURNS)

8.2.1 Which Investment Signals?

The prior three chapters introduced investment frameworks for government bonds, corporate bonds, and emerging market hard currency bonds specifically. There was overlap in the investment themes across these three types of fixed income assets (carry, defensive, momentum, and value themes). We focused on those themes, and simple measures of those themes, not because I believe only in simple measures of these themes, but to help lift the veil on systematic investment processes. You are not limited to these measures. Exhibit 8.2 is a simple visual of the potentially rich set of investment signals that could be part of your forecasted expected returns. Our focus here is the face of the cube that spans breadth and depth across potential investment themes. The usual suspects of carry, defensive, momentum and valuation investment themes are covered on the vertical axis, but additional investment themes like sentiment, smart money, liquidity provision, and so forth, could also be incorporated (the arrow suggests the potential for additional investment insights: that's the research process!)

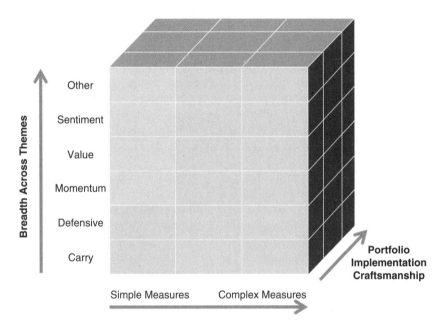

EXHIBIT 8.2   Visualization of the investment model (the investment cube).

Moving across the face of the cube we can add measures of the same investment theme. For example, as we discussed in the prior three chapters measures of momentum can include the asset's own price returns (simple) but can be extended to include measures of related asset returns and a variety of fundamental based momentum measures (complex). Likewise, measures of valuation can range from linear projections of spreads onto credit ratings and return volatility (simple), to structural models and nonlinear machine learning models (complex). It is not the pursuit of complexity alone that is of interest; depth of measures is only useful if they are conceptually additive to your investment process combined with data-based evidence that more complicated measures improve your investment process. Again, the arrow continues to the right (the research process should be continually looking for improvements to existing investment themes). The front face of this investment cube can be useful to distinguish different types of systematic investment processes. Smart beta approaches would cover only the left portion of the face of the cube, and a full systematic investment process would span the entire face and would be looking to increase the size of the front face.

8.2.2 How to Group Investment Signals Together?

In most cases it is clear which signals belong together. Momentum measures are all related to recent performance (price and fundamental versions). Value measures all share similarities in that they compare yields (rate-sensitive assets) or spreads (credit-sensitive assets) to various fundamental anchors. Defensive measures capture measures of low risk or issuer quality. In these cases, economic priors should guide how signals are grouped together. There will, however, be instances where it is not clear how to combine themes together. Do you keep creating new investment themes as new signals are added? In the interest of parsimony, I recommend grouping signals together based on conceptual priors, and supplementing this with statistical analysis that examines how signals are correlated with each other and how the returns linked to signals are correlated with each other (the higher the correlation the more likely you are to group signals together).

Why is grouping signals together important? I view signal grouping as a precursor decision before the signal weighting decision. You could feed all of your signals into a signal weighting algorithm, but I think that is asking too much of the algorithm with too little data.

8.2.3 How to Select Weights for Investment Signals?

Given the prior discussion, there are at least two dimensions of signal-weighting choices. First, for the signals you have grouped together, you need to allocate weights across the signals. I prefer an equal-weighted allocation here unless you have strong conviction. That conviction could come from (relatively) unique data access for a given theme and/or (relatively) unique methodology to convert that data into a signal. For example, within valuation you may allocate a little more weight to the signals that make use of a larger set of fundamental information.

Second, you need to allocate weights across the signal groups. Again, I suggest strongly that you lean on priors here. Start with equal weighting across signal themes and deviate only in two cases: (i) if you have strong conviction of the efficacy of one signal group perhaps based on the depth of insights and number of measures allocate more weight, and (ii) if certain themes are slightly or negatively correlated with each other you will want to increase weights to these signals to help ensure they still matter at the aggregated level. There is a related conceptual topic here about signal correlation: make sure you understand the economic sources of correlation structure across signal categories. As we will see later in this chapter, choices are made to transform raw signals into return forecasts that can affect correlations. Check to make sure your transformations are improving your ability to combine information and not hindering that effort.

The astute reader will notice that I have said nothing about recent performance as the basis for selecting signal weights. As we saw in Chapter 3, tactical investment decisions (timing) is difficult to do successfully at the asset class level. It is also difficult to do well within an asset class across subgroups of assets. These subgroups could be industry groups or factor-mimicking portfolios that target signals. The forecasting challenge is a significant reduction in investment breadth when you move from security selection across the entire eligible investment universe to a small number of subgroups (see, e.g., Grinold and Kahn 2000). Recent signal performance would be a way to "time" your risk allocation across signals (or factors). The topic of factor timing is a large one for asset managers and academics alike (see, e.g., Gupta and Kelly 2019 and references therein). If you are willing to entertain time variation in your weighting across signals, then looking at recent performance is certainly a potential way to do that. I would, however, caution enthusiasm. The evidence for factor timing to date has been in the context of equity markets where it is relatively easier (and cheaper) to trade. So what may look like a modest improvement in risk-adjusted returns for an academic portfolio that ignores real-world implementation challenges may be anything but. Your turnover budget is scarce. Use it on the highest expected return opportunities. I'm not sure factor timing meets that hurdle.

Two final comments on factor timing: valuation and diversification. I have lost count of the number of times that asset owners have suggested that an investment theme has become too expensive and as such you should reduce your weight to that theme (the defensive theme in equity has been a common example for several years). Although that observation and suggested investment decision may have merit, what it fails to fully appreciate is that an investment approach that allocates risk across valuation and other themes is already endogenously timing exposure to other themes based on their prevailing valuation (i.e., the correlation between signals is dynamic and that will be reflected in the final portfolio that maintains strategic weights across investment themes). So, you are getting some value timing for free in a diversified systematic investment approach. Finally, diversification itself is the free lunch that we can risk forgetting at our expense. If your decision to time vary weights across investment themes has a low success rate you will lose the benefit of diversification (i.e., when one of them performs below average another theme is likely to perform above average, it is just hard to tell ex ante which theme will under- or overperform).

My overall recommendation here is to think carefully about factor timing, especially for the more expensive credit sensitive assets. And be wary of commercial vendors offering timing products when their commercial interest is really driven by increased trading activities.

8.2.4 What Units Are These Weights In?

Implicit in all the previous discussion about signal weighting is that we are allocating 100 percent of our signal weights to each investment theme. But 100 percent of what? The systematic investment process is designed to deliver attractive risk adjusted returns. Typically, you are trying to maximize your information ratio, the ratio of excess of benchmark (beta-adjusted) returns scaled by a measure of ex-ante active risk. The denominator of the information ratio (active risk) is the units we are allocating signal weights from. You can think of a risk budget for your investment strategy. For a HY corporate bond portfolio, that might be 2 percent annualized, for an IG corporate bond portfolio that might be 1 percent, and for a long-duration IG corporate bond portfolio that might be 1.5–2 percent. The amount of active risk taken for a given investment vehicle is also an investment choice. Generally, the amount of active risk scales with the risk of the underlying asset class (i.e., an equity portfolio will have more active risk than a core fixed income portfolio).

Signal weighting is typically done in risk terms. If you have a 2 percent active risk budget and are deciding how much (risk) weight to allocate to four investment themes, those weights should be applied to portfolios formed on each investment signal where the weights have been adjusted to allow for comparability across investment themes. Consider carry as an investment theme. Your carry long/short portfolio, like that examined in Chapter 6, would have the long and short side of the portfolio equal each other in dollar terms (i.e., be dollar-neutral), but it will be a very imbalanced portfolio in terms of market exposure *and* it will have more risk than a similar portfolio formed on another theme (say defensive). How to adjust the portfolios to improve comparability? The portfolio weights can be scaled up or down to target a specific level of volatility. This requires a measure of risk, which could be as simple as DTS or could be a more advanced common factor risk model (more on that later in the chapter).

8.2.5 Could/Should You Vary Active Risk Through Time?

Separate from the strategic versus tactical weighting decision across signals (e.g., the choice to increase or decrease your exposure to a certain signal due to recent performance), there is a related decision on whether to allow the aggregate amount of active risk to vary through time or not. This may not be immediately obvious the first time you are asked this. What causes temporal variation in active risk across a combination of investment themes if I am targeting a fixed set of risk weights across the set of investment themes? The individual thematic portfolios may take the same amount of risk at each point in time, but the combination is not guaranteed to do so because of time varying correlation structures across the investment themes. At certain times, signals will be more positively correlated to each other. At certain times, some themes will like a similar set of securities. When this happens, the aggregate active risk across themes will be greater. This is your choice: Do you want to allow that time variation of active risk in your investment process or not? If you believe that risk-adjusted returns are stronger when there is greater agreement across investment themes, then allow that time variation in active risk.

8.2.6 Signal-Specific Investment Choices

- Ordinal/Cardinal: Although each signal has a natural unit, do you want to keep that natural scale (cardinal) or are you mostly interested in the rank ordering across bonds (ordinal)? Perhaps you want to use both dimensions.
- Missing values: How do you want to treat missing values? Excluding bonds with missing values will be very restrictive, especially when you are integrating across many signals. If you have no information for a given signal this is equivalent to a neutral view. Assigning a neutral value may be appropriate. But note that zero is not necessarily a neutral value. It all depends on the scale of the signal and any other treatment you have made to the signal (e.g., group demeaning). In class assignments this choice perplexes students as they can make the neutral value (zero) replacement too early in the process. For example, if your signal was leverage (preference for corporate issuers with lower leverage) then if you assign a value of zero for firms where you could not measure leverage (say private issuers where you are unable to source financial statement data), that choice means you maximally like firms with

missing data to compute leverage. I doubt that was your investment view. Alternative treatment for missing values could be imputation based on available data for similar firms (we will see an example of this in Chapter 10 for carbon aware portfolios).

■ Group neutrality: The investment signals discussed in Chapters 5–7 were designed to capture idiosyncratic return sources either across or within issuer. They were not specifically designed to identify attractive groups of issuers. What do I mean by this? For corporate issuers, we can group them in various dimensions (e.g., rating categories, industry or sector membership, maturity groupings, and country or region of domicile for global portfolios). If your investment theme is not to take active risk across these dimensions, you may want to remove unintended exposure on these dimensions. Your value signal may have a bias toward lower rated issuers or a bias toward certain sectors (e.g., financials). What could you do to remove these biases? A simple regression can be a useful fix. From Statistics 101 we know that a regression of $Y = \alpha + \beta X + \varepsilon$ will produce a regression residual, ε, that has the following property: $COV(X, \varepsilon) = 0$. So, if we regress our signal onto sets of indicator variables that capture the various groupings (rating, industry, domicile, etc.) the residual will be orthogonal to those groupings. Demeaning is equivalent when you are looking to remove the influence of one group, but regression is more efficient when dealing with multiple groupings.

■ Beta neutrality: A key criticism of active risk taking by incumbent fixed income managers (across all fixed income categories), as discussed in Chapter 4, was the passive exposure to traditional market risk premia, especially credit markets. We do not want to be guilty of repackaging beta as alpha. We can use the same technique we used for group neutrality. We can regress our signal onto beta (which, of course, requires a measure of beta for every bond in your eligible investment universe), and the residual from that regression is your signal with any beta effect removed. Unlike a grouping, demeaning does not work for beta neutralizing. An added benefit of regression is that you could also remove beta across your groupings as well. As students work through examples, they appreciate how quickly you can lose degrees of freedom here. Choices will need to be made on the granularity of groupings, and typically you will be disappointed (i.e., you will have some ability to neutralize to rating, sector, country, and so forth, but not for fine categories especially when there are multiple dimensions you are trying to neutralize to).

Let's try to make this discussion of signal-specific investment choices concrete using the example of equity momentum as a signal for a corporate bond long/short portfolio. We have a universe of 195 sufficiently liquid five-year on the run credit-default swap (CDS) contracts for North

American reference entities (spanning both IG and HY markets). For this set of assets, we have a measure of trailing six-month equity returns as our signal. Let's see what happens to this signal as we transform it along the various dimensions just discussed.

One approach to create a signal out of a raw momentum measure could be to Z-score the signal across the entire cross-section (this means subtract the average momentum for all 195 issuers and divide by the standard deviation of momentum across the 195 issuers). Exhibit 8.3 shows what this does to the signal. You preserve the rank ordering across issuers, and the scale is adjusted (it is normalized). But note the negative association with DTS (beta) as better-performing issuers tend to have lower spreads, and the imbalance in long and short positions across sectors. Are these intended?

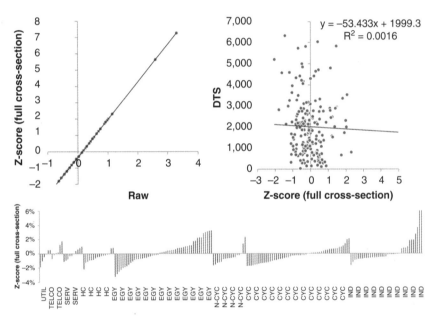

EXHIBIT 8.3   Z-scored (entire cross-section) momentum signal for a liquid corporate universe.

An alternative treatment for the momentum measure would be to Z-score (ranked values) at the sector level rather than across the entire cross-section. This would ensure there is no sector imbalance across the long and short side of the portfolio. And that is exactly what you see in Exhibit 8.4. There is a perfect balance in negative and positive bars in the sector chart,

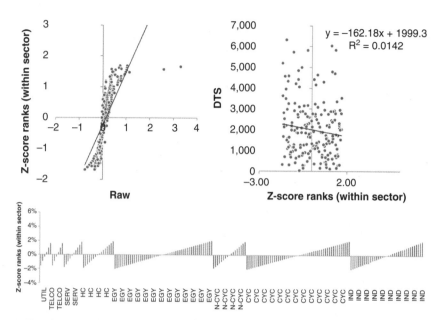

EXHIBIT 8.4   Z-scored ranks (within sector) momentum signal for a liquid corporate universe.

but there is still a negative tilt to DTS. Even after these adjustments, the modified momentum signal still retains the bulk of the information content of the raw momentum signal (correlation of 0.77).

To remove the negative beta tilt, we can regress the Z-score within sector momentum measure onto DTS (proxy for beta). Exhibit 8.5 shows how this removes the beta tilt completely but now introduces a small sector imbalance. The solution would then be to regress the Z-scored within sector momentum measure on a set of indicator variables for sector membership and DTS. A useful exercise for students.

8.3   CHOICES IN THE PORTFOLIO CONSTRUCTION PROCESS (OPTIMIZATION, REBALANCING, TRADING)

Everything in this section speaks to the backward dimension of the investment cube in Exhibit 8.2. Academic research is largely ignorant of this dimension. A simple correlation of a characteristic with future excess return is not a sufficient statistic for success. Let's discuss the many related aspects of portfolio construction that we need to master.

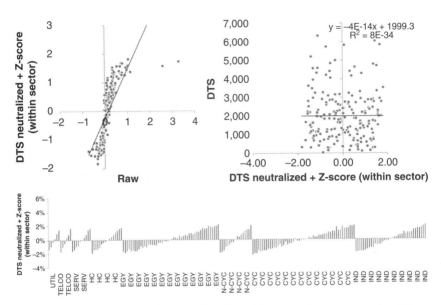

EXHIBIT 8.5 Beta-neutralized Z-scored ranks (within sector) momentum signal for a liquid corporate universe.

8.3.1 Objective Function

At the core of any systematic investment process is an objective function. This will typically be seeking to maximize (net of transaction cost) returns while targeting a given level of risk (tracking error) and satisfying various intuitive constraints. An example objective function for corporate bond security selection was introduced in Israel, Palhares, and Richardson (2018), which I reproduce here with some simplifications:

$$Maximize : \sum_{i=1}^{I} w_i.ER_i$$

subject to :

$$w_i \geq 0, \forall i \ (no \ shorting \ constraint)$$

$$| \ w_i - b_i \ | \leq 0.25\%, \forall i \ (deviation \ from \ benchmark \ constraint)$$

$$\sum_{i=1}^{I} w_i = 1 \ (fully \ invested \ constraint)$$

$$\sum_{i=1}^{I} |w_{i,t} - w_{i,t-1}| \leq 10\% \; (\textit{turnover constraint})$$

$$\sum_{i=1}^{I} |(w_i - b_i).OAS_i| \leq 0.50\% \; (\textit{deviation from benchmark spread constraint})$$

$$\sum_{i=1}^{I} |(w_i - b_i). \; Duration_i|$$

$$\leq 0.50 \; (\textit{deviation from benchmark duration constraint})$$

This linear program captures the essential features for our purpose. It is not a mean-variance optimization. There is no formal modeling of risk via a common factor model (more on that later). But it summarizes what the systematic process is doing. First, the program is solving for a vector of portfolio weights, w. Those weights need to sum to one and all be positive (in the case of a long-only portfolio). For long-short portfolios, those constraints would be different. Second, risk is handled here via three separate constraints: (i) deviations from benchmark weights are capped at 0.25 percent (forced diversification), (ii) deviations from benchmark weights are capped in spread units (50 basis points), and (iii) deviations from benchmark weights are capped in spread duration units (0.5 years). Third, the portfolio wants to hold bonds with the highest expected returns, ER. Additional constraints could be added to limit active risk across various groupings (e.g., sector, rating, country of domicile etc.) and incorporate awareness of liquidity (e.g., portfolio weights may be restricted to be no more than a certain multiple of typical daily trading volumes). This is all very intuitive.

How does a portfolio look once inputs are fed into the objective function? Let's continue with our example of momentum for the corporate universe. We can solve for a set of portfolio weights that maximizes exposure to the beta-neutralized Z-scored within sector version of momentum (i.e., *maximize* : $\sum_{i=1}^{I} w_i.Z_i$) while also requiring all portfolio weights to be positive, no weight to exceed 5 percent of the overall portfolio, portfolio weights cannot exceed four times average daily trading volume, and the portfolio must be fully invested. Exhibit 8.6 shows a scatter plot of the optimized portfolio weights against the beta-neutralized Z-scored ranks (within sector) momentum signal.

At first glance this correlation looks low (it is 0.60) and students initially are uncomfortable. This is not surprising. Your ability to take large positions is limited by liquidity in this optimization setup. If you used additional constraints (e.g., instead of only a 5 percent market capitalization weight limit, also require a risk weight limit) you would see further distance between

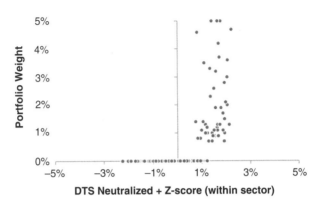

EXHIBIT 8.6   Scatter plot of optimized portfolio weights and the beta-neutralized Z-scored ranks (within sector) momentum signal for a liquid corporate universe.

portfolio weights and your signal. This is the challenge of systematic investing; you want that correlation (called a transfer coefficient as per Grinold and Kahn 2000) to be 1. In the real world, a variety of frictions impede your ability to do so. What can the systematic investor do? Reduce the frictions by preselecting an eligible investment universe that is neither too costly to trade nor too difficult to source liquidity, and improve trading execution. A benefit of visual tools like Exhibit 8.6 is the ability to look at each individual position and understand which constraint is binding, and this can help focus research effort to improve the process (e.g., Do we need better liquidity data to avoid chasing after illiquid bonds? Do we need to enhance modeling of risk to avoid chasing after bonds that have too large a contribution to active risk?)

8.3.2   Getting the Units Correct

The objective function does not specify units. The researcher needs to do this. This is important. In our linear program we are trying to maximize expected returns, ER. But we are using a combination of transformed signals to generate an aggregate score for each bond. Who knows what unit that aggregate score is expressed in. Grinold and Kahn (2000) introduced the equation $ER = Z * IC * \sigma$, which allows for Z-scored signals to be converted to an expected return by multiplying with your skill (IC, information coefficient) and the volatility of the asset (σ). This presupposes that your signal is in risk-adjusted units. It may not be. Consider carry, which is already in expected return units. Some thought is needed to map individual signals into return space. An alternative approach is to empirically calibrate how your combination of signals predicts future excess returns (on average). This reduced form approach will get your signal collection into the correct unit. Why is this important? Other constraints in the objective function (e.g., expected transaction costs) will be in return units, so you want the constraints to behave as expected when trade-offs are made.

8.3.3 Modeling Risk

Risk modeling is a topic worthy of its own book. All I want to introduce here are some of the different types of risk models I have seen used by systematic fixed income investors. By risk model I mean the identification of the volatility and correlation structure across the set of assets in your eligible investment universe. If you have 2,000 bonds in your universe, then we are talking about 2,000 measures of volatility and many, many more correlations! These types of risk models are central to the systematic investment process, as they allow investors to target a level of risk in their portfolios, and constraints can also be specified for specific bonds or combinations of bonds to limit active risk (e.g., groupings on sector, rating, etc.).

While there are advocates of purely statistical models of risk that extract information from the time series of returns using the principal components approach, which we covered in Chapter 5, I find them less useful because they are difficult to interpret. Instead, the most common type of risk models will generate $[N \cdot N]$ covariance matrices, where N is the number of assets in your eligible investment universe. The elements of the matrix can be identified using (i) asset- level historical returns (commonly used for small cross-sections like government bond portfolios), and (ii) common factor historical returns (commonly used for large cross-sections like corporate bonds).

Armed with a risk model, it is possible to move backward and forward between a portfolio and the expected returns that are implied by that set of portfolio weights. A regular mean-variance objective function maximizes the following: $R^T w - \lambda w^T \Sigma w$, where the first expression, $R^T w$, is the portfolio level expected return and the second expression, $w^T \Sigma w$, is portfolio level risk (Σ is the covariance matrix for the returns of the assets in the portfolio), with an aversion parameter, λ. This function is written in matrix form, so the superscript T refers to transpose. The general solution to this type of objective function is: $w \propto \Sigma^{-1} R$. Your collection of signals can represent a desired set of portfolio weights, w, and, using this solution, those portfolio weights imply a set of expected returns, R. Risk models are versatile tools that are useful not only in optimizations but also in constructing your return forecasts.

There are many choices involved in the modeling of risk, including: (i) look-back periods for the estimation of return volatility and correlation structure (shorter for volatility and longer for correlations),

(ii) inclusion of economic priors on the magnitude of volatilities and correlations (various types of shrinkage estimators can be used, with shrinkage to a peer group average quite common), (iii) separately modeling common factor and idiosyncratic return volatility, and (iv) selection of common factors to include in a cross-sectional risk model (e.g., which industry classification schema; consistency of investment signals used in your return forecast; and your risk forecast, liquidity, rating, etc.). Estimating your own risk model has the enormous benefit of transparency and flexibility. You know the structure you have imposed to estimate volatilities and correlations. If you want to modify something, it is easy to do so. The downside is the effort to develop and maintain the risk model infrastructure. Commercial third-party data providers exist for fixed income risk models including BARRA, Axioma, and Northfield.

8.3.4 Rebalancing (Turnover Budget)

A systematic investment process is run in discrete time. That means you look to rebalance your portfolios at periodic intervals. Traditionally, systematic benchmark-aware, long-only portfolios were rebalanced at approximately a monthly frequency. With the advent of liquidity provision strategies, rebalancing is now more frequent and spread over the month. A rebalance is trigged by (i) flows (i.e., redemptions or subscriptions to the fund), (ii) cash flow accumulation (i.e., receipt of coupons from bonds or early receipt of principal due to tenders, calls, and other corporate actions), and (iii) drift in your portfolio from the optimal portfolio. The first two types of rebalance triggers are easy to track (simply look at the amount of uninvested cash in your portfolio and when that gets too large you rebalance). The third type of trigger is an ongoing assessment. We mentioned the term "transfer coefficient" (TC) earlier in this chapter. In a rebalancing context, the TC is a (risk-weighted) measure of distance between the portfolio you hold and the portfolio that you would like to hold (the optimal portfolio). As that distance grows, the utility from rebalancing increases. Portfolio managers watch measures of TC to decide when to rebalance. Of course, rebalances should also be timed to correspond to normal periods of liquidity (i.e., don't rebalance a portfolio on Wednesday prior to Thanksgiving holiday, and don't rebalance a rate-sensitive asset portfolio the morning of a Federal Open Market Committee meeting).

What is the optimal amount of turnover? This is a difficult question to answer, because it is highly endogenous. Your combination of signals will have a natural horizon over which returns are forecasted (typically higher returns in the short horizon and lower returns in the longer horizon). All else equal, the faster your signal (i.e., the quicker the speed of decay of your return forecast) the higher the turnover needed for your portfolio. But, how do you determine the speed of your return forecast? By looking at the data (in-sample or via live experience). The speed of your model should also respect the underlying liquidity of the market. There is a reason that high-frequency trading is limited to equity markets and liquid futures markets. You need low latency (i.e., the ability to trade within a micro-second). As we will see in Chapter 9, corporate bond markets do not have anything close to that type of latency. Furthermore, as noted in Israel, Palhares, and Richardson (2018), expected trading costs for corporate bonds are high relative to the underlying volatility of the asset class (see also Harris 2015). This means that turnover needs to be carefully assessed against the expected transaction costs (the positive utility from increased expected returns needs to be traded off against the negative utility from increased costs paid to trade toward the optimal portfolio). This is where improvements to order management and trade execution systems can have a large impact on the portfolio: they allow you to trade more aggressively toward the optimal portfolio and increase the TC.

8.3.5 Constraints

There are various other constraints that could be incorporated into a systematic investment process, and I discuss them briefly here.

- Beta constraints: Typically, a long-only benchmark-aware portfolio targets beta = 1 and an unconstrained long/short portfolio targets beta = 0. Other beta levels could also be targeted. Whatever the target, a portfolio level constraint can be incorporated (e.g., $w^T\beta = 1$) that ensures your portfolio weights match the beta of the benchmark. Note that this type of constraint can also be expressed in active weight space (i.e., $w^T_{ACTIVE}\beta = 0$). Beta constraints can operate at the portfolio level or could also operate at a subgroup level within the portfolio (e.g., you may want to limit the active risk taken across rating categories or across industry groups).
- Trade-size constraints: Unlike equity markets most fixed income securities do not trade on electronic exchanges where orders can be broken up into small pieces (e.g., 100 shares). Instead, there are socially acceptable regular trade sizes. Although these have trended down over time as electronification of the markets has increased (more on this in the next chapter), there is still a need to trade at minimum sizes. This type of constraint is nonlinear and can cause challenges for efficient solutions, but it is a topic that needs to be addressed.
- Position size constraints: The optimal portfolio weights should also be a function of the underlying liquidity of the market, so the weight for a given bond will typically be capped at a multiple of expected trading

volumes. Risk officers also carefully look at portfolio level statistics based on these measures: How many days would it take to liquidate the portfolio in regular market conditions? Capacity considerations are directly related to this type of constraint. The tighter you make this constraint (perhaps because the investment vehicle allows for daily dealing), then the smaller the positions you can build in any one bond. Combined with other constraints (especially issuer weight limits) this naturally caps the size of the portfolio you can manage.

■ Sustainability: This is a multifaceted term that can mean many different things and asset owners are increasingly paying attention to aspects of sustainability (ESG). We have an entire chapter dedicated to this topic. For now, note that constraints are often an efficient way to incorporate sustainability considerations into a portfolio with the objective of not sacrificing risk-adjusted returns. This is where systematic investment processes are strictly superior to traditional discretionary approaches. When you have multiple objectives for a portfolio, it quickly becomes very difficult to keep track of the correct trade-offs.

■ Other constraints: Systematic investment processes evolve over time, and without fail you will learn things along the way. Beware the knee-jerk reaction of blindly adding constraints to the portfolio in response to an unintended exposure that generated a negative return realization. Yes, you do want to mitigate tracking error coming from sources that are not well compensated, but such constraints do not come for free, they lower your TC. You need to be convinced that every constraint is necessary for your portfolio, otherwise as time passes you will be adding more constraints, and be solving for those constraints, and drifting away from your primary objective: chasing bonds with the highest expected returns. As Richard Grinold used to say, beware the "whack a mole"!

8.3.6 Mixing or Integrating Signals

Our analysis of portfolio construction has worked with one portfolio. It is formed based on integrating across *all* investment insights. This has the benefit of utilizing information across return forecasting sources, especially the correlation structure across investment signals. An alternative approach would be to invest capital (or risk) across separate portfolios that targeted each investment theme separately. This has the benefit of very clean attribution: you can see the performance of each theme very clearly. However, it suffers from a distinct drawback insofar as you will be buying and selling securities across these portfolios due to canceling views (i.e., you may like a bond in a value portfolio but dislike the same bond in a momentum portfolio). In asset classes, where trading costs are high, such as corporate bonds, mixing across separate portfolios seems to be inefficient. For a full examination of this topic in the context of equity markets see Fitzgibbons, Friedman, Pomorski, and Serban (2017).

8.4 OTHER TOPICS

8.4.1 Crowding

Any discussion of systematic investing seems to be incomplete without talking about "crowding." Why this fear seems to be unique to systematic investors is a bit of a mystery. Anyhow, the concern seems to be that as more people know about the investment thesis, the worse it will be. Although that sounds compelling, there are multiple issues with this. Asness (2016) provides an excellent discussion and summary of the key issues. I will just restate a couple of elements of that paper. First, simple knowledge of an investment thesis is insufficient to erode its return potential. Capital needs to be invested to erode that expected return edge. Second, while the capital is invested, to chase the investment thesis the return experience would be very positive (flow induced). But going forward, returns may be lower. Third, capital chasing an idea may not remove its return potential if the basis for the return relation is linked to nondiversifiable risk (as opposed to cognitive errors by capital market participants). Fourth, the presence of levered investors coupled with the risk of crowding introduces an element of deleveraging risk (see also Richardson, Saffi, and Sigurdsson 2017).

As Asness (2016) neatly summarized, a rational forecast of the risk of crowding, at least directionally, is a reduction in expected returns and an increase in risk. The combined effect is a lowering of risk-adjusted returns, not to zero, but a lowering. But does this type of risk apply to systematic fixed income investing? Not yet. Wigglesworth and Fletcher (2021) note that estimates of the quantitative strategies in fixed income are tiny relative to the size of the fixed income markets and quantitative fixed income strategies account for about 3 percent of the assets invested in quantitative equity strategies. So, while crowding is a risk to monitor, it does not seem to be top of the list now.

8.4.2 Beta Completion

My final discussion point on portfolio construction speaks to beta completion. Chapter 4 had noted a systemic shortcoming of beta repackaged as alpha for many active fixed income managers. To avoid that criticism in our systematic approach, we need to be sure that our active risk is not driven by beta views. At the same time, for long-only benchmark-aware portfolios, we need to be sure to give the asset owner the beta embedded in their benchmark. For fixed income investments, that is a multidimensional challenge. All fixed income assets inherit exposure to the local currency-yield curve (risk-free component), all credit-sensitive assets have additional exposure to the local credit curve (risky component), and for global mandates there are multiple currencies reflected in the benchmark.

Our systematic investment process is designed to solve for a set of portfolio weights consistent with the objective function (inclusive of constraints). That portfolio also needs to match the risk-free, risky, and currency exposure of the benchmark. This can be achieved via additional constraints that limit active risk across those dimensions. Or, and what I would strongly recommend, is to use derivatives to complete the beta of the portfolio, especially for credit-sensitive assets that are expensive to trade individually. Why would you want to distort your optimal portfolio to balance interest rate risk, currency risk, or credit risk? There are much cheaper instruments to adjust positioning along these dimensions (e.g., interest rate derivatives, typically swaps and futures, to manage rate risk; credit index derivatives to manage overall credit risk; and currency forwards to manage currency risk). Of course, this means that investment guidelines need to be structured to allow the use of these derivatives. The process of beta completion across these dimensions requires estimation of (i) the beta contribution of each asset to rate and credit risk, and (ii) the sensitivity of your elected derivative to the beta you are completing. Again, more choice and estimation is needed, but these are essential ingredients for a successful systematic investment process.

REFERENCES

Asness, C. (2016). How can a strategy still work if everyone knows about itt? AQR working paper.

Fitzgibbons, S., J. Friedman, L. Pomorski, and L. Serban. (2017). *Journal of Investing*, 26, 153–164.

Grinold, R., and R. Kahn. (2000). *Active Portfolio Management*. McGraw-Hill.

Gupta, T., and B. Kelly. (2019). Factor momentum everywhere. *Journal of Portfolio Management*, 45, 13–36.

Harris, L. (2015). Transaction costs, trade throughs, and riskless principal trading in corporate bond markets. University of Southern California, working paper.

Israel, R., D. Palhares, and S. Richardson. (2018). Common factors in corporate bond returns. *Journal of Investment Management*, 16, 17–46.

Richardson, S., P. Saffi, and K. Sigurdsson. (2017). Deleveraging risk. *Journal of Financial and Quantitative Analysis*, 52, 2491–2522.

Wigglesworth, R., and L. Fletcher. (2021). The next quant revolution: Shaking up the corporate bond market. *Financial Times* (December 7).

CHAPTER 9

Liquidity and Trading Considerations

OVERVIEW

This chapter discusses the implementation challenges related to sourcing and providing liquidity. Although these issues are common to all asset classes (fixed income, stocks, and currencies), they are particularly acute for credit-sensitive assets within the fixed income asset class. This is due to a combination of the over-the-counter nature of trading and the huge breadth of issues to choose from and the venues to trade in. We will focus on the evolving microstructure of credit-sensitive assets and highlight opportunities for systematic investing approaches within this challenged liquidity environment.

9.1 SOME CONTEXT FOR THE LIQUIDITY CHALLENGES OF FIXED INCOME ASSETS

We will start by looking at high-level data on transaction costs across the main asset classes (fixed income, stocks, currencies, and commodities). Exhibit 9.1 shows high-level information on market capitalization, average daily trading volumes, turnover, number of securities, bid–ask spreads, and volatilities. I show this only for US markets covering (i) US government bonds (Treasury), (ii) US corporate bonds inclusive of investment-grade (IG) and high-yield (HY) bonds (corporate), and (iii) US equities inclusive of stocks listed on NYSE, Nasdaq, and over-the-counter exchange (OTCQX, stocks).

Exhibit 9.1 makes it clear that despite similar relative sizes of government bond, corporate bond, and stock markets (all exceed $10 trillion USD) there are large differences in the relative trading activity, both in terms of

EXHIBIT 9.1   Overview of relative liquidity and trading challenges across stock and bond markets. Data approximations are as of 2020.

	Treasury	Corporate	Stocks
Market Capitalization	≈$20 trillion USD	≈$10 trillion USD	≈$40 trillion USD
Daily Volumes	≈$600 billion USD	≈$40 billion USD	≈$500 billion USD
Turnover	3%	0.4%	1.2%
# Securities	≈100	≈10,000	≈4,000
Idiosyncrasies	No	Yes	No
Bid–Ask Spreads	<0.05%	0.3–0.5%	<0.1%
Volatility	4%	6-8%	≈20%
Spread/Volatility	1%	6%	0.5%

Sources: Securities Industry and Financial Markets Association (SIFMA), Siblis Research, TRACE, Bloomberg Indices.

average daily trading volumes and typical bid–ask spreads. As discussed earlier in the book, there is also considerable heterogeneity in the corporate bond markets. There are multiple bonds issued by the typical corporation, and those bonds differ in terms of maturity, seniority, and embedded options. This high degree of idiosyncrasies adds operational complexity to trading credit-sensitive assets, but a systematic investment process with the capability to model thousands of corporate bonds may be uniquely positioned, relative to traditional discretionary investment approaches, to be nimble and capitalize on the opportunities that arise from idiosyncrasies (we will discuss the role of substitutions at the end of this chapter).

The final row in Exhibit 9.1 is perhaps the most telling. Explicit transaction costs from crossing the bid–ask spread are largest in corporate bond markets, and when scaling that expected transaction cost by the volatility of the asset class, corporate bonds are the most expensive asset class to trade by a wide margin. Our focus in this chapter will be on credit-sensitive assets. Most of the discussion will center on corporate bonds, but I will cover credit index instruments (derivatives, exchange-traded funds (ETFs), and swaps) as well.

9.2   BASICS FOR TRADING CREDIT-SENSITIVE ASSETS

9.2.1   Over-the-Counter Markets

Single-name credit-sensitive securities trade in what is called an "over-the-counter" manner. Exhibit 9.2 visualizes the traditional dealer-intermediated over-the-counter market.

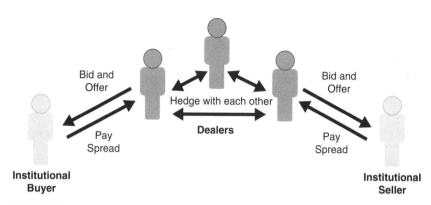

EXHIBIT 9.2 Visualization of the corporate bond market structure with dealers acting in a principal capacity.

In this traditional model, dealers are said to be acting in a principal capacity, which refers to their core role of holding inventory. Over the last decade, the value of corporate bond inventory held by the dealer community has fallen enormously. The New York Fed maintains data on primary dealer statistics (https://www.newyorkfed.org/markets/counterparties/primary-dealers-statistics). The purpose of this data is to allow the Fed to monitor the activities of the main broker-dealers through which it implements its monetary policy. Although this is not a complete set of all dealers making markets in corporate bonds, the temporal trend of primary dealer involvement is still very useful to understand the changing dynamic of corporate bond trading. As of December 31, 2007, primary dealers held nearly $265 billion USD of IG-rated corporate bonds. As of December 31, 2013, that number had fallen to nearly $73 billion USD, and by December 31, 2020 it had fallen to a little over $4 billion USD. There has been a massive reduction in the primary-market-making capabilities of the broker-dealer community. This is due to a combination of regulatory capital pressures and the ongoing electronification of the corporate bond markets. (More on this in the next section.)

Consequently, agency trading has become more common. This is where the dealer acts as a matchmaker and brings together buyer and seller through their own networks or increasingly via electronic platforms (more on that later). Agency trading is a boon for systematic investors in credit-sensitive assets as they possess the unique capability of having (i) a view on many corporate bonds, and (ii) the ability to respond quickly to expressions of interest from other market participants. This makes systematic investors powerful liquidity providers to credit sensitive markets.

9.2.2 Trading Convention for Investment-Grade Corporate Bonds

Investment-grade-rated corporate bonds are typically quoted on a spread basis. Dealers will send their indicative quotes to interested parties. Exhibit 9.3 shows a hypothetical dealer run (where a dealer expresses their interest in trading a given asset or set of assets) for an IG corporate issuer. There are multiple useful things to note about this run. First, it covers many corporate bonds from the same issuer. This is efficient from a portfolio management perspective as you can quickly see the pricing and indications of interest of potential substitute bonds. You will find, on occasion, that a specific bond you find attractive will not be available either in terms of the quantity you are seeking or the price is far from what you have based your expected return forecast on. In that case, you need an efficient way to identify potentially suitable substitutes (more on this at the end of the chapter). Second, the "prices" are not prices but spreads. Spreads to what? There will be market consensus on what the closest Treasury bond (Bench column in Exhibit 9.3) is for a given corporate bond, and the spread will be the yield difference between those two bonds. Let's be sure we understand what bid–ask means in this context. Traditionally, when we speak of bid–ask we naturally think in price terms, and the bid–ask spread covers the bid side (lower price at which you could sell the asset to the dealer who is "bidding") and the ask side (higher price at which you could buy the asset from the dealer who is "asking"). However, in the case of market-pricing convention with spread assets, we need to remember the inverse relation between yields (spreads) and price. The dealer is still going to charge a spread to trade the spread asset (yes, deliberately confusing!), but they quote that in terms of the higher spread (lower price) at which they are willing to buy (their bid) and the lower spread (higher price) at which they are willing to sell (their ask). For the first bond in Exhibit 9.3 the dealer is willing to buy (sell) at a spread of 83 (78) basis points. We can convert the bid–ask spread that is quoted in spread terms into price terms by multiplying it by the duration of the asset (this will be useful later when we compare trading costs of IG to HY corporate bonds). The final two columns in Exhibit 9.3 provide an indication of the potential depth in the market for each bond (these are indications of how much the dealer is willing to buy or sell).

The quantity information is an indication of the dealer's willingness to transact in size on either side of the indicative bid–ask spread. In practice, these runs are indications not commitments. There is a growing trend for quotes to be color coded as firm or to-be-confirmed. Not all quotes are two sided; they can be one sided (i.e., only buy or sell interest from the dealer). Typically, the lack of two-sided markets across multiple dealers at institutional trade sizes (read more than $1 million) is an indication of an

y		Bid Ask Sprd Sprd	Sp 1D	Bench	BSz ASz (M) (M)
3.35	02/09/27	83/78	+2	10YR	10mx10m
4.65	02/23/46	114/109	-5	T 2⅞ 46	10mx5m
4¼	02/09/47	110/105	-4	T 2⅞ 46	10mx5m
3.3	02/01/27	93/89	+0	10YR	10mx5m
3.4	07/15/46	122/117	-1	T 2⅞ 46	7500x7500
2.4	08/08/26	65/61	+0	10YR	7500x7500
3.3	02/06/27	69/66	+0	10YR	10mx5m
4.1	02/06/37	80/76	-1	T 2⅞ 46	10mx5m
3.7	08/08/46	100/96	-1	T 2⅞ 46	10mx5m
4¼	02/06/47	104/100	-1	T 2⅞ 46	7500x7500
4½	02/06/57	127/123	-1	T 2⅞ 46	10mx5m
2.65	07/15/26	81/77	+0	10YR	5mx10m

EXHIBIT 9.3 Quoting and trading conventions for IG corporate bonds. Hypothetical Bloomberg screenshot.

illiquid bond. This is one type of data that could be used as part of the liquidity prefiltering that was discussed in Chapter 8.

To help complete the picture of the typical liquidity profile of corporate bonds, Exhibit 9.4 includes screenshots from the "QMGR" (Quote Manager) feature in Bloomberg for two IG-rated corporate bonds (GE as an

GE 4.418 11/15/35 $↑119.840 -.402 123.8 bp vs T 1.375 11/15/2031
At 14:50 Source BMRK
GE 4.418 11/15/35 Corp vs <Enter Security> 11) Actions 12) Settings
1 Criteria Applied View Last by Dealer Date Range 5 Days 99) Buy 98) Sell

Time	Time	Sender	Dlr	B Px / A Px	B Yld / A Yld	B Sprd / A Sprd	B Sz A Sz
14:48	14:48			119.876 / 120.134	2.70 / 2.68	123.00 / 121.00	20MM X
14:43	14:43			119.837 / 120.353	2.70 / 2.66	125.00 / 121.00	10MM X 10MM
14:39	14:39			119.632 / 120.053	2.71 / 2.68	124.00 / 121.00	5MM X 5MM
14:31	14:31			119.312 /	2.74 /	127.70 /	300M X
14:19	14:19			119.812 / 120.069	2.70 / 2.68	124.00 / 122.00	
13:51	13:51			/ 120.224	/ 2.67	/ 122.00	X 1MM
13:49	13:49			120.198 / 120.846	2.67 / 2.62	122.00 / 117.00	X 1,500M
13:10	13:10			/ 120.230	/ 2.67	/ 122.00	X 8,837M
13:06	13:06						
11:39	11:39			120.056 / 120.560	2.68 / 2.64	124.00 / 120.00	
11:23	11:23			/ 120.211	/ 2.67	/ 123.00	
10:01	10:01			119.837 / 120.250	2.70 / 2.67	125.00 / 122.00	
09:51	09:51			120.060 / 120.440	2.68 / 2.65	123.00 / 120.00	
08:37	08:37			120.100 / 120.740	2.68 / 2.63	124.00 / 119.00	
08:00	08:00			119.729 /	2.71 /	125.00 /	10MM X
07:56	07:56			120.392 / 120.911	2.66 / 2.62	124.00 / 120.00	
12/14	15:48			119.918 / 120.564	2.69 / 2.64	125.00 / 120.00	5MM X 5MM
12/13	12:48			/ 121.220	/ 2.59	/ 117.00	X 10MM
12/13	07:07			120.334 / 120.853	2.66 / 2.62	119.00 / 115.00	

CENT 4 ⅛ 10/15/30 $↑99.919 -.403 Yld 4.136
At 14:52 Source BMRK
CENT 4 ⅛ 10/15/30 Corp vs <Enter Security> 11) Actions 12) Settings
1 Criteria Applied View Last by Dealer Date Range 5 Days 99) Buy 98) Sell

Time	Time	Sender	Dlr	B Px / A Px	B Yld / A Yld	B Sprd / A Sprd	B Sz A Sz
13:38	13:38			99.625 / 100.375	4.18 / 4.06	272.60 / 261.10	
13:23	13:23			/ 100.250	/ 4.08	/ 263.39	X 700M
10:50	10:50			99.625 / 100.375	4.18 / 4.06	272.68 / 261.20	2MM X 2MM
08:26	08:26			100.125 / 100.875	4.10 / 3.98	265.51 / 252.87	
07:51	07:51			99.625 / 100.375	4.18 / 4.06	272.30 / 260.80	
07:45	07:45			100.000 / 100.500	4.12 / 4.04	[illegible]	
07:28	07:28			99.750 / 100.750	4.16 / 4.00	271.14 / 255.05	
06:47	06:47			99.875 / 100.375	4.14 / 4.06	269.82 / 261.82	
12/14	09:04			99.750 / 100.750	4.16 / 4.00	272.00 / 256.00	
12/14	08:58			99.625 /	4.18 /	273.78 /	2MM X
12/10	12:23						

EXHIBIT 9.4 Example of liquid (GE) and illiquid (CENT) IG corporate bonds. Hypothetical Bloomberg screenshot.

example of a more liquid corporate bond and CENT as an example of a less liquid corporate bond) filtering on only the most recent quote from each dealer.

It should be immediately clear the vast difference in liquidity across these two corporate bonds. GE has multiple dealers willing to make markets in the 2035 bond with these indicative quotes closely aligned in calendar time and bid–ask space. This GE bond has both depth of trading opportunities across many dealers and also relatively tight bid–ask spreads (less than 5 basis points wide in spread space) and substantial trade sizes (MM is Bloomberg units for millions). In contrast, although the CENT 2030 bond is also quoted by multiple dealers, there are fewer indicative quotes, and they are less concentrated in time (i.e., less recent), have wider bid–ask spreads (typically more than 10 basis points in spread space), and are for smaller trade sizes (M is Bloomberg units for thousands).

9.2.3 Trading Convention for HY Corporate Bonds

HY corporate bonds are generally quoted on a price basis as opposed to spread basis. Exhibit 9.5 shows a hypothetical dealer run for a HY corporate issuer. A general dealer run for the HY market may aggregate multiple issuers together that are closely related to each other, or, in the case of issuers with multiple bonds outstanding, the run may be issuer specific. Exhibit 9.5 simply shows indicative quotes on the bid and ask sides. Alongside, there is equivalent information in yield terms (the YAS, Yield Analysis, screen in Bloomberg facilitates this). As with the IG dealer runs there may also be information on indicative sizes on the bid or ask side. I've excluded these here for brevity.

curity		Price		YTW	
		Bid	Ask	Bid	Ask
$5\frac{3}{8}$	02/21	$101\frac{3}{4}$	$102\frac{1}{4}$	2.96	2.28
$5\frac{1}{2}$	02/22	104	$104\frac{3}{4}$	3.17	2.75
$5\frac{3}{4}$	03/24	$108\frac{3}{4}$	$109\frac{1}{2}$	3.29	3.09
$5\frac{7}{8}$	02/25	$110\frac{3}{8}$	$110\frac{7}{8}$	3.50	3.39
$3\frac{5}{8}$	06/25	$101\frac{1}{4}$	$101\frac{3}{4}$	3.36	3.25
$4\frac{3}{8}$	11/26	105	106	3.51	3.34
$4\frac{7}{8}$	04/28	$106\frac{1}{4}$	107	3.95	3.84
$5\frac{7}{8}$	11/28	$112\frac{7}{8}$	$113\frac{5}{8}$	4.07	3.98
$6\frac{3}{8}$	05/29	$116\frac{3}{8}$	$117\frac{1}{8}$	4.18	4.09
$5\frac{3}{8}$	11/29	$110\frac{1}{8}$	$110\frac{7}{8}$	4.08	3.99
$4\frac{7}{8}$	06/30	107	$107\frac{3}{4}$	4.01	3.92

EXHIBIT 9.5 Quoting and trading conventions for HY corporate bonds. Hypothetical Bloomberg screenshot.

The IG and HY dealer runs may create the illusion of liquidity in corporate bond markets. It is useful to remember the staggering differences in actual liquidity across bond and stock markets. For example, the largest 50 stocks in the SP500 index trade more than 50,000 times per day, whereas the largest 50 IG or HY corporate issuers may trade around 20 times per day.[1] These trades are also vastly different across stock and bond markets. The typical stock trade is for less than $20,000 USD and the typical IG or HY bond trade is closer to $2 million USD.[2] Corporate bonds trade at a much lower frequency, but when they do trade in traditional over-the-counter markets the trade size is much larger. There are significantly more corporate bonds to choose from for a given corporate issuer, and each bond has a small market capitalization relative to the total equity market capitalization of the issuer (for public issuers).

To help complete the picture of the typical liquidity profile of corporate bonds, Exhibit 9.6 includes screenshots from the "QMGR" feature in Bloomberg for two high-yield-rated corporate bonds (CHTR as an example of a more liquid bond and HCC as an example of a less liquid bond) filtering on only the most recent quote from each dealer.

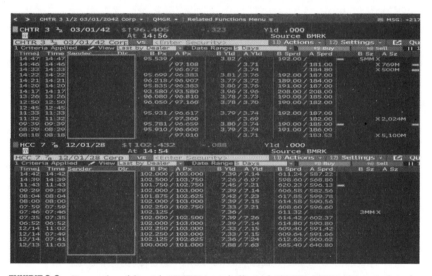

EXHIBIT 9.6 Example of liquid (CHTR) and illiquid (HCC) HY corporate bonds. Hypothetical Bloomberg screenshot.

---

[1]*Source*: SIFMA, TRACE.
[2]Ibid.

Again, it should be immediately clear the vast difference in liquidity across these two corporate bonds. CHTR has multiple dealers willing to make markets in the 2042 bond with these indicative quotes closely aligned in calendar time and bid–ask space. This CHTR bond has both depth of trading opportunities across many dealers but also relatively tight bid-ask spreads (less than five basis points wide in spread space) and substantial trade sizes (noting that trade sizes are generally smaller in HY markets relative to IG markets). In contrast, although the HCC 2028 bond is also quoted by multiple dealers, there are fewer indicative quotes, they are less concentrated in time (i.e., less recent), have wider bid–ask spreads (typically more than 20 basis points in spread space), and are for smaller trade sizes (only one indicative quote has a size indication and that is only a one-sided market).

9.2.4 Trading Conventions and Liquidity for Credit Indices

Investment views on the credit market itself (either strategic asset allocation decisions discussed in Chapter 2 or tactical asset allocation decisions discussed in Chapter 3) are typically implemented via credit index derivatives (e.g., CDX contracts for North American corporate issuers, or iTraxx contracts for European corporate issuers, where both are equally weighted default baskets of a predefined set of IG- or HY-rated corporate issuers), ETFs (e.g., JNK or HYG tickers for HY market exposure or LQD ticker for IG market exposure), or total return swaps from banks linked to specific corporate bond indices.

There are trade-offs that must be made in selecting the instrument for market-level investment views. Total return swaps have the advantage that they have very low tracking error relative to the index, but they come at a high cost and heightened counterparty risk. ETFs have the benefit that they trade like a regular stock with exchange traded liquidity and streaming prices. There is an ongoing management fee charge for the ETF (can be as high as 0.5 percent per year). And the returns of the ETF are known to lag the underlying indices, especially for the HY market. The combination of high management fee charges and negative return slippage relative to the underlying index can make an ETF less suitable for strategic asset allocation choices.

Finally, the credit index derivatives (CDX/iTraxx) have the benefit of trading on swap execution facilities (SEFs) that provide ready access for multiple market participants to execute trades from open pricing. The latency of trading for credit index derivatives is very low (i.e., you can trade easily within a minute at relatively large sizes). The main limitation of credit index derivatives is the tracking error relative to corporate bond indices. Asvanunt and Richardson (2017) note the higher risk-adjusted returns from long positions selling protection on CDX and iTraxx contracts relative to long positions in the corresponding corporate cash bond indices. Desclee, Maitra, and Polbennikov (2015) list the many reasons for this return difference including: (i) seniority (CDS indices include only senior unsecured whereas corporate bond indices also include subordinated), (ii) sector composition (CDS indices have lower weights on financial companies for example), (iii) maturity (CDS indices have 5-year maturity, whereas corporate bond indices include bonds between 1- and 30-year maturity), (iv) quality (CDS indices tend to include lower-rated issuers due to a combination of hedging demands for riskier names and less frequent reconstitutions leading to fallen angels staying in the index for longer), and (v) issuer selection (even after controlling for the previous four differences, not all issuers are included in CDS indices). These structural differences could explain the differences in credit-excess returns of CDS indices and corporate bond indices.

In summary, there are a variety of instruments for the investor to choose from to express a market level view on credit sensitive assets. The appropriate instrument will be dependent on the use case. I have found the credit index derivatives to be very useful for beta completion of portfolios due to the ease of trading and extremely low trading costs.

Exhibit 9.7 contains screenshots of the "ALLQ" Bloomberg function for CDX.HY (top) and CDX.IG (bottom) toward the end of 2021. The quotes

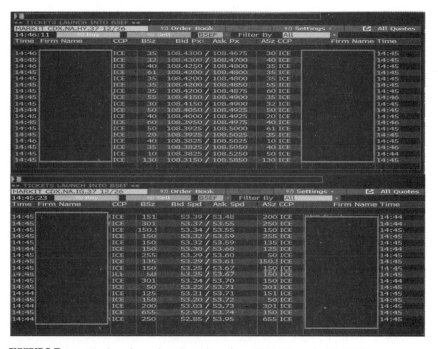

EXHIBIT 9.7 Example of market liquidity for CDX.IG and CDX.HY contracts. Hypothetical Bloomberg screenshots.

here are ordered in terms of pricing competitiveness on the bid and ask side. Notice how in both markets the quotes are all tightly clustered in time (i.e., many dealers are willing to make markets in credit index derivatives), have exceptionally tight bid–ask spreads (less than 1 basis point when aggregating across dealers), and are for very large trade sizes relative to single-name corporate bonds.

A final discussion point on liquidity for credit index derivatives relates to the concentration of liquidity (both trading volumes and open interest) in the 5-year "on-the-run" contract. Every six months a new CDX and iTraxx contract is developed (a committee comprising buy-side and sell-side market participants decides the constituents of the new series). These contracts are offered with different tenors (e.g., 1-year, 3-year, 5-year, 7-year, and 10-year). Therefore, at any point in time there can be many such contracts outstanding. For example, the US HY market will have 10 CDX.HY contracts for the 5-year tenor outstanding and smaller (larger) numbers for CDX.HY contracts with shorter (longer) tenors. Most of the trading volume and open interest is, however, concentrated in the 5-year recent vintage. Older vintages can be of interest to express views on distressed names in an efficient way (e.g., sell or buy protection across vintages to gain exposure to different constituents).

Liquidity in exchange-traded funds (ETFs) is also high relative to the underlying single name corporate bonds. Exhibit 9.8 shows a Bloomberg screenshot for market making in JNK (US HY ETF).

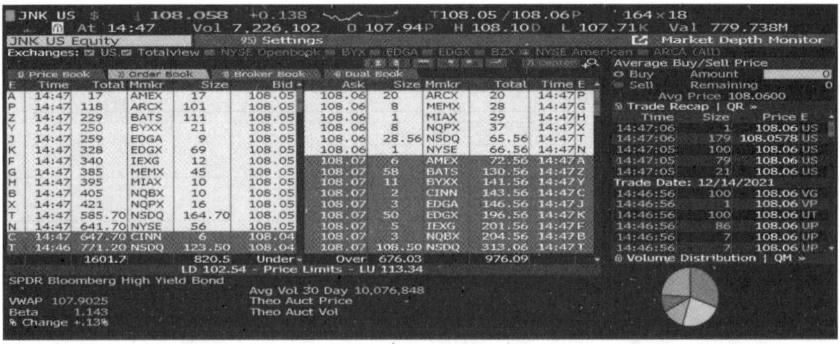

EXHIBIT 9.8 Example of market liquidity for JNK ETF contract. Hypothetical Bloomberg screenshots.

The bid–ask spread of the JNK ETF is very tight (1 cent), and the order book has large sizes potentially executable. Transacting in the ETF market has a primary and secondary component. Exhibit 9.8 shows pricing in the secondary market where you can buy/sell the ETF itself, which gives exposure to a broad set of securities designed to track the underlying corporate bond index (Bloomberg High Yield Very Liquid index in the case of JNK). There is also a primary market where the ETF security is created and redeemed. Each day there is an agreed upon basket of corporate bonds that, if presented to an authorized participant, can be converted to an ETF unit. Likewise, an ETF unit can be converted to a basket of underlying corporate bonds. For active credit managers, the create-and-redeem process can be an effective way to trade into and out of a portfolio of corporate bonds. Of course, there is the potential for adverse selection in the create-and- redeem process, and that could be one reason why the ETFs tend to lag the performance of the underlying bond indices. However, a benefit of ETFs relative to total return swaps is the perpetual nature of the ETF. You do not need to roll the contract, thereby removing uncertainty about future pricing and sizing.

9.3 ELECTRONIFICATION OF TRADING FOR CREDIT-SENSITIVE ASSETS

Exhibit 9.9 is an excellent way to summarize the vast differences in trading protocols and use of electronic platforms for trading fixed income securities.

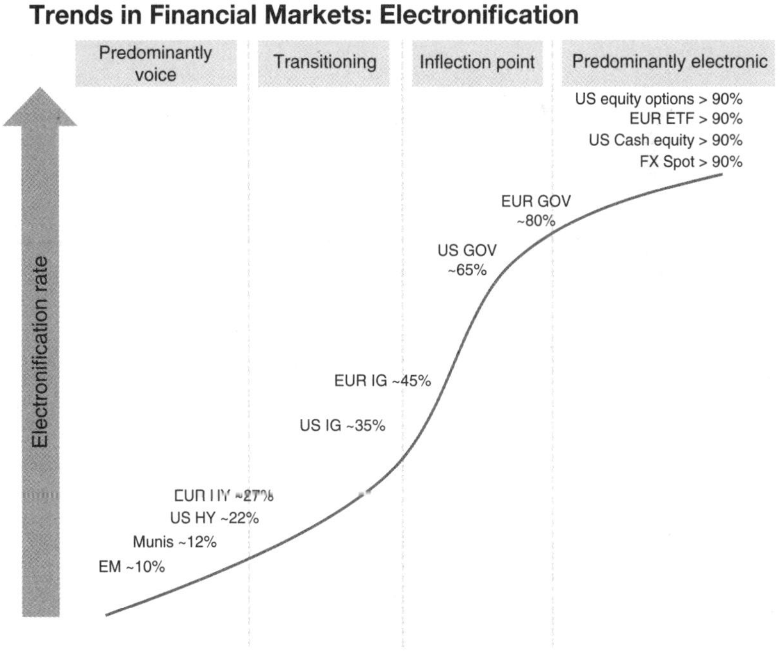

Trends in Financial Markets: Electronification

EXHIBIT 9.9 Differences in electronic trading across asset classes.
Source: MarketAxess, Flow Traders Data 2021.

The bottom left covers municipal bonds, emerging-market bonds, and risky HY corporate bonds, which we have already seen, have limited liquidity, and are characterized by bilateral, noncleared, voice-based trading activity. The secondary (and primary) markets for corporate bonds have, for a long time, been heavily intermediated by the broker-dealer community but are slowly transitioning to greater use of electronic trading protocols. Moving to the far right of Exhibit 9.9 are government bonds and equity and currency markets, which are essentially all exchange traded instruments. The credit index derivatives we discussed in the previous section could also be placed to the right of this exhibit.

The last few years have seen considerable disruption in primary and secondary market trading with a push toward electronic platforms. While corporate bond trading may never end up with the latent liquidity of stock markets, due to the idiosyncratic nature of corporate bond issuance and large number of highly substitutable bonds, there is still a lot that can be done to further improve pre- and post-trade price transparency and develop true market access for a broad set of participants.

Greenwich Associates (2021) notes that as of December 2020 38 (27) percent of US IG (HY) corporate bond trading volumes were executed on electronic platforms. These percentages are drawn from survey data, because there is still not yet a great, centralized data source for electronic trading. These percentages have been increasing significantly over the past five years. By way of comparison electronic trading for US interest rate markets is around 65 percent.

How many electronic trading platforms exist? The primary platforms are Bloomberg, MarketAxess, TradeWeb, TruMid, and LiquidNet. Most of the market share is concentrated in Bloomberg for European corporate bonds (60–70 percent over the past two years) and MarketAxess for North American corporate bonds (around 80 percent over the past two years).

What trading protocols are used on the electronic platforms, and how do these protocols differ from regular over-the-counter trading? A fully developed electronic market would contain a central limit order book (CLOB) in which all market participants are able to enter their desired limit orders (i.e., a buy or sell order at a specific price or better), and the exchange would aggregate that information. A CLOB could also show sizes, thereby aggregating information on bid–ask spread and market depth. Electronic platforms for trading corporate bonds are generally not yet CLOBs. Greenwich Associates (2021) notes that trading protocols include, in descending order of executed trading volumes in the US IG corporate bond markets: (i) 51 percent for anonymous RFQs (request for quote), (ii) 20 percent for disclosed RFQs, (iii) 10 percent for auctions, (iv) 8 percent for CLOBs, (v) 7 percent for portfolio trading, and (vi) 4 percent for streaming. Dealer to client disclosed RFQs is the original protocol for corporate bond e-trading and is still the major protocol, but more avenues are developing. Portfolio trades allow for sets of corporate bonds to be bought or sold as a package that can help with immediacy and reduce time commitment to source quotes/sizes for individual bonds.

Electronic trading has the potential to be a boon for systematic investors. Your ability to form views on the entire set of individual corporate bonds can make you an excellent liquidity provider in the various electronic markets. Rather than trading your portfolio at a discrete interval (e.g., every month) you may be able to stand ready and respond to liquidity takers who express their needs via RFQs or limit orders, allocating your turnover more continuously through time.

What about single-name CDS contracts? This market has evolved a lot more quickly in part because of the standardized nature of the contract (one security for the reference entity and market acceptance for liquidity at the five-year tenor at senior unsecured level). Single-name CDS contracts are centrally cleared removing counterparty risk and greatly facilitating liquidity (Intercontinental Exchange (ICE) clears virtually all US single-name CDS contracts and about 90 percent for Europe). The Depository Trust & Clearing Corporation (DTCC) provides regular data updates on the trading volumes and open interest of CDS contracts, making it easier to monitor liquidity. Interestingly, and perhaps because of the concentrated nature of liquidity, systematic strategies are thought to account for as much as 25 percent of single name CDS trading volumes. The majority of single name CDS trading remains voice based, as opposed to the growth in e-trading seen for corporate bonds.

9.4 PRIMARY MARKETS – LIQUIDITY PROVISION

9.4.1 The New Issue Concession

As was discussed in Chapter 4, corporations are continually issuing debt to maintain the financing needs of their operating and investing activity. As old bonds mature, new bonds need to be issued to take their place. When bonds are newly issued, they do not enter indices until the month after their issuance. This creates a liquidity provision opportunity for asset owners who can participate in the primary market and collect what is known as the "new issue concession" (see e.g., chapter 7 in Ben Dor, Desclee, Dynkin, Hyman, and Polbennikov 2021).

It can be difficult to source reliable data on the existence, magnitude, and persistence of this new issue concession. Access to new issue data and the new issue market is heavily relationship dependent and attempts to measure the new issue concession are model dependent. For example, what do you compare the spread of the new bond to for measuring the concession? Is it the most recently issued bond by the same issuer? What if they differ in terms of maturity or seniority? What if the issuer has not issued a bond for a long time?

One way to quantify the new issue concession is to track daily price changes of the corporate bond using data from multiple data sources over the month before the bond is added to an index. Pricing sources could include trades printed on TRACE, dealer runs as captured by Bloomberg or Markit, or pricing data directly from Bloomberg, Reuters, or IDC. Daily beta-adjusted credit excess returns can be computed from these daily prices. Exhibit 9.10 shows the average returns for US IG and US HY bonds that were newly issued over the 2016–2020 period. The average return on the first couple of days is about 0.25 (0.85) percent for IG (HY) bonds, respectively. Returns are positive for 72 (86) percent of the roughly 5,500 (1,200) new issues in the US IG (HY) corporate bond markets, respectively. This investment opportunity is not trivial. For example, new issues in the US IG market over the 2016–2020 period account for about $1 trillion USD of corporate bonds (annually).

So which new issues should a systematic investor participate in? One approach is simply to try to participate in all new issues and capture the short-term concession. This would require selling the new issue back into the market in the days following issuance. Although feasible, this would require a cash allocation from the overall portfolio, participation rates may be too low to turn the dial, and there is a risk of adverse selection where you receive small allocations on performing deals and larger allocations on struggling deals. An alternative approach might be to limit your participation only to those bonds (or issuers) that meet your regular liquidity thresholds and for which your view on that new issue is sufficiently attractive. In so doing, you can focus your interest in the primary market and may be able to be a better counterparty to the underwriters by helping to support certain deals.

A variety of refinements could be applied to primary market participation. Although there is an attractive on-average positive return for new issues, this is not guaranteed. The magnitude of the new issue concession should be a function of net demand from primary market participants, so when net demand is expected to be lower you may expect a higher new issue concession. However, your focus should not be simply on the one- to two-day return around the new issue date, especially for investors that hold the new issues past the seasoning period. Such investors face an adverse selection risk, and attempts to mitigate that risk might involve examining relative size of issues, use of proceeds, and market/sector sentiment leading into the new issue.

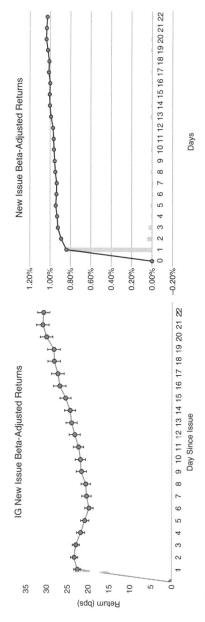

EXHIBIT 9.10 Cumulative returns of corporate bonds in the first month after issuance.
Sources: TRACE, Bloomberg, Reuters.

In summary, awareness of the primary market is important for all active fixed income investors. For systematic fixed income investors, this can be a particularly useful venue to gain exposure to attractive corporate bonds. Not only may there be a concession to capture from participation, there are two other benefits. First, you can transact at the new issue price thereby avoiding the need to cross any bid–ask spread. Second, as a systematic investor, you may be able to communicate the nature of your investment horizon (i.e., the horizon of your expected returns is typically measured in months), and thereby credibly communicate to the underwriting desk that you are not a "flipper." If successful, this may translate into higher participation rates in the primary market.

9.4.2 Primary Market Mechanics

The primary market for corporate bonds remains a predominantly heavily intermediated and compressed market. By that I mean (i) a small number of broker-dealers account for the majority of underwriting services for corporate entities (Bloomberg notes that during 2021, of the 151 credit managers underwriting US IG corporate bond primary market issuance, the top five dealers accounted for 49.3 percent of the $1.5 trillion USD issued, and the concentration is only slightly smaller for the US HY market with the top five dealers accounting for 31.7 percent of the $0.52 trillion USD issued), and (ii) your interest in participation needs to be decided and communicated in a very short time period. Exhibit 9.11 shows a stylized timeline for the new issue market.

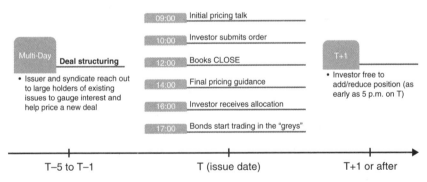

EXHIBIT 9.11 Timeline for primary markets.

At the start of the process, the corporate issuer coordinates with the underwriting syndicate to ensure sufficient appetite for the desired fund raising and associated terms (maturity, coupon, use of proceeds etc.). This happens in the days leading up to the issue date. On the issue date, an investor needs to submit an order based on initial pricing talk. Final pricing and allocations are not decided until after the full demand is revealed from primary market participants. Investors find out their allocation late on the issue date and can sell those bonds back into the secondary markets (as early as late on the day of issue). There is typically a lot of secondary-market trading activity in the one to two days surrounding the new issue date, but that quickly drops off to more normal levels.

The European IG primary market is a little different from the US, primarily due to the nature of corporate bonds at time of issue (Reg S bearer bond status) and the heavy retail participation (unlike an almost exclusive institutional participation in the United States). United States securities laws prevent US investors from participating in the sale of Reg S bearer bonds, which can limit primary market participation for an investor or asset owner if they don't have a presence in Europe.

Successful primary market participation has at least two key ingredients. The first ingredient is sufficient scale. You need to be large enough for the syndicate desks to make the effort to include you in pricing and allocation discussions. Scale can also encompass breadth of the investment opportunity set. It helps if you are interested in many corporate issuers, not just a small handful. The second ingredient is credibility. Primary market participation is a repeated game. The investor can monitor returns for the corporate bonds where they participated (relative to similar bonds where they did not) and quantify adverse selection issues. Likewise, the syndicate members will quickly learn of your true intent (flipping or holding). A systematic investing approach operating at scale can be very successful in the primary market.

Electronification is also starting to develop in primary markets. Direct-Books (https://www.directbooks.com/) was founded in 2019 as a consortium of dealers to help optimize the communications process and workflow around the primary issuance of securities. The platform was launched in late 2020 and covers IG primary market issuance across the main developed markets. Most of the large primary market dealers are participating on DirectBooks. The platform allows institutional investors and underwriters involved in primary issuance to coordinate the gathering of information and optimize pricing and allocation decisions. This development of electronification, like what we see elsewhere in corporate bond markets, naturally lends itself to a systematic investment process. If you can form investment views across thousands of corporate entities and bonds, then you are a natural liquidity provider to the primary corporate bond market, and you will make for a reliable partner with the dealer community.

9.5 SECONDARY MARKETS – LIQUIDITY PROVISION

Active investors in fixed income markets, whether they be traditional discretionary or systematic, all want to improve trading execution. This will include avoiding unnecessarily disclosing trade intent (side and size of order) and trying to trade in a liquidity-providing manner. Liquidity provision requires patience and the willing acceptance of opportunity costs by waiting for execution. The electronic platforms that we described earlier in the chapter are all venues in which liquidity provision is possible, especially with trading protocols where you are responding to requests for liquidity.

The traditional systematic investment process suggested by academic research suggests that the investor is a liquidity taker (i.e., your investment process suggests a trade list of buys and sells). The underlying assumption is that all those trades can be executed relatively quickly once the trade list is generated and close to the prices at the time the trade list is generated. If only life was that easy! Such trading would require either a deep two-sided market and/or large aggregate dealer corporate bond inventory to facilitate principal trading. As we have seen earlier in the chapter, it is rare to see deep two-sided markets and dealers currently hold only a small amount of corporate bond inventory. Forcing dealers to act in a principal capacity will be costly. What else can an investor do to become a better liquidity provider? Work with the dealers to be a liquidity provider to them and help them with agency trading.

9.5.1 Axes

We use the term *axes* to cover these liquidity-providing opportunities with the dealer community broadly defined. There can be multiple ways to become informed of dealer positioning (i.e., are they "axed" long or short on a given security). Approaches can include (i) aggregating trades through time to see whether dealers are likely to be net long or short, (ii) aggregating dealer runs through time to see how a dealer is axed, and (iii) engaging directly with dealers to be shown 1→1 or 1→many axes (or indications of interest). Exhibit 9.12 shows hypothetical examples of 1→many axes where

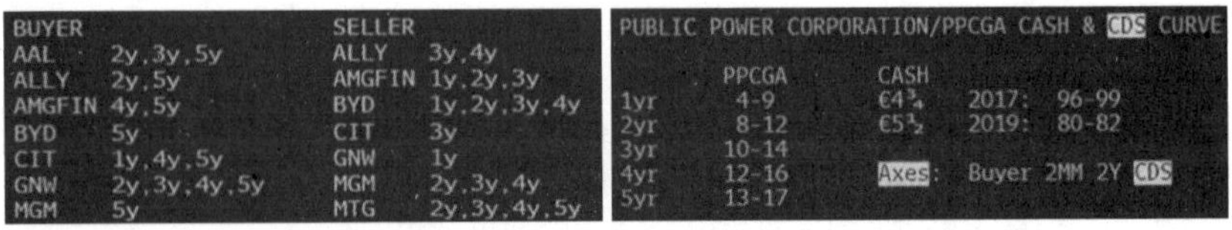

EXHIBIT 9.12 Hypothetical Bloomberg 1→many axes.

dealers communicate broadly their interest in a specific bond, specific issuer, or specific set of bonds.

In both examples of 1→many axes you see only high-level information. Sometimes you see potential sizes (right example in Exhibit 9.12) but not always. These axes are communicated broadly in the market and are a standard way for dealers to solicit orders and show their preference for side of trade. In contrast, 1→1 axes are communicated to a much smaller audience. Although you can never be sure that an axe you are shown has not been shown simultaneously to another market participant, the repeated game nature of trading limits this type of behavior. The axes tend to provide pricing that is inside the prevailing bid–ask spread and are client driven by a liquidity taker (the dealer has another client who needs to buy or sell something). Speed is critical for these opportunities. A systematic process can be uniquely positioned here. The investment process is scalable and is updated frequently so at any point if a buy or sell axe is shown to you it does not take long to decide if the side and size of that axe improves the utility of your portfolio.

An axe participation program can be built by the systematic investor and it brings multiple benefits. First, it will directly lower transaction costs due to trading inside the prevailing bid–ask spread but also by avoiding slippage costs by communicating to the market if you were a liquidity taker. Second, it can improve the alpha capture (i.e., increase the transfer coefficient we discussed in Chapter 8) of your investment process by timelier portfolio turnover. Rather than rebalancing at a discrete interval the portfolio can be continuously rebalanced over the course of the year. Third, it can enhance the capacity of your investment strategy by fully utilizing all available liquidity.

The design of an axe participation program is an entire research undertaking to itself. Just think about the degrees of freedom here. You don't know which axe opportunities will arrive tomorrow, but you do know the marginal gains from participating in buys and sells via improvements to expected returns and/or utility gains that come from relaxing various constraints (e.g., you may prefer to sell a bond with positive expected returns if it relaxes a guideline constraint). These trade-offs are exceptionally difficult to think through but are natural extensions of a systematic investment process.

9.5.2 Electronification of Axes

As with regular corporate bond trading, electronification is moving into the interdealer market and broadening access to axe opportunities. Project Neptune is a data connectivity effort designed to enable real-time connectivity between dealers and investors to increase trade immediacy and volumes.

Initial coverage for this network is quite broad and it is likely to succeed as a liquidity platform. Why? The dealers control access to the underlying data (i.e., the client relationship). Project Neptune can be thought of as an effort to build a moat and protect that valuable data. The dealers can therefore maintain ownership of the client relationships and hence the source of the data (the client's desire for liquidity), and monetize that via selective participation with investors.

9.6 ANCILLARY TOPICS

9.6.1 Sustainable (Labeled) Issuance

A growing area of corporate bond issuance relates to "labeled" bonds. In our next chapter we will explore sustainability broadly for the fixed income asset class. Here, I just want to note the development of labeled corporate bonds that include: (i) green bonds with a stated use of proceeds dedicated to a "green" business activity; (ii) social bonds, typically used to fund eligible projects aimed at underserved and/or underprivileged groups, including projects aimed at providing or improving essential services and basic infrastructure; (iii) sustainability bonds with a stated use of proceeds that covers both green and social purposes; and (iv) sustainability-linked bonds whose coupon is typically linked to a specific environmental or social target. Bank of America (2021) forecasts issuance of labeled bonds of between $650 billion and $750 billion for 2021. This is relative to issuance of $450 billion in 2020, $250 billion in 2019, and around $50 billion in 2016. Although this is clearly a growing area, it is important to note that these bonds are issued by sovereigns, supranationals, government agencies, local authorities, as well as corporate issuers. Exhibit 9.13 (sourced from Bloomberg) shows a rapid growth in "green" bonds (a subset of the broader category of "labeled" bonds).

For example, in November 2021, Ford Motor Co. sold a $2.5 billion corporate bond where the proceeds will be used to "benefit the environment" via zero-emission vehicles and associated infrastructure (Mutua 2021). Such issuance will become more commonplace as corporations globally join pledges for carbon neutrality and other environmental targets. Although green bonds are currently in their own climate-aware indices, expect this to evolve as labeled bonds become increasingly common.

9.6.2 Substitutions

Implicit in most of the discussion in this chapter is the liquidity challenges faced when trading corporate bonds (and single-name CDS). In practice,

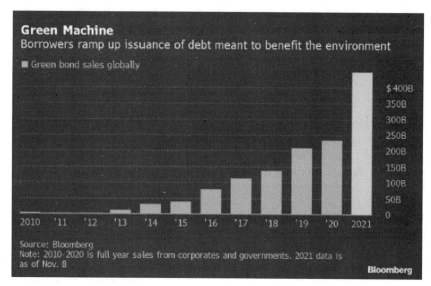

EXHIBIT 9.13 Growth in green bond issuance.
Source: Bloomberg.

despite your best attempts at (i) prefiltering your investment universe to focus on what you think are liquid bonds, and (ii) developing access to a variety of trading protocols and trading venues, you may still be unable to trade. This could be due to lack of quantity (i.e., there is no other side to our trade) or price (i.e. the price at time of trade has moved too far from what you thought the price was when you created the trade list).

What to do in this situation? You must do something unless you wish to become a buy and hold investor by force. One effective approach is to build a systematic process for substitutions. In this way traders become an integral part of the investment process by providing live information on liquidity (prices and quantities) and with a predefined set of rules (e.g., prices move by more than X percent or available quantity is less than Y percent of the original ask) to stop seeking to trade that particular bond and, instead, look for a substitute trade. This means systematically identifying the next-best bond for the portfolio (i.e., the bond that has the next highest marginal utility from trading). This substitute bond may be another bond from the same issuer or a bond from a different issuer. The desired size of the substitute will be different because the risk contribution will differ as you make substitutions (you can think of a DTS ratio as a crude way to adjust the desired trade size for your substituted bond). This is all modeled ex ante in a systematic way. It does not require discretionary trader investment choices at time of trade.

9.6.3 Transaction Cost Analysis

Systematic investors thrive on incorporating data into the investment process. Your skill at trading should be subject to the same level of data analysis as you would undertake for modeling returns and risk. Successful transaction cost analysis requires careful data storage. Ideally, you should have available continuous pricing across your potential trading venues.

A key benefit of measuring the quality of your trade execution is that you then know where to allocate your scarce resources to improve execution. For example, a simple focus only on the executed price relative to the prevailing mid-price immediately before execution may drastically understate trading costs. The concern is the slippage between the time your systematic investment process had decided the trade list and the time your trader executed. Depending on the communication strategy employed for trading, prices may move in the direction of your desired trade if that communication strategy is poor. How might you be able to confirm that?

Exhibit 9.14 shows a stylized example of a trade relative to a variety of prices. This stylized example is exaggerated to make it easy to discuss the different sources of "shortfall" that reduce investor returns. In this Exhibit, shortfall is the difference between the executed price, $P_{EXECUTED}$, and the price at the time the systematic process was completed to generate a trade list, P_{OPT}. This shortfall is comprised of two main components: (i) trading costs (t-costs) measured as the difference between the executed price,

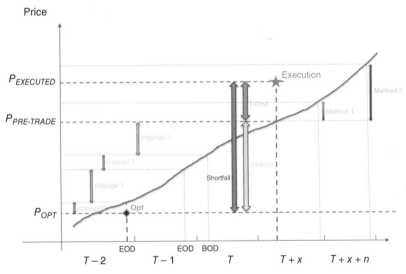

EXHIBIT 9.14   Visualizing of transaction cost analysis (TCA).

$P_{EXECUTED}$, and the prevailing market price immediately before execution, $P_{PRE-TRADE}$, and (ii) slippage measured as the difference between the prevailing market price immediately before execution, $P_{PRE-TRADE}$, and the price at the time the systematic process was completed to generate an optimized trade list, P_{OPT}.

The aim of any investment process is to minimize both slippage and transaction costs. It is critical not to convince yourself you have execution skill only by looking at transaction costs. Shortfall can be large due to communicating your side and size to the market prior to trading (and prices moving against you). But we can examine the sources of slippage in more detail to try to improve the investment process. For example, the initial price at time of optimization, P_{OPT}, may be from one data source and the end-of-day pricing for the portfolio uses a price from a different data source (labeled as Slippage 0). Work with consistent high-quality pricing sources to limit this type of slippage. There may be time required after the systematic investment process is run before the traders receive the list (e.g., data checking, corporate action checking) labeled as Slippage 1 and 2. Working to improve speed of data loading, data checking, and systematizing corporate action checks will shorten the time period between time of optimization and arrival time for the traders. Finally, there is the additional slippage due to the passage of time during which the trader did not immediately execute (labeled as Slippage 3). It is difficult to shorten this time when you want to be a liquidity provider.

Evaluation of trade execution will typically adjust for market movements due to the passage of time (e.g., if the market rallied during a period when you were looking to buy bonds, your shortfall would be large) but beta adjusting can mitigate this affect. What you care about most is mitigating idiosyncratic returns from poor execution.

One final point on transaction cost analysis is what is labeled as "markout" in Exhibit 9.14. Assessing how price moves after our trade can be very useful for at least two reasons. First, if you were a liquidity taker, you would expect some reversal in the price after your trade. Second, if there is adverse selection (either from regular over-the-counter trades or axes), you would see prices move against your trade. This is critical for measuring the success of and managing the axe program.

All these transaction costs can be estimated for individual trades and then aggregated across trades to make assessments on relative trader execution quality, relative counterparty execution quality, and relative trading protocol execution quality. This needs to be a standard component of a successful systematic strategy but will need commitment early on to store the timing of trade information and develop a real-time pricing source. You cannot go back in time and timestamp all steps of the order management and execution process.

REFERENCES

Asvanunt, A., and S. Richardson. (2017). The credit risk premium. *Journal of Fixed Income*, 26, 6–24.

Bank of America. (2021). *ESG in Fixed Income Quarterly*. Q2 2021.

Ben Dor, A., A. Desclee, L. Dynkin, J. Hyman, and S. Polbennikov. (2021). *Systematic Investing in Credit*. Wiley.

Desclee, A., A. Maitra, and S. Polbennikov (2015). Synthetic vs corporate bond indices: Why CDX and iTRaxx have outperformed bond indices. Barclays Quantitative Portfolio Strategy.

Greenwich Associates. (2021). All-to-all trading takes hold in corporate bonds. White paper.

Mutua, C. (2021). Fore breaks green bond record with $2.5 billion debut sale. Bloomberg News (November 8, 2021).

CHAPTER 10

Sustainability

OVERVIEW

How can I write about investing in 2022 and not discuss sustainability? This chapter discusses the measurement of sustainability for the fixed income asset class, with a primary focus on credit-sensitive assets. Systematic investment approaches are naturally suited to the joint challenge of fulfilling the fiduciary obligation to deliver attractive risk-adjusted returns and simultaneously deliver on sustainability objectives. Although the direct investor relevance of measures of sustainability is modest (i.e., measures of sustainability only exhibit weak correlations with measures of credit-excess returns or risk), a systematic investment approach can deliver economically meaningful improvements in sustainability without sacrificing risk-adjusted returns. The reader should note that this chapter is an introduction to sustainable fixed income investing. Sustainable investing can be a book, and course, unto itself.

10.1   INTEREST IN ESG/SUSTAINABILITY

Interest from investors, asset owners, regulators, and the public generally on responsible/sustainable investing has increased enormously over the last decade. Because there is no clear, generally accepted definition of what qualifies as "responsible" or "sustainable" investing, it can be hard to quantify precisely what fraction of assets are managed in a responsible or sustainable manner. One could argue that an asset manager is responsible simply by attempting to generate the highest risk-adjusted returns possible for their asset owners, responsible in the sense of fulfilling their fiduciary duty to the asset owner. But that is not what people generally mean when they talk about "sustainable" or "responsible" investing. As we work through this chapter, measures of sustainability that are potentially relevant from an investor perspective will be covered. Note to reader: for the rest of this chapter I will use the term *sustainable* to span responsible investing and ESG (environmental/social/governance) investing approaches. Before we get into precise measures let's discuss the breadth of interest in this space.

One data point consistent with the drastic increase in sustainable investing is the rising prominence of the United Nations Principles for Responsible Investing (PRI). The PRI was launched in 2006 and was designed to be a proponent for sustainable investing. The PRI has a set of principles that signatories (investors) commit to follow in their investment processes. These commitments (paraphrased) include: (i) incorporating sustainability issues directly into the investment process, (ii) incorporating sustainability issues into ownership policies and decisions, (iii) seeking improved disclosure on sustainability issues from investee entities, and (iv) promoting sustainable investing practices generally. From 2006 to 2020 the signatory base has grown significantly, and as of 2020 around $100 trillion USD of assets are committed to PRI. Sustainable investing is here to stay.

Originally, the focus on sustainable investing was public equity markets, but there are now thousands of sustainable indices tracking public equity and public fixed income markets. The Global Sustainable Investment Alliance (http://www.gsi-alliance.org/) collects data on assets under management that follow sustainable investing practices (covering everything from simple exclusions to fully integrated sustainable investment processes), and as of 2020 they note that $35.3 trillion USD was invested in a sustainable manner representing 35.9 percent of the total assets managed. The interest in sustainability has even led to the development of index futures contracts (across developed equity markets) that are linked to ESG equity indices, and these now have open interest of more than $10 billion USD (as of September, 2021). Although these numbers are very small relative to trading volumes and open interest for regular equity (or fixed income) index futures, the direction of travel from asset owners is increasing demand for broad market exposures that are sustainable.

Let's explore how sustainability is influencing active investment management for fixed income. Given the historical emphasis of sustainable investing on public equity markets, the most natural extension in fixed income is the senior claims in the corporate capital structure (our credit-sensitive assets). Although we will spend most of this chapter discussing sustainable investing for corporates, it is useful to remember the growing interest in sustainable investing at the macro level. This is still very much a nascent area with no agreed upon solutions at present. But we will cover, at least conceptually, the choices that would need to be made and thought through to have a successful sustainable investment process at the country level (e.g., sustainable developed or emerging market country selection).

10.2   SUSTAINABLE INVESTING WITH CREDIT-SENSITIVE ASSETS

This section draws heavily on analysis in Diep, Pomorski, and Richardson (DPR; 2021). DPR conduct two primary sets of empirical analyses. First, they assess the direct investment relevance of sustainability measures for corporate bonds. Second, they examine how sustainability measures can be incorporated in an investment process to help achieve the joint objective of maximizing risk-adjusted returns and a sustainability target.

DPR use data across four distinct categories of corporate bonds: (i) US IG includes all CAD and USD denominated bonds issued by corporate issuers domiciled in developed markets within the ICE/BAML G0BC index, (ii) US HY bonds (ICE/BAML H0A0 index), (iii) European (EU) IG includes all GBP and EUR denominated bonds issued by corporate issuers domiciled in developed markets within the ICE/BAML G0BC index, and (iv) EU HY bonds (ICE/BAML HP00 index). All the bonds they examine are issued by corporations domiciled in developed markets.

For sustainability measures, they use MSCI ESG data, who measure each issuer's ESG score relative to industry peers, from 0 (worst) to 10 (best in class). MSCI ESG data is designed to give users a holistic assessment of companies' ESG risks, leveraging a range of company disclosures (e.g., corporate filings, corporate social responsibility [CSR] reports, etc.) and information from sources not controlled by the company (e.g., news media, government data, etc.). The scores reflect ESG risk exposures based on issuers' business and geographic segments, and reflect if, and how, the issuer manages such underlying ESG risks. There are many third-party data providers of sustainability measures including Sustainalytics, Refinitiv, Reprisk, Truvalue Labs, Vigeo-Eiris, Standard & Poor's, ISS, and MSCI (see e.g., Berg, Koelbel, Pavlova, and Rigobon 2021 for a discussion of consistency in sustainability measurement across these providers). For measures of an issuer's greenhouse gas emissions, expressed in terms of carbon dioxide (CO_2) equivalents, DPR use data from Trucost, focusing on Scope 1 plus Scope 2 emissions. Scope 3 data, while very important in principle, is not currently measured precisely enough for many asset owners to rely upon (see e.g., Callan 2020). The time period examined by DPR is limited to 2012–2020 due to the limited cross-sectional coverage of sustainability measures further back in time.

One important consideration for sustainable investing in corporate bonds is the issue of missing data. Data vendors like MSCI have traditionally serviced equity investors, and naturally their data coverage is better for corporate issuers who also have publicly traded equity. For example, DPR notes that the typical coverage of MSCI ESG data for their US (EU) IG corporate bond universe is about 85 (75) percent on average. This coverage is less than 100 percent for two reasons: (i) MSCI does not compute ESG scores for all public issuers (coverage is excellent for constituents of large cap indices like SP500 or R1000), and (ii) private issuers tend to be less well covered (especially historically). The coverage is lower in the EU, where there is a higher concentration of private issuers. Explicit decisions need to be made for issuers with missing data. For the academic analysis linking measures of sustainability to credit spreads and credit excess returns discussed in the next section, DPR limits the sample to corporate issuers (and their bonds) with nonmissing MSCI ESG data. In practice, active fixed income investors cannot simply ignore issuers with missing data, so an explicit decision needs to be made for these cases of missing data. Treatment of missing sustainability data for portfolio construction is a little more involved and we will discuss that later in this chapter.

10.2.1 Direct Investment Relevance

Let's first explore the ways in which representative measures of sustainability may be useful from an investment perspective. There are two broad ways by which sustainability measures might improve investment performance: (i) improved modeling of expected returns, and (ii) improved modeling of risk. We can assess this investment relevance from an ex ante (i.e., how useful are sustainability measures in explaining cross-sectional variation in credit spreads, which can be viewed as a measure of expected returns but also risk) and an ex post perspective (i.e., how useful are sustainability measures in explaining cross-sectional variation in future credit excess returns and/or the volatility of future credit excess returns). Let's look at the evidence.

DPR start their analysis by exploring whether measures of sustainability help explain cross-sectional variation in (option-adjusted) credit spreads across their four corporate bond universes. They estimate regression equation (10.1) using their full panel of data (the i subscript reflects each bond, and the t subscript reflects each month).

$$Spread_{i,t} = \alpha + \beta_{SUST}SUST_{i,t} + \beta_{PD}PD_{i,t} + \varepsilon_{i,t} \qquad (10.1)$$

$SUST$ is the MSCI industry adjusted sustainability score, and PD is a default probability forecast based on a combination of linear, structural, and machine learning models discussed in Chapter 6 (see e.g., Correia, Richardson, and Tuna 2012 and Correia, Kang, and Richardson 2018 for full details). Exhibit 10.1 is a visualization of the regression results allowing an assessment of both the statistical significance (color of bars) and economic significance (height of bars). There are eight bars corresponding to two sets of four regressions. For each of the four corporate bond universes

(US IG, US HY, EU IG, and EU HY), Equation (10.1) is estimated with and without PD. The specifications without PD give the greatest chance for measures of sustainability to explain credit spreads, but they are naïve specifications, because any active fixed income investor will already have their own internal measure of credit risk (e.g., ratings, default forecasts, etc.). It is more natural to see how measures of sustainability provide incremental explanatory power for credit spreads.

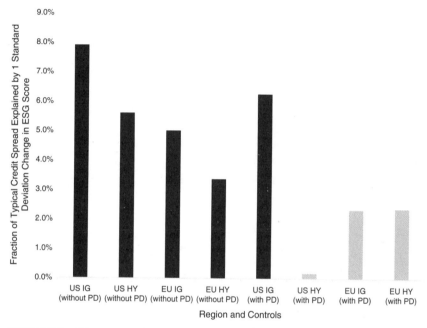

EXHIBIT 10.1 Histogram showing the fraction of variation in credit spreads explained by a one standard deviation change in measures of sustainability. Dark (gray) bars indicate statistical significance (insignificance) at conventional thresholds. The four corporate bond universes are US IG, US HY, EU IG, and EU HY. *Source*: Diep, Pomorski, and Richardson (2021).

When there is no control for measures of credit risk, measures of sustainability are significantly associated with credit spreads (and in the expected direction where corporate issuers with higher sustainability scores have lower credit spreads). The first five bars in Exhibit 10.1 are dark, indicating statistical significance. The height of the bars is, however, small in economic terms. A one standard deviation change in sustainability scores is associated with a 3–8 percent change in credit spreads. Once fundamental measures of credit risk are included (the second set of four bars), the statistical and economic strength of the relation between measures of sustainability and credit spreads is considerably weaker. Only the US IG bar is dark in the last four bars.

A common question that I have heard raised from asset owners is whether the relation between measures of sustainability and credit spreads has become stronger in recent years as investor attention to sustainability has increased. The panel regressions in DPR utilize the full sample of data and mask any temporal patterns. DPR note that across all four universes, with or without controlling for default forecasts, they do not find reliable evidence of a temporal trend in the relation between measures of sustainability and credit spreads. Exhibit 10.2 summarizes these results. Instead of estimating Equation (10.1) over the full sample, it is estimated each month and the monthly β_{SUST} regression coefficient is volatility scaled to allow for comparability through time. There is not a strong temporal trend, but there was a large increase in the negative association between measures of sustainability and credit spreads at the start of the global pandemic (March 2020) for US IG and EU IG. Outside of that spike, there is little to suggest a trend consistent with increasing importance given to sustainability considerations in the determination of credit risk.

EXHIBIT 10.2 Temporal variation in the relation between measures of sustainability and credit spreads. The lines capture the volatility scaled β_{SUST} regression coefficient from estimating Equation (10.1) across the four corporate bond universes (US IG, US HY, EU IG, and EU HY).
Source: Diep, Pomorski, and Richardson (2021).

Another limitation of Equation (10.1) is that it is agnostic to the maturity dimension of credit risk. It is possible that any issues related to sustainability may take considerable time to manifest and impact corporate issuers. Specifically, the relation between measures of sustainability and credit spreads might be more muted for corporate bonds that mature in the near term, but that relation may be stronger for bonds that mature in the longer term. The fact that we have multiple bonds issued by the same corporate issuers provides a powerful setting to examine whether measures of sustainability impact credit spreads differentially based on the duration of that credit risk. DPR discuss unreported results where they estimate Equation (10.2) across their four corporate bond universes (subscripts omitted here for brevity).

$$\frac{Spread_{LONG} - Spread_{SHORT}}{Maturity_{LONG} - Maturity_{SHORT}} = \alpha + \beta_{SUST}SUST + \varepsilon \qquad (10.2)$$

For each corporate issuer that has at least two bonds outstanding, DPR select the bond with the longest remaining time to maturity (call that the *LONG* bond). DPR then select another bond with the same seniority as the *LONG* bond but with the shortest remaining time to maturity (call that the *SHORT* bond). You can then compute the difference in spreads across the two bonds ($Spread_{LONG} - Spread_{SHORT}$). To ensure comparability in pairs of bonds across issuers, this spread difference needs to be scaled by the difference in remaining time to maturity across the two bonds ($Maturity_{LONG} - Maturity_{SHORT}$). The dependent variable in Equation (10.2) captures the slope of the corporate issuer's credit curve. If measures of sustainability matter more for longer-dated corporate bonds, you would expect to see $\beta_{SUST} < 0$ (i.e., corporate issuers with higher sustainability scores should have lower longer-term credit spreads and hence flatter credit-term structure). DPR estimate Equation (10.2) for each of their four corporate bond universes and only find a significant negative relation for the US IG universe, suggesting there is some evidence that the relation between measures of ESG and credit risk is attributable to longer-term risks.

The empirical relation between measures of sustainability and future credit excess returns can be estimated by Equation (10.3).

$$\frac{XS\_RETURNS_{i,t+1}^{Beta-Adjusted}}{DTS_{i,t}} = \alpha + \beta_{SUST}SUST_{i,t} + \beta_{ER}ER_{i,t} + \varepsilon_{i,t} \qquad (10.3)$$

The dependent variable in Equation (10.3) is beta adjusted *DTS* scaled 1-month ahead of credit-excess returns. Yes, a bit of a tongue twister. The dependent variable is a measure of risk-adjusted idiosyncratic returns. The beta is estimated using historical returns between the issuer and the respective corporate bond universe. The *DTS* deflation is to mitigate issues of heteroskedasticity and facilitates better comparison across issuers that vary in risk terms (as discussed in Chapter 6, the product of spread duration and spread, DTS, is a useful heuristic for risk, Ben Dor et al. 2007). DPR estimate Equation (10.3) separately for each of their four corporate bond universes with and without controlling for expected returns, ER. The ER is based on the full set of systematic signals described in Chapter 6.

Exhibit 10.3 shows the test statistics for the β_{SUST} regression coefficient across the eight regression specifications (four corporate bond universes, with and without ER). The relation between credit-excess returns and sustainability measures is virtually nonexistent (all bars are gray scaled, and test statistics are far from conventional thresholds of significance). This inference is true whether we include ex ante forecasts of expected returns or not.

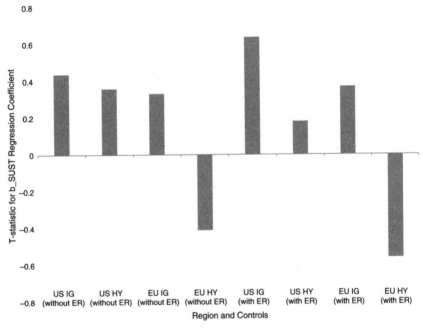

EXHIBIT 10.3   Histogram showing the statistical significance of measures of sustainability in explaining future beta adjusted credit-excess returns. Dark (gray) bars indicate statistical significance (insignificance) at conventional thresholds. The four corporate bond universes are US IG, US HY, EU IG, and EU HY.
Source: Diep, Pomorski, and Richardson (2021).

The final empirical assessment of the direct investment relevance of sustainability measures for credit investors in DPR is the assessment of return volatility (ex post risk). Equation (10.4) is estimated for each of the four corporate bond universes.

$$\sigma_{\beta-adj\ XS-RET_{i,t+12}} = \alpha + \beta_{SUST}SUST_{i,t} + \beta_{DTS}DTS_{i,t}$$
$$+ \beta_{RISK}\sigma_{\beta-adj\ XS-RET_{i,t-12}} + \varepsilon \qquad (10.4)$$

The dependent variable in Equation (10.4) is the volatility of beta adjusted credit-excess returns (estimated at the issuer level by averaging credit-excess returns across bonds linked to the issuer). These returns are not *DTS* scaled, because that would be using future information (i.e., the return for each month is scaled by *DTS* at the start of that month). Instead, DPR add *DTS* as an explanatory variable (which is measured at the start of the 12-month period over which volatility is estimated, so there is no look-ahead bias). Except for EU HY, measures of sustainability are consistently negatively associated with the volatility of future idiosyncratic credit-excess returns. Even after controlling for lagged volatility and *DTS*, there is still reliable evidence of measures of sustainability helping to explain variation in the volatility of future idiosyncratic credit excess returns. Exhibit 10.5 provides an assessment of both the statistical significance (color of bars) and economic significance (height of bars).

Although most of the bars are black (statistically significant as per Exhibit 10.4), the height of the bars is, however, small in economic terms. A one-standard-deviation change in sustainability scores is associated

EXHIBIT 10.4 Regression results of Equation (10.4). The four corporate bond universes are US IG, US HY, EU IG, and EU HY. Regression coefficients are reported above italicized test statistics.

	US IG		US HY		EU IG		EU HY	
	I	**II**	**I**	**II**	**I**	**II**	**I**	**II**
α	0.0294	0.0069	0.0994	−0.0076	0.0232	0.0071	0.0665	0.0071
	23.27	*6.07*	*15.63*	*−1.23*	*15.29*	*5.58*	*7.16*	*1.14*
β_{SUST}	−0.0008	−0.0003	−0.0059	−0.0019	−0.0009	−0.0003	−0.0021	−0.0006
	−3.69	*−2.08*	*−4.49*	*−2.47*	*−4.19*	*−2.26*	*−1.48*	*−0.59*
β_{DTS}		0.1151		0.4620		0.0726		0.1948
		14.40		*10.49*		*8.80*		*4.72*
β_{RISK}		0.4086		0.3396		0.4038		0.5290
		7.34		*5.05*	·	*7.80*		*4.66*
R^2	30.0%	48.7%	11.2%	38.1%	14.9%	37.3%	11.7%	36.8%

Source: Diep, Pomorski, and Richardson (2021).

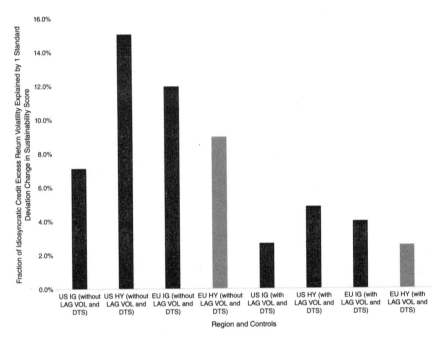

EXHIBIT 10.5 Histogram showing the fraction of variation in credit spreads explained by a one standard deviation change in measures of sustainability. Dark (gray) bars indicate statistical significance (insignificance) at conventional thresholds. The four corporate bond universes are US IG, US HY, EU IG, and EU HY.
Source: Diep, Pomorski, and Richardson (2021).

with a 7 to 15 percent change in future idiosyncratic credit excess return volatility (relative to the average level of volatility in the respective corporate bond universe). Once measures of credit risk are also included (the rightmost set of four bars), the economic strength of the relation between measures of sustainability and credit spreads is considerably weaker. A one-standard-deviation change in sustainability scores is associated with a 2 to 5 percent change in future idiosyncratic credit excess return volatility (again, relative to the average level of volatility in the respective corporate bond universe).

It is important to emphasize the optimistic take-away in DPR. Although the set of empirical evidence linking measures of sustainability to (i) credit spreads, (ii) credit spread term structure, (iii) future credit excess returns, and (iv) future idiosyncratic credit excess return volatility, was generally modest, this does not necessarily mean that sustainability is not of direct use to investors and asset owners. The empirical analysis is limited by (i) sample period (2012–2020), (ii) breadth of measures (only one third-party commercial provider was examined), and (iii) context (aggregate measures of sustainability were examined across all corporate issuers). It is possible with different time periods, different data sets, and more tailored measures of sustainability relevant for each corporate issuer that the inferences might be different. But caution is needed; do not exhaust all possible measures and samples looking for a result and then claim victory. For the true systematic investor, that is called in-sample data mining, and such behavior is a cardinal sin.

10.2.2 Incorporating Sustainability Awareness into the Portfolio

The second, and more commercially relevant, part of DPR is the analysis of how awareness of sustainability can be incorporated into a systematic investment process. Think of the scale of the investment challenge here. The investor is still trying to achieve the best risk-adjusted returns possible utilizing the full breadth and depth of signals discussed in Chapter 6 and all the portfolio construction choices discussed in Chapters 8 and 9. Now you are asking the investor to also consider multiple aspects of sustainability when building the portfolio. How an individual following a traditional discretionary process can adequately handle the various trade-offs here is beyond my understanding. I think systematic investment processes generally are uniquely suited to solving the joint challenge of maximizing risk-adjusted returns in a liquidity challenged asset class while achieving multiple sustainability targets. Also note that the original portfolio that maximizes risk-adjusted returns should already include any measure of sustainability that the investor is convinced, both conceptually and empirically, improves the portfolio (e.g., Fitzgibbons, Pedersen, and Pomorski 2021).

What are the dimensions of sustainability that could be incorporated into a systematic investment process? DPR examine the following dimensions. First, DPR incorporate static screens to remove issuers whose business models cover controversial weapons, fossil fuels, and tobacco. Second, they incorporate tactical/dynamic screens that exclude the *worst* corporate issuers from a sustainability perspective (defined as belonging to the bottom 10 percent of MSCI scores). Third, they explicitly tilt the portfolio to achieve an overall sustainability score that is 10 percent better than the benchmark. Fourth, they ensure that the final portfolio always has a carbon intensity that is at least 25 percent below that of the benchmark. Their analysis looks at a global high-yield benchmark (ICE/BAML Developed Markets High Yield Index, ticker: HYDM). The approach has equal efficacy in IG corporate bond markets as well.

There are two sets of exclusions (static in the case of business models and tactical in terms of relative sustainability scores) in this sustainable portfolio. The static exclusions remove corporate issuers in (i) tobacco (defined as corporations with more than 5 percent of revenue generated from tobacco), (ii) controversial weapons (defined as corporations involved in the production of, or key components to, or generating revenue from controversial weapons including cluster munitions, landmines, chemical and biological weapons), and (iii) fossil fuels (defined as corporations with any fossil fuel reserves or deriving more than 10 percent of their revenue from either thermal coal or oil sands). The tactical exclusion removes corporate issuers who have industry-adjusted sustainability scores in the bottom 10 percent of the region (i.e., US and EU separately). This exclusion requires a nonmissing sustainability score to be available from MSCI. They retain issuers that do not have a sustainability score from MSCI. This is equivalent to assuming the issuer is "average" relative to its peer group. In the absence of issuer-specific sustainability information, it is difficult to justify any alternative treatment.

Both the static and tactical exclusions reduce investment breadth. DPR note that the combined impact on breadth for the US (EU) HY universe is a loss of 18.1 (12.8) percent of market capitalization and a loss of 11 (7) percent of corporate issuers. The exclusions do not make a portfolio solution unfeasible; there are still enough liquid issuers across sectors to engage in security selection.

The tilting of the portfolio toward a higher sustainability score relative to the benchmark also involves a choice for missing data. In this case, DPR do not reward corporate issuers with missing sustainability scores. So, the tilting can only be operationalized for those corporate issuers with available sustainability scores.

The carbon awareness screen involves many choices. DPR consider only Scope 1 and Scope 2 carbon emissions. These emissions are measured relative to the revenue of the corporate issuer (what is called carbon intensity). An imputation method is used for corporate issuers with missing data from TruCost; DPR use the average carbon intensity for all companies with available data in the same industry group. Alternative choices could be made here including (i) approaches to estimate Scope 3 carbon emission from knowledge of the customers and suppliers of each corporate entity, and (ii) scaling carbon emissions by a measure of enterprise value rather than sales to ensure a complete allocation of carbon emissions across all capital providers to the corporation (this measure is not widely used but is starting to gain traction in Europe).

What is the impact of the tactical sustainability exclusions, sustainability tilts, and carbon reduction? How should the thresholds be set for each of these portfolio constraints? Given all of these sustainability constraints move the portfolio away from the original optimal solution (remember the original portfolio already includes any measure of sustainability the investor has both conceptual and empirical support for improved risk-adjusted returns), the rational expectation for adding these constraints is a reduction in expected returns. Exhibit 10.6 illustrates the extent of this expected return reduction.

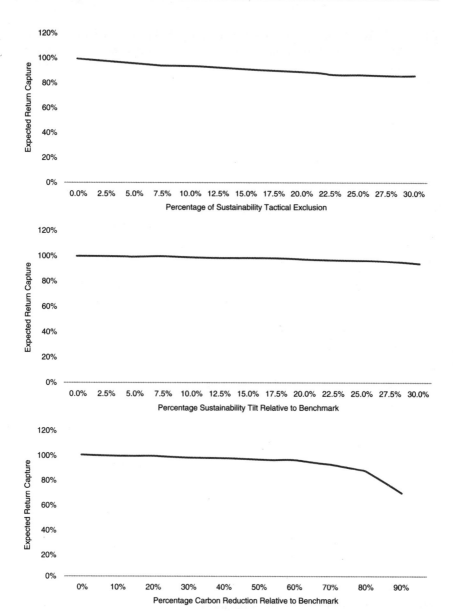

EXHIBIT 10.6 Reduction in portfolio level expected returns from increasing sustainability awareness across (i) tactical exclusions, (ii) sustainability tilts, and (iii) carbon intensity reduction. Zero percent corresponds to the base case systematic global HY portfolio that ignores these sustainability considerations. A frontier of portfolio-level expected returns is shown for different levels of sustainability awareness.
Source: Diep, Pomorski, and Richardson (2021).

This analysis is all ex ante (i.e., the portfolio level expected return is the sum-product of portfolio weights and expected returns for each corporate issuer in the portfolio). It is not based on realized returns (that may lead to deficient portfolio choices if flows or investor attention to sustainability distort returns in this sample period). The expected returns include the full breadth and depth of systematic measures for credit-sensitive assets covered in Chapter 6.

For both the sustainable tactical exclusion and sustainability tilts, the expected return frontier is downward sloping but relatively flat. That means a meaningful amount of tactical exclusions and tilts is possible. At first glance, this seems too good to be true. It is possible because (i) there are still enough nonexcluded corporate issuers to engage in security selection (and maintain beta exposure across sector, rating, and maturity categories as was discussed in Chapter 8), and (ii) the original portfolio is not seeking out exposure to corporate issuers that score poorly on sustainability measures. The return frontier is not guaranteed to be flat; it will be steeply declining for a portfolio that targeted exposure to those issuers with the lowest sustainability scores or those that operated in controversial lines of business.

The expected return frontier for carbon intensity reduction is initially flat and then quickly declines beyond a 70 percent reduction. It is possible to have significant improvements in the carbon emissions profile without meaningfully impacting portfolio returns because carbon intensity (at least measured using Scope 1 and Scope 2 emissions) is currently concentrated in a small number of industries. This inference is not generally true. With a broader measure of carbon emissions and as technology evolves to be less carbon intensive, it may become very difficult to have such large reductions in carbon intensity relative to the benchmark. For this reason, many institutional investor guidelines commit to carbon reduction relative to a fixed level of carbon emissions (e.g., as of 2019 or 2020) rather than the prevailing carbon intensity in the benchmark.

What does a sustainable systematic global HY corporate bond portfolio look like relative to a standard systematic global HY corporate bond portfolio? Exhibit 10.7 shows the cumulative returns for both portfolios relative to the global HY benchmark. Yes, there are three lines in Exhibit 10.7. The return profile (realized not ex ante here) for the regular systematic portfolio and the sustainable systematic portfolio are just very similar to each other. This is not too surprising, as the thresholds for sustainability awareness were selected such that there was not much of an ex ante reduction in portfolio returns. This is no guarantee that integrating sustainability would not affect portfolio returns for different time periods, different sustainability measures, or different thresholds for sustainability awareness.

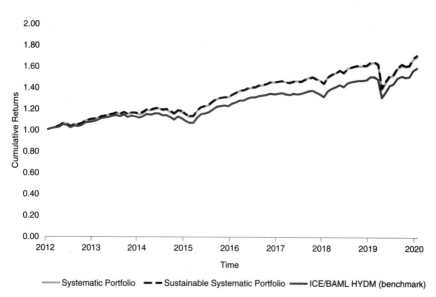

EXHIBIT 10.7 Cumulative performance of sustainable systematic global high yield portfolio, regular systematic global high yield portfolio, and global high yield benchmark (ICE/BAML Global High Yield Developed Markets, ticker: HYDM).
Source: Diep, Pomorski, and Richardson (2021).

DPR also note that the characteristics of the two portfolios (number of bonds, rating breakdown, sector breakdown, maturity breakdown) are all very similar. Overall, the results suggest that the static sustainability exclusions, tactical sustainability exclusions, sustainability tilts, and economically meaningful reductions in carbon intensity can be achieved without sacrificing return potential. This leaves the asset owner with a favorable outcome: although pursuing sustainability objectives in and of themselves may not improve performance, incorporating sustainability awareness, up to a point, may not be detrimental to risk-adjusted returns.

10.2.3 Other Topics

- Are there measures of sustainability that are relevant from an investment perspective?

  There are credible measures of "sustainability" that have both conceptual and empirical evidence supporting their inclusion into an active investment process. These measures tend to fall within the "governance" component of ESG/sustainability. For example, reduced-form measures like aggregate accruals reflect the quality of the senior management team of a company and their strategic use of discretion within the financial reporting system. Corporate issuers with higher levels of aggregate accruals have been shown to experience lower levels of future profitability, more negative analyst revisions, higher risk of earnings restatements and class action lawsuits, and lower future stock returns (see e.g., Sloan 1996; Bradshaw, Richardson, and Sloan 2001; Richardson, Sloan, Soliman, and Tuna 2006). Bhojraj and Swaminathan (2009) demonstrated that corporate-bond credit-excess returns are negatively associated with measures of accruals (i.e., corporate issuers with higher levels of accruals, as a proxy for poorer governance, experience lower future credit-excess returns). Exhibit 10.8 shows this result using a more recent dataset for a combined US and EU IG universe. Corporate issuers with poor governance, as measured by high level of accruals, do experience lower future credit-excess returns. There will be other measures of governance that may improve risk-adjusted returns for active fixed income investors.

■ Distinguishing flows from expected returns.

As discussed in Pedersen, Fitzgibbons, and Pomorski, (2021), the relation between measures of sustainability and expected returns is nuanced. If investors shun securities with poor sustainability attributes, these securities will experience low returns while investors remove these securities from their portfolios. However, going forward those securities may earn a high return as compensation for the relative investor neglect. The dynamics depend on the mix of investor types and their trading decisions. Unfortunately, this can greatly complicate empirical analysis on the relation between sustainability measures and future returns due to the impact of in-sample flows into or out of securities with high or low sustainability scores. Specifically, it may be the case that flows into securities with favorable sustainability scores

EXHIBIT 10.8   Measures of governance and their relation to corporate bond returns. Governance measure is aggregate accruals from Richardson, Sloan, Soliman, and Tuna (2005).
Sources: AQR (2019), ICE/BAML indices.

experience positive returns while that net flow is occurring, but once a new equilibrium of holdings has been reached, those same securities will experience a lower future return. Indeed, this is the exact point made in Pastor, Stambaugh, and Taylor (2021). This is important as it directly affects the potential usefulness of recent empirical studies attempting to show how sustainability measures affect future security returns. This is a challenge for all investors, not just fixed income investors and not just systematic investors.

- Role of labeled bonds

    A discussion of labeled bonds can be found at the end of Chapter 9. In the context of building sustainable corporate bond portfolios the role of labeled bonds is likely to increase going forward. The supply of labeled bonds is growing, and although these bonds are typically not included in the standard corporate bond indices, this may change in the future, and security selection choices within the corporate issuer (labeled vs nonlabeled bonds) may become an additional investment consideration.

10.3 SUSTAINABLE INVESTING WITH RATE-SENSITIVE ASSETS

I close this chapter with a conceptual discussion of integrating sustainability awareness into a government bond portfolio. Why? To date, there is not yet general acceptance on how to (i) operationalize measurement of sustainability at the country level, and (ii) think about trade-offs of tracking error from exclusions and tilts in a very concentrated asset class. As we have discussed in earlier chapters, the universe of corporate bonds contains thousands of issuers, and excluding a small set of corporate issuers based on sustainability considerations does not greatly reduce the effective breadth of the investment opportunity set. However, for government bond portfolios (both developed and emerging markets) there is a far greater concentration in market capitalization and number of bonds among a very small number of sovereign entities. This makes integrating sustainability into government bond portfolios more challenging and more limiting (i.e., it is often not possible to exclude issuers).

10.3.1 What Might Some Measures of Sustainability Be at the Country Level?

Robeco (2021) provides an excellent summary of one approach to incorporate country-level sustainability into macroportfolios. Exhibit 10.9 is

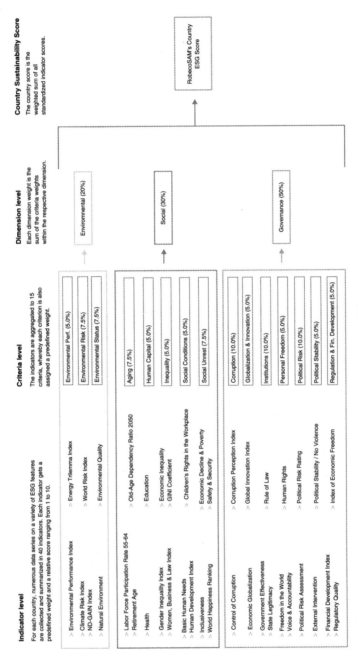

EXHIBIT 10.9 A framework for measuring country-level sustainability.
Source: Robeco (2021).

taken from the Appendix of Robeco (2021) and describes how Robeco thinks of the multiple dimensions of sustainability (environmental, social, and governance). Within each category they have multiple measures with a highly diversified overall country sustainability score. I'm not suggesting the Robeco approach is the best or only approach, but it is a very useful illustration of the breadth of dimensions that may need to be considered (many other asset managers publish white papers describing how they think about sustainability at the country level including PIMCO, AQR, Acadian, JP Morgan, Bridgewater Associates, Schroders, and GMO). There are many differences in the types of data utilized across asset managers and the weights assigned to different dimensions of sustainability across countries. Berg, Koelbel, and Rigobon (2019) have commented on the divergence of sustainability scores across third-party data providers for corporate issuers; the divergence in scores across countries is also likely to be considerable. Exhibit 10.10 shows a global map with a breakdown of current country sustainability scores using the Robeco framework.

Although I am personally happy to see Australia score highly on broad measures of sustainability, it is useful to contrast this with narrower measures of carbon intensity/emissions. How to measure carbon emissions at the country level? Like corporate bonds there is considerable choice here. Most measures will look something like $\frac{Emission}{Scalar}$, where *Emission* could reflect (i) emissions from what is produced in that country (export perspective), (ii) emissions from what is consumed in that country (import perspective), or (iii) a combination of what is produced and what is used in that country (territorial perspective). This latter approach is like the Scope 3 idea for corporates. As with all attempts to measure carbon emission at this aggregate level, there will be double counting. The scalar is designed to adjust for the size of the country (like the carbon intensity measure used for corporates) and could include (i) country level GDP, (ii) population, or (iii) total amount of sovereign debt outstanding. Depending on the scalar chosen (e.g., debt outstanding), Australia can look very poor on country emission criteria. Choices on sustainability measurement can have a very large influence on the final portfolio weights.

10.3.2   What Portfolio Approaches Have Been Adopted for Government Bonds?

There are many approaches taken by asset managers to incorporate sustainability at the country level. In this section, I will discuss one approach used by Bridgewater Associates because it makes use of a different approach

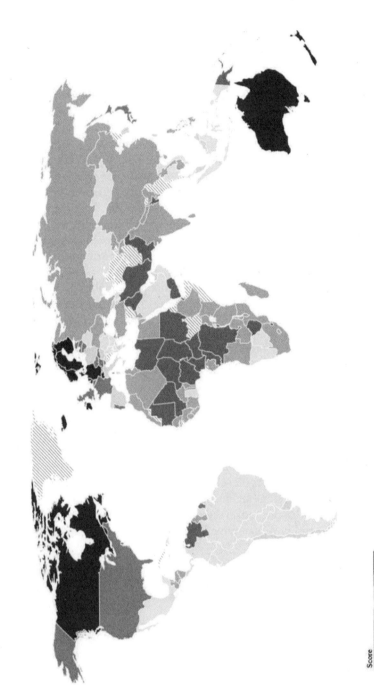

Scores as of April 2021
Score Range from 1 to 10 (best)

Score
0 1 2 3 4 5 6 7 8 9 10

EXHIBIT 10.10 Global map showing country-level sustainability scores.
Source: Robeco (2021).

to incorporate sustainability. Bridgewater Associates is an investment management company located in Westport, Connecticut, that manages about $140 billion USD. They have a well-known strategy called "All Weather" that is designed to harvest risk premium across multiple asset classes, and they have recently launched a sustainable version of All Weather. At the core of this sustainable strategy are the United Nations sustainable development goals. Exhibit 10.11 illustrates the set of 17 sustainable development goals (SDGs).[1]

Integrating sustainability in this way requires (i) identification of SDGs that are relevant for your investment objective (asset owners will have different views on which of the 17 SDGs matter most for them), and (ii) estimating country level sensitivity to those SDGs. This sensitivity needs to be estimated and there is no generally agreed way to do this (examples might include text analysis of company business models rolled up to the country level for country equity investment decisions, or analysis of some of the data sources mentioned in Robeco (2021)).

APG Asset Management, a Dutch entity, responsible for the pension assets of 4.5 million participants covering over €575 billion in assets, are also strong advocates of integrating SDGs into the investment process. As of the start of 2021, APG had around €80 billion of their assets invested consistent with SDGs, with a large focus on SDG7 (clean and affordable energy). Why do I single out APG? They have been developing a rich taxonomy of company-level alignment with investment-relevant SDGs, and this matrix of company-SDG alignment is starting to be utilized in equity portfolios. Going forward, there may be an adoption of common SDG alignment scores both at the corporate and sovereign level. Such movements would help provide structure to the discussion of sustainability. Of course, it may prove too difficult to get general agreement on sustainability, because asset-owner views on which dimensions are important and how they should be weighted might simply be too heterogenous for any common solution to emerge.

10.3.3 Other Topics

■ Screening versus tilting

Although exclusions were feasible in the large corporate bond universes, they are not typically used for government bond portfolios. A typical developed-market bond portfolio (e.g., W0G1 from ICE/BAML) might contain over 1,000 bonds, but those bonds are issued

---

[1] https://sdgs.un.org/goals

EXHIBIT 10.11 United Nations sustainable development goals.

Source: United Nations (https://sdgs.un.org/goals).

by a small number of sovereigns. As of December 31, 2020, the 10 largest sovereign issuers in W0G1 accounted for 95 percent of the total market capitalization of W0G1, and of that the United States and Japan accounted for 63 percent. If your measure of sustainability excluded the United States or Japan, that would *greatly* affect your tracking error relative to a standard developed-market government-bond index. Concentration is also high in emerging-market bond portfolios (e.g., although the JP Morgan EMBIGD index that we covered in Chapter 7 contained 861 bonds as of December 31, 2020, across 87 distinct sovereign issuers, a small number of issuers account for a large share of this index notably Brazil, Mexico, Indonesia, and Turkey). Again, a sustainability criterion that excluded Brazil or Mexico would have an outsized impact on tracking error relative to a standard emerging market government bond index. For this reason, tilting is far more common for sustainable government bond portfolios.

- Developed-market versus emerging-market tilts

A related consideration is how to deal with portfolios that have allocations to both developed and emerging market sovereign bonds. Although typical long-only fixed income allocations separate developed- and emerging-market government bonds, other macrostrategies will typically include allocations to both developed- and emerging-market rate-sensitive assets. In these portfolios, choices need to be made about how to score on the sustainability dimension. There can be drastic differences in sustainability across developed and emerging markets, and comparing across these groups may cause heavy tilts away from emerging markets. At a conceptual level, this may be the correct response if absolute standards of sustainability are important. However, in practice, to moderate the tracking-error impact of screens and tilts, developed- and emerging-market sovereigns are typically evaluated within their respective universes.

- What measures might work?

There are credible measures of "sustainability" that have both conceptual and empirical evidence supporting their inclusion into an active investment process for government bonds. These measures tend to fall within the "quality" or "governance" component of sustainability. For example, Brooks, Richardson, and Xu (2020) note that a credible reduced-form measure of quality for emerging governments is their ability to achieve low and stable levels of inflation. This is a reduced-form measure reflecting the quality of macroeconomic policy of the sovereign entity (a lower level of forecasted inflation is an indicator

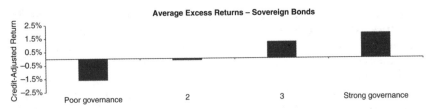

EXHIBIT 10.12 Measures of governance and their relation to government bond returns. The governance measure is the level of inflation and expected level of inflation as used in Brooks, Richardson, and Xu (2020).
Sources: AQR (2019), JP Morgan Indices, Consensus Economics.

of higher-quality macroeconomic risk management by the sovereign). Exhibit 10.12 shows the relation between inflation level and future emerging-government bond credit-excess returns. Emerging sovereigns with higher governance scores (lower levels of inflation) have higher excess returns.

REFERENCES

AQR. (2019). Responsible asset selection: ESG in portfolio decisions. White paper.
Ben Dor, A., Dynkin, L., Hyman, J., Houweling, P., Van Leeuwen, E., and Penniga, O. (2007). DTS (Duration Times Spread). *Journal of Portfolio Management*, 33, 77–100.
Berg, F., J. Koelbel, and R. Rigobon. (2019). Aggregate confusion: The divergence of EGS ratings. Working paper, MIT.
Berg, F., J. Koelbel, A. Pavlova, and R. Rigobon. (2021). ESG confusion and stock returns: Tackling the problem of noise. Working paper, MIT.
Bhojraj, S., and B. Swaminathan. (2009). How does the corporate bond market value capital investment and accruals? *Review of Accounting Studies*, 14, 31–62.
Bradshaw, M., S. Richardson, and R. Sloan. (2001). Do analysts and auditors use information in accruals? *Journal of Accounting Research*, 39, 45–74.
Brooks, J., S. Richardson, and Z. Xu. (2020). (Systematic) investing in emerging market debt. *Journal of Fixed Income*, 30, 44–61.
Callan (2020). Callan 2020 ESG Survey.
Correia, M., S. Richardson, and İ. Tuna. (2012). Value investing in credit markets. *Review of Accounting Studies*, 17, 572–609.
Correia, M., J. Kang, and S. Richardson. (2018) Asset volatility. *Review of Accounting Studies*, 23, 37–94.
Diep, P., L. Pomorski, and S. Richardson. (2021). Sustainable systematic credit. Working paper, AQR.
Pastor, L., R. Stambaugh and L. Taylor. (2021). Dissecting green returns. Working paper, University of Pennsylvania.

Pedersen, L., Fitzgibbons, S., and L. Pomorski. (2021). Responsible investing: The ESG-efficient frontier. *Journal of Financial Economics*, 142, 572–597.

Richardson, S., Sloan, R., Soliman, M., & Tuna, İ. (2005). Accrual reliability, earnings persistence, and stock prices. *Journal of Accounting and Economics*, 39, 437–485.

Richardson, S., Sloan, R., Soliman, M., & Tuna, İ. (2006). The implications of accounting distortions and growth for accruals and profitability. *The Accounting Review*, 81, 713–743.

Robeco. (2021). Country sustainability ranking – summer 2021 update. White paper.

Sloan, R. (1996). Do stock prices fully reflect information in accruals and cash flows about future earnings? *The Accounting Review*, 71, 289–316.

CHAPTER 11

Putting It All Together

OVERVIEW

Our final chapter is a short one. Our journey through the book started with a discussion of the size of fixed income markets and the (currently) small presence of systematic investors in fixed income. Might a systematic approach be successful? The book has introduced the various tools for modeling expected returns, risks, liquidity, and ultimately building portfolios in a systematic manner. A systematic approach could be successful. We also discussed how incumbent fixed income managers have, as a group, beaten their benchmarks, but have done so by leaning into traditional risk premia rather than security selection. In this chapter we will discuss how a well-implemented systematic approach may beat a benchmark and do so not by loading up on traditional market risk premia, but, instead, via security selection opportunities. A well-implemented systematic investment approach can be a powerful diversifier.

11.1   WHAT MIGHT A SUCCESSFUL SYSTEMATIC FIXED INCOME INVESTING PROCESS LOOK LIKE?

Let's examine the return properties of representative systematic fixed income portfolios. We will look at many of the active fixed income categories examined in Chapter 4. These portfolios are hypothetical representations of what might be possible from well-implemented systematic portfolio construction (i.e., putting together everything we have discussed throughout the book). Revisiting the investment cube, this means mastery of the front face of the cube (breadth and depth of measures) and also of critical skills in implementation and portfolio construction. All strategy returns examined in this chapter are gross of any management fees but include estimates of transaction costs.

11.1.1   Investment Grade Corporate

A systematic long-only (benchmark-aware) IG corporate bond portfolio might select a global IG corporate bond index as its benchmark (e.g., Bloomberg Barclays Global Aggregate Corporate Total Return Index or ICE/BAML Global Corporate Bond Index). The systematic portfolio would select a level of active risk (tracking error that we discussed in Chapter 8) to offer investors (e.g., 1.0 percent). The amount of active risk is an investment choice and, as discussed in Chapter 8, it is a function of the volatility of the asset class itself (i.e., lower active risk for asset classes with less volatility) and parameters of your investment process (e.g., maximum position constraints at the issuer level may limit the total risk you are able to generate).

That active risk budget is then "spent" by the systematic investment process. It would include return forecasts spanning the various sources of returns (e.g., carry, defensive, momentum, value, sentiment, and other investment themes) covered in Chapter 6. It would seek to capture return potential in an idiosyncratic way identifying attractive issuers relative to a peer group (e.g., within industry) and attractive issues for a given issuer. The primary objective of the systematic investment process is to maximize the returns for the active risk taken. This is typically done while providing the beta of the benchmark. In the case of a global IG corporate bond portfolio, that beta includes a rate and a spread component across multiple currencies, so beta completion (covered at the end of Chapter 8) becomes an important part of the portfolio construction process. As you buy the most attractive corporate bonds based on your process, you need to keep track of the rate and spread exposure across countries, currencies, rating categories, industries, maturity buckets, etc. If done well, the final portfolio should isolate well-compensated sources of idiosyncratic returns.

So, what might a systematic IG corporate bond portfolio look like? Exhibit 11.1 shows a scatter plot of the excess of benchmark returns for a systematic global IG corporate bond portfolio compared to the credit premium, CP (the same 50%/50% blend of Barclays U.S. High Yield Corporate Bond Index returns in excess of Duration-Matched Treasuries, and S&P Leverage Loan Index in excess of three-month LIBOR used in Chapter 4). This visualizes the following regression:

$$R_{IG\ SYSTEMATIC} = \alpha + \beta_{CP}CP + \varepsilon \qquad (11.1)$$

It is clear there is no positive association between the excess of benchmark returns for the systematic IG corporate bond portfolio and the credit premium. The regression equation is reported in Exhibit 11.1 and the R^2 is

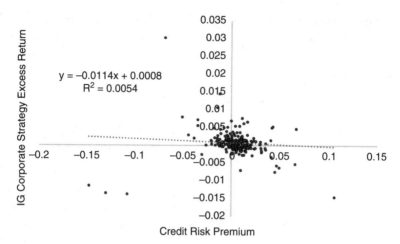

EXHIBIT 11.1   Scatter plot of excess of benchmark returns for a systematic IG corporate bond portfolio against the credit premium (50/50 blend of US HY credit-excess returns and US Loan excess returns).
Sources: ICE/BAML indices, S&P indices, and author calculations. The period examined was 2003–2020.

very low (0.54 percent). The slope coefficient is negative (−0.0114) but not significantly so (t-statistic of −1.08). The (annualized) intercept of 0.0097 and the (annualized) volatility of regression residuals (1.29 percent) suggest an information ratio (IR) of 0.75 for a systematic global IG corporate bond portfolio. If this systematic portfolio was run with an active risk of 100 basis points, this would translate to 75 basis points of alpha (0.75 × 1.0 percent). The IR is similar to the Sharpe ratio (0.71) due to the effort in portfolio construction where (i) all signals were built to be neutral to traditional market risk premia, and (ii) the optimization process, via constraints and completion, helped ensure the final portfolio had the greatest chance to provide alpha instead of beta.

11.1.2   Long Duration IG Corporate

Although this chapter is emphasizing the diversifying potential of systematic investment approaches, it is useful to remember the scalability of systematic investment processes generally. Long duration corporate bond mandates are a classic example. Public and corporate pension plans in North America have an almost insatiable appetite for long duration corporate bond portfolios. Pension plans have a desire to match expected future cash flows on their investments with expected future cash flows on their liabilities. Long-dated corporate bonds issued in USD help fill this demand. It is an easy extension to tailor the global IG corporate bond portfolio to focus on USD long-dated corporate bonds.

What might a systematic long-duration IG corporate bond portfolio look like? A typical long-duration corporate benchmark (e.g., Bloomberg US 10+ Year Corporate Bond Index or ICE/BAML 10+ Year US Corporate Index) will contain a smaller set of corporate issuers. This is because not all IG rated corporate issuers have bonds with more than 10 years of remaining maturity and, for those that do, only their longest bonds are eligible for the long-duration benchmark. That said, there are still over 3,000 bonds in the typical long-duration benchmark, which is more than enough opportunity to engage in security selection. The tracking error (active risk) for a long-duration corporate bond portfolio is typically a little higher than a regular IG corporate bond portfolio (around 1.5 percent).

Exhibit 11.2 shows a scatter plot of the excess of benchmark returns for a systematic long duration IG corporate bond portfolio compared to the credit premium, *CP*. This visualizes the following regression:

$$R_{LONG\ DURATION\ IG\ SYSTEMATIC} = \alpha + \beta_{CP}CP + \varepsilon \qquad (11.2)$$

It is clear there is no positive association between the excess of benchmark returns for the systematic long duration IG corporate bond portfolio

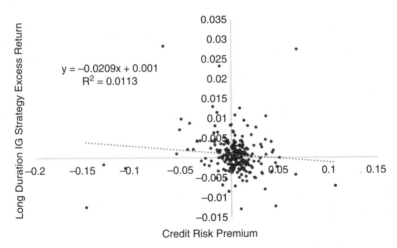

EXHIBIT 11.2   Scatter plot of excess of benchmark returns for a systematic long-duration IG corporate bond portfolio against the credit premium (50/50 blend of US HY credit-excess returns and US Loan excess returns).
Sources: ICE/BAML indices, S&P indices, and author calculations. The period examined was 2000–2020.

and the credit premium. The regression equation is reported in Exhibit 11.2, and the R^2 is very low (1.13 percent) and the slope coefficient is negative (-0.0209) but not significantly so (t-statistic of -1.69). The (annualized) intercept of 0.0118 and the (annualized) volatility of regression residuals (1.61 percent) suggest an information ratio of 0.73 for a systematic long-duration IG corporate bond portfolio. If this systematic portfolio was run with an active risk of 100 basis points this would translate to 110 basis points of alpha (0.73×1.5 percent). Again, the IR is similar to the Sharpe ratio (0.69) due to the effort in portfolio construction where (i) all signals were built to be neutral to traditional market risk premia, and (ii) the optimization process, via constraints and completion, helped ensure the final portfolio had the greatest chance to provide alpha instead of beta.

11.1.3 HY Corporates

A systematic long-only (benchmark-aware) US HY corporate bonds portfolio might select the Bloomberg US Corporate High Yield Index or the ICE/BAML US High Yield Index as its benchmark. The choice of specific benchmark does not really matter and is typically a preference of the asset owner. The indices are typically very highly correlated, and while they do have differences (e.g., minimum face value, liquidity filters, issuer concentration limits, etc.), they are more similar than they are dissimilar. Compared to the IG corporate bond portfolios examined earlier, the amount of active risk for HY corporate bond portfolios tends to be closer to 2 percent.

Exhibit 11.3 shows a scatter plot of the excess of benchmark returns for a systematic US HY corporate bond portfolio compared to the credit premium, *CP*. This visualizes the following regression:

$$R_{HY\ SYSTEMATIC} = \alpha + \beta_{CP}CP + \varepsilon \tag{11.3}$$

There is a small positive association between the excess of benchmark returns for the systematic US HY corporate bond portfolio and the credit premium. The regression equation is reported in Exhibit 11.3. The R^2 is very low (1.26 percent) and, although the slope coefficient is positive (0.0354), it is not significantly so (t-statistic of 1.79). The (annualized) intercept of 0.0226 and the (annualized) volatility of regression residuals (2.58 percent) suggest an information ratio of 0.88 for a systematic US HY corporate bond portfolio. If this systematic portfolio was run with an active risk of 200 basis points, this would translate to 176 basis points of alpha ($0.88 \times 2.0\%$). Again, the information ratio is similar to the Sharpe ratio (0.91) due to the effort in portfolio construction where (i) all signals were built to be neutral to traditional market risk premia, and (ii) the optimization process, via

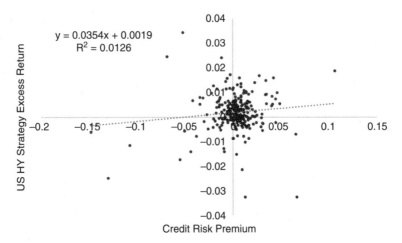

EXHIBIT 11.3 Scatter plot of excess of benchmark returns for a systematic US HY corporate bond portfolio against the credit premium (50/50 blend of US HY credit excess returns and US Loan excess returns).
Sources: ICE/BAML indices, S&P indices, and author calculations. The period examined was 2000–2020.

constraints and completion, helped ensure the final portfolio had the greatest chance to provide alpha instead of beta.

11.1.4 Credit Long/Short

A systematic approach to security selection can also be applied to a broader set of credit-sensitive assets. Long/short implementations of single-name corporate selection can be applied via derivatives (CDS contracts) and cash instruments in developed markets. Aggregate-level credit risk could also be traded outright, as mentioned in Chapter 3. Investment decisions around aggregate credit markets might include views on (i) North American vs. European corporate indices, (ii) IG vs. HY corporate indices, (iii) developed vs. emerging market corporate indices, and (iv) credit curve positioning (e.g., 5-year relative to 10-year exposures). Capital structure approaches could also be applied at the corporate and index level, allowing for additional investment opportunities within the full spectrum of credit-sensitive assets. The amount of *active* risk taken in long/short portfolios is much larger than that for benchmark-aware portfolios (though the total risk of benchmark-aware portfolios may be higher than long/short portfolios). The set of 51 credit long/short funds we examined in Chapter 4 had an average annualized return of 8.66 percent and a corresponding Sharpe ratio of 1.09, suggesting an active risk of around 9 percent for the current credit long/short manager. The systematic credit long/short portfolio that we will examine next will target an active risk of around 6–8 percent annually but importantly will seek to minimize exposure to traditional market risk premia.

What might a systematic credit long/short portfolio look like? Exhibit 11.4 shows a scatter plot of the excess of cash returns for a systematic credit long/short portfolio compared to the credit premium, *CP*. This visualizes the following regression:

$$R_{CLS\ SYSTEMATIC} = \alpha + \beta_{CP}CP + \varepsilon \qquad (11.4)$$

There is a small positive association between the excess of cash returns for the systematic credit long/short portfolio and the credit premium. The regression equation is reported in Exhibit 11.4 and the R^2 is very low (0.93 percent) and, although the slope coefficient is positive (0.0945), it is not significantly so (t-statistic of 1.34). The (annualized) intercept of 0.1069 and the (annualized) volatility of regression residuals (8.44 percent) suggest an information ratio of 1.27 for a systematic credit long/short portfolio. If this systematic portfolio was run with an active risk of 700 basis points, this would translate to 889 basis points of alpha (1.27 × 7.0 percent). The IR is

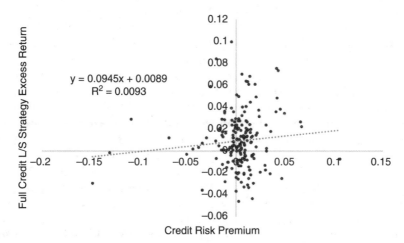

EXHIBIT 11.4 Scatter plot of excess of cash returns for a systematic credit long/short portfolio against the credit premium (50/50 blend of US HY credit excess returns and US Loan excess returns).

Sources: ICE/BAML indices, S&P indices, and author calculations. The period examined was 2004–2020.

similar to the Sharpe ratio (1.30) due to the effort in portfolio construction where (i) all signals were built to be neutral to traditional market risk premia, and (ii) the optimization process, via constraints and completion, helped ensure the final portfolio had the greatest chance to provide alpha instead of beta.

The difference between a systematic credit long/short portfolio and the typical discretionary credit long/short fund examined in Chapter 4 is striking. Although all funds are run at similar levels of risk and are able to generate similar excess of cash returns (i.e., Sharpe ratios are above 1), there is a striking difference in the amount of beta packaged as alpha in this category. More than half of the excess of cash returns for the typical credit long/short fund is attributable to passive beta exposure. A systematic approach, in contrast, preserves its excess of cash returns after controlling for passive exposure to traditional market risk premia.

11.1.5 Emerging Markets

Emerging market fixed income covers a broad set of bonds: (i) local currency bonds issued by emerging sovereign, quasi-sovereign, and corporate issuers, and (ii) hard currency bonds issued by emerging sovereign, quasi-sovereign, and corporate issuers. A systematic approach can be applied to all these bond categories, but our focus here, as it was in Chapter 7, is on hard currency bonds issued by emerging sovereign and quasi-sovereign entities.

Our systematic emerging market hard currency bond portfolio engages in security selection opportunities on both the country and maturity dimensions described in Chapter 7. The portfolio targets about 2 percent active risk (relative to the JP Morgan Emerging Market Global Diversified Index). This amount of risk is lower than the typical discretionary emerging market bond manager (Chapter 4 showed that the typical emerging market bond fund had a Sharpe ratio of 0.29 and average excess of benchmark return of 1.04 percent, suggesting a tracking error of around 3.5 percent).

What might a systematic emerging market bond portfolio look like? Exhibit 11.5 shows a scatter plot of the excess of benchmark returns for the systematic emerging market bond portfolio compared to the credit premium, CP. There is a small positive association between the excess of benchmark returns for the systematic emerging market bond portfolio and the credit premium. The regression equation is reported in Exhibit 11.5. The R^2 is very low (0.12 percent) and, although the slope coefficient is positive (0.0069), it is not significantly so (t-statistic of 0.49). The (annualized) intercept of 0.0171 and the (annualized) volatility of regression residuals (1.68 percent) suggest an information ratio of 1.02 for a systematic emerging market bond portfolio. If this systematic portfolio was run with an active risk of 200 basis

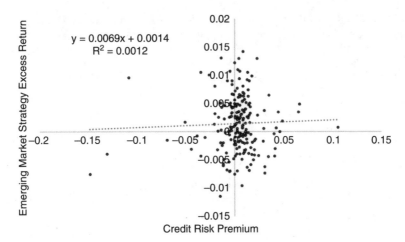

EXHIBIT 11.5 Scatter plot of excess of benchmark returns for a systematic emerging market bond portfolio against the credit premium (50/50 blend of US HY credit excess returns and US Loan excess returns).
Sources: JP Morgan indices, S&P indices, and author calculations. The period examined was 2004–2020.

points, this would translate to 204 basis points of alpha (1.02 × 2.0 percent). The information ratio is similar to the Sharpe ratio (1.03) due to the effort in portfolio construction where (i) all signals were built to be neutral to traditional market risk premia, and (ii) the optimization process, via constraints and completion, helped ensure the final portfolio had the greatest chance to provide alpha instead of beta.

To ensure fairness in the comparison to the set of 117 emerging market bond funds examined in Chapter 4, we can run the same regression specification:

$$R_{EM\ SYSTEMATIC} = \alpha + \beta_{USTP}USTP + \beta_{EMD}EMD$$
$$+ \beta_{EMCORP}EMCORP + \beta_{EMFX}EMFX + \varepsilon \tag{11.5}$$

$R_{EM\ SYSTEMATIC}$ is the monthly excess of benchmark return for the systematic emerging market bond fund, and the right-hand side variables are all as defined in Exhibit 4.3. Exhibit 11.6 summarizes the regression analysis.

The (annualized) intercept from regression (11.5) of 1.63 percent is marginally lower than the simpler analysis controlling only for the credit premium (note that the correlation to the credit premium, ρ_{CP}, is only 0.03). The information ratio, after adjusting for term premium, emerging

EXHIBIT 11.6   Regression analysis for systematic emerging market bond fund. Regression coefficients are reported on top of (italicized) t-statistics.

Active Return	Sharpe Ratio	β_{USTP}	β_{EMD}	β_{EMCORP}	β_{EMFX}	α	IR	ρ_{CP}
1.74%	1.03	0.07	−0.06	0.05	−0.03	1.63%	0.98	0.03
		(2.10)	*(−1.47)*	*(3.19)*	*(−1.19)*	*(13.63)*		

Sources: Bloomberg indices, JP Morgan indices, and author calculations. The period examined was 2004–2020.

premium, emerging credit premium, and emerging currency exposure, is 0.98. A well-implemented systematic emerging market bond portfolio has the potential to be a powerful diversifier.

11.1.6   Global Aggregate and Unconstrained

The final systematic portfolio that we will evaluate in this chapter is one that combines security selection for rate and credit-sensitive assets. We will explore these broad systematic fixed income portfolios in two ways. First, we will examine long-only portfolios that use the Bloomberg Global Aggregate Index. Second, we will examine an alternative investment solution that takes active risk in an unconstrained benchmark agnostic manner. In both cases, the underlying systematic investment process is the same. Security selection for rate-sensitive assets is expressed via country level and maturity views as described in Chapter 5. Security selection for credit-sensitive assets is expressed across and within corporate issuer. Global fixed income portfolios also allow for active currency investment views to be incorporated. Although we have not focused on active currency management in this book, that is a commonly used additional lever for return enhancement on global fixed income portfolios. Finally, the unconstrained version allows for additional sources of return potential including tactical timing of the term and credit premium (as covered in Chapter 3) and extensions into emerging market bonds and HY corporate bonds (the "Plus" categories). The challenge will be whether a systematic approach can avoid the strong tendency of most existing active approaches in the unconstrained category to simply use the breadth enhancement as an excuse for more credit beta exposure. Can the additional breadth be harnessed in such a way to add security selection benefit without doubling down on credit beta?

A systematic Global Aggregate benchmarked portfolio could target about 1.5 percent of active risk, diversifying that active risk budget across credit-sensitive asset security selection, rate-sensitive asset security selection, and possibly active currency management. The systematic unconstrained portfolio (benchmarked to cash) could target a higher level of active risk (e.g., 4–5 percent annualized). This requires use of leverage, derivatives, and shorting to build positions that are large enough to offer attractive idiosyncratic returns. Consequently, a systematic unconstrained portfolio may not be for all asset owners (a levered strategy in the fixed income part of the asset owner's portfolio is not always the easiest sell). Let's examine how successful each portfolio might be.

Exhibit 11.7 shows a scatter plot of the excess of benchmark returns for a systematic Global Aggregate portfolio compared to the credit premium, CP. There is a small positive association between the excess of benchmark returns for the systematic Global Aggregate portfolio and the credit premium. The regression equation is reported in Exhibit 11.7. The R^2 is very low (1.23 percent) and, although the slope coefficient is positive (0.0148), it is not significantly so (t-statistic of 1.63). The (annualized) intercept of 0.0101 and the (annualized) volatility of regression residuals (1.11 percent) suggest an information ratio of 0.91 for a systematic Global Aggregate portfolio. If this systematic portfolio was run with an active risk of 150 basis points, this would translate to 137 basis points of alpha (0.91 × 1.5 percent). The information ratio is similar to the Sharpe ratio (1.03) due to the effort in portfolio construction where (i) all signals were built to be neutral to traditional market risk premia, and (ii) the optimization process, via

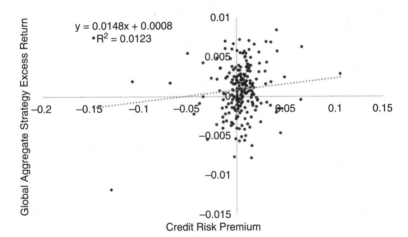

EXHIBIT 11.7 Scatter plot of excess of benchmark returns for a systematic Global Aggregate portfolio against the credit premium (50/50 blend of US HY credit-excess returns and US Loan excess returns).

Sources: ICE/BAML indices, S&P indices, and author calculations. The period examined was 2003–2020.

constraints and completion, helped ensure the final portfolio had the greatest chance to provide alpha instead of beta.

Again, to ensure fairness in the comparison to the set of 94 Global Aggregate funds examined in Chapter 4, we can run the same regression specification:

$$
R_{GAGG\ SYSTEMATIC} = \alpha + \beta_{GTP}GTP + \beta_{CP}CP + \beta_{EMD}EMD
$$
$$
+ \beta_{EMFX}EMFX + \beta_{VOL}VOL + \varepsilon \tag{11.6}
$$

$R_{GAGG\ SYSTEMATIC}$ is the monthly excess of benchmark return for the systematic Global Aggregate strategy, and the right-hand side variables are all as defined in Exhibit 4.3. Exhibit 11.8 summarizes the regression analysis. The (annualized) intercept from regression (11.6) of 0.77 percent is lower than the simpler analysis controlling only for the credit premium (note that the correlation to the credit premium, ρ_{CP}, is 0.11). The information ratio, after adjusting for term premium, credit premium, emerging premium, emerging currency exposure, and the volatility premium is 0.71. A well-implemented systematic Global Aggregate portfolio has the potential to be a powerful diversifier.

EXHIBIT 11.8 Regression analysis for systematic Global Aggregate strategy. Regression coefficients are reported on top of (italicized) t-statistics.

Active Return	Sharpe Ratio	β_{GTP}	β_{CP}	β_{EMD}	β_{EMFX}	β_{VOL}	α	IR	ρ_{CP}
1.07%	0.96	0.07	0.03	−0.01	0.01	0.01	0.77%	0.71	0.11
		(2.36)	*(1.26)*	*(−0.26)*	*(0.13)*	*(0.40)*	*(2.76)*		

Sources: Bloomberg indices, JP Morgan indices, and author calculations. The period examined was 2003–2020.

Exhibit 11.9 shows a scatter plot of the excess of cash returns for a systematic Unconstrained Bond portfolio compared to the credit premium, CP. There is a positive association between the excess of cash returns for the systematic Unconstrained Bond portfolio and the credit premium. The regression equation is reported in Exhibit 11.9. The R^2 is a little higher than we have seen with other systematic strategies (6.58 percent) and the slope coefficient is positive (0.1612) and significant (t-statistic of 4.20). Part of the unconstrained strategy includes a small capture of fixed income risk premia (inclusive of term premium, credit premium, emerging premium, and prepayment risk premium). Some exposure to traditional risk premia is expected in this category, and importantly, as we will see shortly, the extent of that traditional risk premia capture is small (especially compared to the incumbent

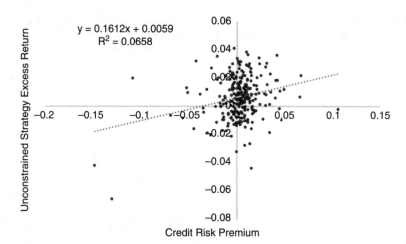

$y = 0.1612x + 0.0059$
$R^2 = 0.0658$

(y-axis label: Unconstrained Strategy Excess Return)
(x-axis label: Credit Risk Premium)

EXHIBIT 11.9 Scatter plot of excess of cash returns for a systematic Unconstrained Bond portfolio against the credit premium (50/50 blend of US HY credit-excess returns and US Loan excess returns).
Sources: ICE/BAML indices, S&P indices, and author calculations. The period examined was 2000–2020.

Unconstrained Bond funds examined in Chapter 4) and it does not erode alpha. The (annualized) intercept of 0.0704 and the (annualized) volatility of regression residuals (5.00 percent) suggest an information ratio of 1.41 for a systematic Unconstrained Bond portfolio. If this systematic portfolio was run with an active risk of 500 basis points, this would translate to 705 basis points of alpha (1.41 × 5 percent).

Again, to ensure fairness in the comparison to the set of 103 Unconstrained Bond funds examined in Chapter 4, we can run the same regression specification:

$$R_{SYS\ UNCON} = \alpha + \beta_{GAGG}GAGG + \beta_{INF}INF + \beta_{CP}CP$$
$$+ \beta_{EMD}EMD + \beta_{EMFX}EMFX + \beta_{VOL}VOL + \varepsilon \quad (11.7)$$

$R_{SYS\ UNCON}$ is the monthly excess of cash return for the systematic Unconstrained Bond strategy, and the right-hand side variables are all as defined in Exhibit 4.3. Exhibit 11.10 summarizes the regression analysis. The (annualized) intercept from regression (11.7) of 3.99 percent is lower than the simpler analysis controlling only for the credit premium (the correlation to the credit premium, ρ_{CP}, is 0.26), primarily due to the embedded capture of term premium and credit premium. The information ratio, after

EXHIBIT 11.10   Regression analysis for systematic Unconstrained Bond strategy. Regression coefficients are reported on top of (italicized) t-statistics.

Active Return	Sharpe Ratio	β_{GAGG}	β_{INF}	β_{CP}	β_{EMD}	β_{EMFX}	β_{VOL}	α	IR	ρ_{CP}
7.51%	1.45	0.86	−0.02	0.16	−0.01	0.02	0.13	3.99%	0.91	0.26
		(4.55)	*(−0.20)*	*(2.73)*	*(−0.11)*	*(0.29)*	*(1.79)*	*(3.84)*		

Sources: Bloomberg indices, JP Morgan indices, and author calculations. The period examined was 2000–2020.

adjusting for term premium, credit premium, emerging premium, emerging currency exposure, and the volatility premium is 0.91. A well-implemented systematic Unconstrained Bond portfolio has the potential to be a powerful diversifier.

11.2   SOME FINAL THOUGHTS

I would like to close this book with some thoughts about careers in investment management, especially for systematic investors. This advice is largely parroting, perhaps not as eloquently, what I have been told over the past 20 years.

11.2.1   Failure Is Success

Anyone entertaining a career in systematic investments (fixed income or otherwise) needs to appreciate the importance of failure. A lot of investment ideas that you try will not work out as originally intended. This may not be because the idea had no merit, but, rather, the idea may not have been additive to what the investment process is already doing, or perhaps the market is more efficient with respect to your investment idea than you originally thought. Do not despair if the fruits of your effort only make marginal impact on the investment process in a given quarter or year. But do despair if someone working at a systematic investment business sets your key performance indicator to change the model by X percent. That is inconsistent with a systematic investment process. You should only take risk on an investment idea if it is conceptually grounded and empirically additive (see the recipe in Chapter 1). A systematic investment professional could have a very productive year yet have had minimal impact on the overall model.

Beware the hidden data-mining risk in the research process. Although the famous quotes of Thomas Edison speak about not failing but finding thousands of ways that won't or don't work lend credence to the "fail and succeed" model, there is a serious risk of trying many things and focusing only on the positive results. This is an age-old problem with all fields of research (not just investing). Keep track of the graveyard where all the failed ideas are buried. Not only is this good practice for efficient management of scarce investment resources (i.e., an idea that someone suggests today is usually related to an idea that someone else had tried years ago), it will also help the governance process. How many ideas or variants were examined? How robust are results across different, but defensible, research design choices? Absent knowledge of the graveyard, it is impossible to know how good a given research result is.

11.2.2 Culture Clash

Over the years, tensions between investment professionals (like any other workplace) need to be well managed. For a systematic investor, that means shared belief in the investment philosophy described in Chapter 1. At the same time, a good investment team needs individuals with a deep fundamental knowledge of the asset class (i.e., an ability to understand and model the return data-generating process). It is unusual to find excellence in asset class domain knowledge and excellence in data analytics in the same individual. Herein lies the tension, as you need excellence across both dimensions to have a successful systematic investment process. And individuals typically want to be responsible for risk-taking decision rights.

There are two potential solutions to this process. First, individuals can improve the dimension in which they are weaker (domain knowledge or data analytics skill). That is challenging, given the benefits of specialization and the limits of time. Second, the team can hire for excellence across dimensions. This is more common in practice. To be successful, however, individuals who join a systematic investment team should ensure expectations management are set both when they join and when their career develops. Exactly what skill set are you bringing to the table? How does your employer expect to utilize that skill set? Is that use consistent with what you are really passionate about? A similar thought process needs to be followed by the investment management company as well to ensure that the skill set acquired and the individual's career aspirations fit with the strategic plans. A lot of time and effort from both employee and employer are required to make an investment effort successful. It is a shame when there are expectations mismatches about roles and responsibilities.

Before starting a career in systematic investing, ask yourself what you really want to do. If it is the ability to have your own P&L and (ultimately discretionary) investment decision rights, then a career in collaborative systematic investing is not for you. There are differences in investment business models (for both systematic and discretionary processes) ranging from more collaborative efforts to more siloed and "eat what you kill" (smaller) teams. Systematic approaches can flourish across this spectrum. Think carefully what model is best suited for your personality.

11.2.3 Importance of Communication

Communication is an important part of success in all walks of life. For the systematic investor communication is, arguably, even more important than it is for a typical discretionary-approach investor. Why? As we discussed in Chapter 1, a discretionary investment approach is characterized by a smaller number of positions with a clear narrative for each position in the portfolio. The discretionary portfolio manager is able to articulate the investment thesis for each key position in the portfolio. This "narrative" is important because it brings the asset owner into the investment process, and that shared understanding makes it easier to explain performance (both good and bad). A systematic portfolio manager, on the other hand, tends to find it challenging to provide a clear and compelling narrative for portfolio positions. Yes, this is a challenge, but it is a huge opportunity to bring your investors into the investment process. Simply stating that your systematic investment process seeks exposure to a set of characteristics like carry, defensive, momentum, and value, will work for some asset owners but not for all. How do you explain what you do to an asset owner if there are over 500 positions in the portfolio and all you have in front of you are four investment labels? An asset owner is going to want to know a lot more about the corporate bonds and government bonds in their portfolio. But that's okay. Leverage the power of data analytics to look through the portfolio positions down to the signals that gave rise to the positions (it is a deterministic process mapping data inputs to portfolio weights after all). There is considerable variety across systematic managers for portfolio attribution, and this is very much a nascent area. The successful systematic fixed investors will be those who are able to (i) generate positive excess of benchmark returns (a necessary condition for all investors), (ii) generate positive excess of benchmark returns that are lowly correlated with traditional risk premia (close to a sufficient condition), and (iii) clearly explain their investment process and provide deep levels of attribution to the portfolio.

The opportunity is there for systematic fixed income investors. As we noted in Chapter 1, only a very small portion of active fixed income funds are managed in a systematic way. The first section of this chapter showed how a systematic investment approach can be very different from, and very diversifying to, traditional discretionary fixed income managers. Part of that difference stems from lower exposure to traditional market risk premia, but part of that difference is also attributable to a different approach to security selection and portfolio construction. Palhares and Richardson (2020) explore the differences in discretionary and systematic investment approaches in the US HY market. That subgroup of fixed income managers is selected due to disclosure of portfolio holdings and the relative homogeneity across funds. The majority of US HY mutual-fund corporate bond funds hold HY corporate bonds, and every quarter they disclose their holdings and their benchmark. It is easy to compute an active view for every corporate issuer and issue in that benchmark. The systematic corporate bond manager has an expected return forecast for every bond in the index. A heuristic similarity measure (labeled TC in Exhibit 11.11) can be computed for every fund quarter. The correlation between active weights and standardized values of the respective investment themes (carry, defensive, momentum, and value) is an efficient way to capture this similarity. It should be clear from Exhibit 11.11 that across the set of 154 HY mutual funds there is little similarity in active risk taking with a systematic investment approach. The vertical line toward the middle of each histogram is the average TC across mutual funds (it is close to zero as the market clears and the set of mutual funds is representative of the overall market).The vertical line at the right reflects the correlation for a systematic fund designed to target exposure to these four investment themes. It is very far to the right of the distribution of discretionary HY bond funds. A systematic investment approach can be a powerful diversifier

11.2.4 Market Efficiency

One final note. Be humble. A career in active investing requires you to challenge market prices. This is a daunting challenge. There is an enormous amount of capital invested in the markets every day. What is your edge? How can you maintain your edge? Always strive to articulate your investment thesis. Does a given measure associate with future returns due to (i) risk, (ii) behavioral/cognitive errors, or (iii) are you exploiting an institutional friction? Anything anchored on (ii) or (iii) should be continually challenged. Is your idea still not fully appreciated by the market? Is the friction still strong enough to be exploited? But note that just because something did not work recently is not, by itself, grounds for dismissing the efficacy of your idea.

Be sure you sleep soundly at night. Your belief in market efficiency should be consistent with (i) your investment career choice, and (ii) your

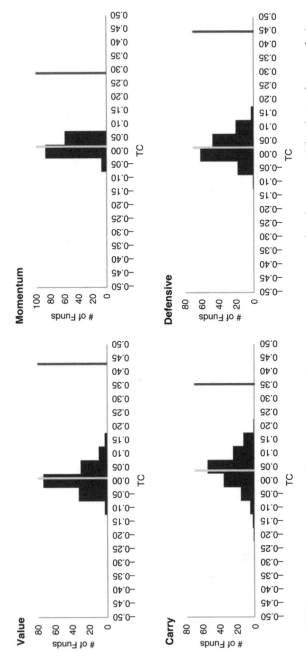

EXHIBIT 11.11 Holdings analysis of discretionary and systematic HY corporate bond managers. The charts show a relative frequency histogram of the transfer coefficient (TC) between fund active weights and standardized systematic measures of bond attractiveness for a set of 154 HY mutual funds. The light vertical line is the average TC across all mutual funds. The dark vertical line is the TC for a systematic HY bond portfolio.
Source: Palhares and Richardson (2020).

personal investing decisions. A die-hard believer in efficient markets should not be working in active investment management and should have all their financial assets with Vanguard. I wish you all the best in your systematic fixed income investing career. Together let's make the systematic share of actively managed fixed income strategies much larger. It will be good for you, and, most importantly, it will be good for your asset owners!

REFERENCE

Palhares, D., and S. Richardson. (2020). Looking under the hood of active credit managers. *Financial Analysts Journal*, 76, 82–102.

Index